EDUARD LOHSE

THE NEW TESTAMENT ENVIRONMENT

EDUARD LOHSE

THE
NEW TESTAMENT
ENVIRONMENT

SCM PRESS LTD

Translated by John E. Steely from the German
Umwelt des Neuen Testaments, revised edition
published by Vandenhoeck & Ruprecht, Göttingen 1974

334 02214 2
First published in English 1976
by SCM Press Ltd
26–30 Tottenham Road London N1
Fourth impression 1985

Printed and bound in Great Britain at
The Camelot Press Ltd
Southampton

CONTENTS

Part II
The Hellenistic-Roman Environment of the New Testament

Contents

TRANSLATOR'S PREFACE

If the translator's work is properly done, the reader will
be unaware of him and will hear only the author whose
words, insights, and suggestions are the justification for the
work. A preface such as this, however, gives the translator
an opportunity to intrude for a moment into the conversation
between author and reader.

The first debt of thanks is owed to the author, to the
publishers of the work in its original German, and to the
editors and publishers of this translation. Only those who
have been the recipients of such support and encouragement
can know the extent of my indebtedness and the warmth
of my gratitude to these whose labors stand behind this
completed work.

I should like to take this opportunity to thank my col-
leagues in the faculty and student body of Southeastern
Baptist Theological Seminary for their interest and for the
inquiries by which they both prompted and sustained this
work.

My wife has shared in the painstaking toil represented by
these pages, as well as in the rewards of a challenging task.
I must say too little by way of thanks to her, lest it appear
that I have thought to say enough.

JOHN E. STEELY
Wake Forest, North Carolina
April 26, 1975

INTRODUCTION

"When the time was fulfilled"—the apostle Paul writes—
"God sent his Son, born of a woman, born under the law"
(Gal. 4:4). Like a vessel filled to its brim, so time was at its
fullest measure when the Son of God came into the world.
Luther, in a lecture on Galatians which he delivered in
1516/17, shed light on this passage, emphasizing that the
"fulfillment" of the times that is spoken of here does not
result from a prerequisite lapse of time but from a prerequisite and unique event, the sending of the Son, which,
having occurred, brought the times to fulfillment. In the
same way, it should be emphasized that the times during
which Jesus of Nazareth preached and the gospel was first
proclaimed among Jews and Greeks were not intrinsically
different from all other moments of history, nor were the
people living in them uniquely different from all preceding
and subsequent humanity. Humanity was not at that time
prepared in a special way for this message of the Son.
Instead, time itself took its shape, its human significance from
the event of which the gospel tells. The people who met
Jesus, who heard the messengers of Christ and became members of the first churches were ordinary people. They had
their daily work to perform; they lived as men and women,
as children and old people, rich and poor. They were
acquainted with anxiety and suffering, but also with joy and
happiness; they wondered about the meaning of life and
sought for a valid answer to this ultimate question. The gospel gives this answer: God sent his Son, who was born of a
woman and experienced the common lot of man even to the

point of death, "that he might redeem those who were under the law, that we might be adopted as sons" (Gal. 4:5).

Jesus of Nazareth was born during the reign of the Emperor Augustus (Luke 2:1). "In the fifteenth year of the reign of the Emperor Tiberius, when Pontius Pilate was governor in Judea, Herod was tetrarch in Galilee and his brother Philip was tetrarch in Iturea and in the country of Trachonitis, and Lysanias was tetrarch in Abilene, when Annas and Caiaphas were high priests" (Luke 3:1), John the Baptist appeared in the wilderness and soon thereafter Jesus of Nazareth began to preach publicly. His preaching did not convey general truths which could be repeated without reference to the situation of the hearers, nor was this true of the proclamation of the primitive Christian community; instead, men were addressed where they were, in the midst of their lives. They heard their anxieties considered in language familiar to them, and their questions were answered in words that they knew. Because the gospel was first given expression at a particular place and a particular time in history, it is indispensable, for a proper understanding of the message, not only to study the languages in which people then spoke—Hebrew, Aramaic, and Greek—but also as precisely as possible to relate to contemporary experience the political conditions, the circumstances of life, and the customs of those people, their hopes and expectations, their conceptions and views. The more precisely we determine where people felt the impact of the Christian proclamation and how they understood and related the gospel to their lives, the better we will succeed in translating the content of this message from the manner of speech and the conceptions of the ancient world into the language of our own time.

The environment of the New Testament affords an extremely varied picture. In the age of Hellenism the Greeks encountered the peoples of the ancient Orient, East and West met, and religions and cultures intermingled. Out of the rich abundance of this world of late antiquity, we plan to set forth here what is of immediate importance for understanding the New Testament. Hence we cannot go into details on Greek history, nor address the particular problems of the cultural history of the Near East. Our task is limited strictly to achieving a contribution to the understanding of the New Testament. Jesus, his disciples, and the first Christians were Jews. But the gospel quickly pushed beyond the boundaries of Palestine into the Hellenistic-Roman environment. The two spheres—Judaism on the one hand and the Hellenistic-Roman environment on the other—cannot be sharply distinguished from each other. For since the time of Alexander the Great, even Palestine had remained under the strong Hellenistic influence that had produced powerful effects everywhere throughout the countryside, and in Jerusalem as well. Since the Christian communities, which were formed in rapid succession along the coastal curve of the Mediterranean Sea, often rose from the circles of Hellenistic synagogues and their adherents, early Christianity formed an acquaintance with the Greek legacy and its Hellenistic extension chiefly through the mediation of Hellenistic Judaism. The tradition of Jesus of Nazareth is written not in Aramaic words but in Greek, and the epistles of the apostle Paul, like the Gospels, were composed in the Greek language. Thus the New Testament itself bears testimony to the extremely far-reaching significance of Hellenism for Palestine, the Near East, and the entire Mediterranean world. The writings of the New Testament are likewise the most important source of information about the New Testament environment; for they contain references to circumstances in Palestine and in the Roman Empire which can be dated exactly. These circumstances will be described more precisely and illustrated through comparison with contemporary literature, inscriptions, and nonliterary documents, as well as with archaeological data.

PART I
Judaism in the Time of the New Testament

CHAPTER 1
The Political History of Judaism in the Hellenistic Period

Judaism in the time of the New Testament is the legacy of its changeful history in the preceding centuries. Like their neighbors, the Jews lived at times under the dominion of the great powers which successively ruled the Near East, and although from time to time they, like other smaller tribes, were allowed a relatively unhindered life of their own, at other times they suffered interference with and dictation of their style of life. Each of these succeeding powers continued to influence the history of the land and its inhabitants, so that in the New Testament period their effects are clearly recognizable. Hence the situation in which Judaism found itself in the time of Jesus can be adequately described only against the background of the historical past by which it was molded.

1. Palestine Under the Rule of the Persians

The history of Judaism begins with the time of the *Babylonian exile*. After the destruction of Samaria by the Assyrians in 722 B.C., the ten tribes of Israel, which had settled in the northern part of the country, disappeared. In 587 B.C. Judea was finally conquered by Babylon, Jerusalem was destroyed, and the upper stratum of the population was deported to Babylon. These Judeans were able to preserve their unity as a people and their belief in the God of Israel. Though they were forbidden to continue the temple cultus, they held fast to the law of their God and obeyed the commandments of the sabbath and of circumcision—signs by which Israel constantly made itself aware of its separation and distinction from all other peoples. This produced the intellectual and spiritual precondition that made possible, after the end of the Babylonian rule, a new beginning in the land of their fathers.

The turning point came with the victory of the Persian king *Cyrus,* who with powerful blows put an end to the neo-Babylonian empire. In 539 B.C. he marched triumphantly into Babylon and thereupon became ruler not only over Mesopotamia but also over Syria and Palestine. The Persians followed a policy toward the foreign nations that came under their dominion different from that pursued earlier by the Assyrians and Babylonians. The latter, after the conquest of the countries, had transplanted entire populations, or at least deported the upper stratum; they had everywhere enforced their cult as the state religion. The Persians, on the other hand, neither forced large-scale resettlements nor required that one single state religion be acknowledged. Instead, they made allowances for various local conditions, permitted any peculiar customs of the people to be continued, let the people conduct their daily lives as previously, and sought thereby to win their allegiance. For official business the Persian government employed not its own language, but the Aramaic language, which was widely used in Syria and Palestine. This policy also afforded Judaism the opportunity to develop its own life with the express support of the government. Shortly after the conquest of Babylon, King Cyrus issued a decree ordering that the house of God in Jerusalem be rebuilt and the furnishings which Nebuchadnezzar had taken from the temple be restored (Ezra 6:3–5). Presumably, however, few of the Jews living in exile at first took advantage of the permission to return to their homeland. And the remnant of the Jewish population in Palestine lived in such modest circumstances that reconstruction of the temple began only slowly and with difficulty.

In the fifth century there arose among the Jews who had remained in Mesopotamia a strong impetus for the consolidation of the Jewish community in Jerusalem. Upon commission of the great king, first Nehemiah, then Ezra came to Palestine to set things in order. Nehemiah undertook to surround Jerusalem with fortified walls and exacted from the Jews a sworn promise not to enter into any marriages with members of alien neighboring tribes. Ezra taught the city's inhabitants the Law and, on order from the king, put it into effect. It can be asssumed, with a high degree of probability, that this Law embraced the five books of Moses, i.e., the Pentateuch, in which the ancient traditions of Israel had been collected and arranged. By virtue of the fact that the Jews were under obligation to obey the law and a royal decree had confirmed its authority, Israel's Law now served as the Persian law of the land in Jerusalem and Judea. Hence the cultus of the Jewish community stood under the protection of the Persian government, and the community could develop its life without hindrance according to the prescriptions of the Law.

These circumstances evoked both envy and jealousy on the part of the neighboring peoples, and in particular among the inhabitants of *Samaria*. In the north of Palestine, after the conquest by the Assyrians, foreign settlers had become residents of the land, and these had mixed with the population that remained (II Kings 17). Their descendants, it is true, worshiped Yahweh as the God of the land, who gave fertility and growth to the soil, but they were not recognized by the Jews as true Israelites. Hence the Jerusalem community, which had been urged by Nehemiah and Ezra not to enter into any alliances with other peoples, separated itself from them and would have no dealings with them. This harsh separation and the king's heavy favoring of Jerusalem created bitterness among the people in the region of Samaria, which led to increased alienation between north and south and finally to the political separation of the provinces of Samaria and Judea. Insofar as the Samaritan people worshiped Yahweh as the God of Israel, they had continued to go to Jerusalem, the capital of the neighboring but unfriendly province, in order to offer sacrifices and to worship in the temple there. Now political dissension gave rise to the desire on the part of the Samaritans to erect a sanctuary of their own so that they might become wholly independent of Jerusalem.

Thus, at first, the Samaritans still belonged to the cultic community of Jerusalem; for only this way is it possible to explain the fact that the Samaritans have in common with the Jews the five books of Moses as Holy Scripture, but not the remaining parts of the Old Testament Canon, the prophetic writings and the books of poetry. The separation between Jews and Samaritans must have come after the completion of the Pentateuch and before the canonical boundaries of the other parts of the Old Testament had been fixed (cf. pp. 167–69). Although the Jewish historian Josephus relates that it was only under Alexander the Great that the Samaritans first received permission to erect a temple on Mount Gerizim (*Jewish Antiquities* XIII. 74–79), their sanctuary had probably already been built by this time. Since before its collapse the Persian Empire suffered serious upheavals, it must have been in this time at the earliest that it became possible to secure the agreement of the great king to the building of the holy places of the Samaritans. The Samaritans proudly point out that in the Law of Moses Jerusalem is not explicitly named, but their holy mountain, Gerizim, is (Deut. 11:29; 27:12-13).

From the time the Samaritans possessed their own sanctuary, such bitter enmity prevailed in their relationship with the Jews, that the eventual result was conflict tantamount to outright warfare, and in the year 128 B.C. the Jews under John Hyrcanus destroyed the temple on Mount Gerizim. Although the Samaritans could not rebuild it, still they clung unwaveringly to Gerizim as their holy place. Even today the small Samaritan community annually celebrates in this place the Passover feast according to the age old usage that it has preserved.

In Jesus' time, Jews and Samaritans had no dealings with each other (John 4:9). To the Jews, the Samaritans were of an alien tribe (Luke 17:18). "Samaritan" was used as a term of abuse and, specifically, was applied to persons considered demented (John 8:48). If Jewish pilgrims on their way to feasts in Jerusalem wished to take a route through Samaritan territory, they could expect hindrances and hostile treatment on the way (Luke 9:51-56). It is true that the Samaritans referred to the patriarchs as their ancestors (John 4:12), but the Jews did not allow this claim. Jesus cited, not the act of a Jew, but that of a Samaritan, as an example of love for one's neighbor unselfishly demonstrated (Luke 10:30-37). And it is told that a Samaritan, not a Jew, after being cured of leprosy, gave praise to God (Luke 17:11-19). After some initial hesitation (Matt. 10:5-6), the primitive community overcame the alienation that existed between Jews and Samaritans and carried the gospel to Samaria (Acts 8:4-25). The old dispute over whether one should worship on Mount Gerizim or in Jerusalem (John 4:20) was now of no importance, "for God is spirit, and those who worship him must worship him in spirit and in truth" (John 4:24).

2. Palestine Under Alexander the Great and the Rule of the Egyptians

In the battle of Issus (333 B.C.), *Alexander the Great* conquered the Persian king Darius III and, by means of this victory, opened the way via Syria and Palestine to Egypt. Only slight resistance could be offered to the rapid advance of the Macedonian forces. The strong island fortress of Tyre was able to maintain itself until a seven-month-long siege brought about its capitulation. Gaza held out for two months; then this city also fell. After overcoming these obstacles, Alexander was able to march along the Mediterranean coast directly to Egypt. The victorious king did not remain for the conquest and occupation of the inland districts, but left this task to his generals. Judea submitted to the commander Parmenio without offering any resistance. Samaria, the seat of the Persian governor, was conquered by Perdiccas and his soldiers. The Jews were deeply impressed by the strength of the Greek army and acknowledged the superior power of the new lords without delay. Since the Jews submitted peaceably, the rights that they possessed under Persian rule were preserved for them. The Jerusalem community was permitted to continue practicing its cult without hindrance.

The lack of outward change occasioned with respect to the legal situation of the Jewish community by the change in rulers contrasted sharply with the later profound effect caused by the entrance of the *Greeks* into the country. Although in earlier times Greek traders, merchants, and travelers had come to Palestine, now the trade and the manner of life of the Greeks reached into all parts of the country. The peoples of the Near East opened themselves to the Greek influence—manners, culture, and intellectual materials—so that the descendants of the ancient Phoenicians and Philistines exchanged their language for Greek, and, thereby, became so completely absorbed into the world of Hellenism that they lost their distinctive culture. Greek settlements and cities were founded, but Greeks also settled in already existing cities. The conquered fortress of Tyre was resettled with Greeks; the city of Samaria, which had offered resistance, received Macedonians as inhabitants. Many cities adopted not only a Greek name but also Greek civil law. From this time on, therefore, the Jews in Palestine lived in close proximity to the Greeks, who enforced their language as the language of trade. Anyone who was not able to speak Greek was regarded as a barbarian. Many Jews learned the language of the aliens (which was spoken in all the countries which Alexander the Great had reached in his triumphal march) so that in New Testament times many people in Palestine could understand and speak Greek. If one had dealings with the representatives of the Roman occupation forces, one could make oneself understood with Greek. When Paul was arrested in Jerusalem and wanted to defend himself before the masses of the people—thus the book of Acts reports—people were surprised that he spoke Hebrew, or Aramaic, and not Greek (Acts 22:2). Apparently people would have been able to understand one language as well as the other without difficulty.

Along with the language there came into the country the Hellenistic civilization as well, for the Greek settlers brought along their own patterns of life and clung to them. Greek buildings appeared, theaters and baths were erected in the cities, and sports were pursued in the gymnasia. *Greek customs* were adopted; in festive meals, people ate while reclining at the table (cf. Mark 14:18 par.; 22 par.). They came to enjoy the medical skill that the Greeks had developed to a high degree (Mark 5:26 par.). As the Greeks sought to develop a train of thought in conversation and through the interplay of question and answer to find the solution to a problem, so now the Jews also learned to debate and, in didactic conversation, to inquire about and to attempt to clarify the truth of the divine will. These examples show how the Jews also learned to adapt themselves to the new conditions and to find their way about in them. The attraction which people in many Jewish circles felt for the superior civilization and culture of the Greeks increased to the extent that in the second century B.C. there were Jews in Jerusalem who in all seriousness believed that they were kinsmen of the Spartans, who were famed for their just laws. I Maccabees tells of a letter which Areus, the king of Sparta, is supposed to have written to the high priest Onias; this letter states that an ancient writing has been discovered which identifies Spartans and Jews as brothers and both as descendants of the tribe of Abraham (I Macc. 12:21). This development might finally have led to complete hellenization of Jerusalem and Judea, as had happened with the land of the Phoenicians and Philistines. But the Law that was received from the fathers and recorded in the Hebrew language obligated the community to keep the old faith, to order its worship according to the law of Moses, and to remain aware that God had set Israel, his people, apart from all the other nations.

The sudden death of Alexander the Great at the age of 33, in 323 B.C., plunged his hastily constructed empire into political confusion. Alexander's military commanders fell into a dispute about their respective jurisdictions, and the unity of the empire collapsed. The governor Ptolemy, who resided in

Egypt, sent forces to occupy Palestine and at first brought it under his control. But Antigonus, who governed Syria, contested Ptolemy's claim to Palestine and usurped his rule (315 B.C.). However, when Antigonus later succeeded in reconquering the old Persian Empire almost in its entirety, the other former governors under Alexander became envious of his success and joined forces against him. As a result, Ptolemy succeeded in regaining control of Palestine and acquired the southern part of Syria, as well. Therewith circumstances were decided which were to prevail for the next one hundred years. Palestine, which so often in its history had been the source of discord between the great powers in Egypt and Mesopotamia, stood under the overlordship of Egypt, now a Hellenistic state, so that the Hellenistic influence in Palestine continued unchanged.

The Ptolemies apparently followed the example of the Persians and Alexander the Great in refraining from meddling in the internal affairs of the cultic community in Jerusalem. The leadership of Judaism lay in the hands of its high priest, who was able to order and guide its interests with the consent of the Hellenistic rulers of Egypt. Standing with him in the Sanhedrin were priests and elders, the heads of the influential families of Jerusalem. It cannot be determined with certainty when this supreme Jewish authority came into existence. Its origin could in fact date from the Persian period, but there is unequivocal evidence for its existence only beginning with the Hellenistic period. In the first century B.C., the priests and elders were joined by a third group (cf. p. 33). The Sanhedrin is frequently mentioned in the New Testament, primarily in the passion narratives, in this context. (Mark 10:33 par.; 11:27 par.; 14:43 par.; *et passim*). When occasionally only two groups are named—the chief priests and scribes (Mark 11:18 par.; 14:1 par.; *et passim*), or the chief priests and elders (Matt. 21:45; 26:3, 47; *et passim*) —or when only the chief priests are cited as representatives of the Sanhedrin (Mark 14:55 par. *et passim*), what is meant is always the supreme Jewish authority which came together under the leadership of the high priest, to regulate all secular and spiritual matters which affected the Jewish population.

3. Palestine Under the Rule of Syria
and the Maccabean Struggle for Freedom

After a first fruitless attempt, about the end of the third or the beginning of the second century B.C., the Syrian king Antiochus III (223–187 B.C.) succeeded in wresting Palestine from Egypt. The Ptolemies were obliged to withdraw and to leave the country to the Syrians. Since the Jews had recognized in time that the scales were tipping in the Syrians' favor and during the hostilities had fought on their side, after the victory they were treated accordingly by the Syrians. Efforts were made to repair the damage which Jerusalem had suffered during the war, and to their existing rights further privileges were added. up to a certain amount, the expenses required for the temple cult were to be defrayed by funds from the state's treasury, and the members of the council of elders and the scribes were granted freedom from taxation.

Yet the friendly relations were not to continue for long. Syria was ruled by the dynasty of the Seleucids, which had been founded by Seleucus after the death of Alexander the Great. The Seleucids strove, by promoting Hellenistic culture, to bind the diverse peoples of their kingdom closer together. Large groups of the Jews were receptive to this policy, and even among the priesthood in Jerusalem there were many who adjusted to the process of hellenization. The high priest, as head of the Jewish people, was responsible for enforcing the laws and decrees of the Syrian king. Since he was also responsible for seeing that the taxes owed were paid on time, the Syrians could also turn to him when they wished to collect more money. When *Antiochus IV* assumed the reign in Syria in the year 175 B.C., the high priest in Jerusalem was *Onias*, a devout observer of the law. Nevertheless he had opponents within the priesthood, above all in the person of his brother Joshua and generally among the adherents to the hellenizing movement. Joshua rendered his name into Greek as Jason, offered the Syrians a considerable sum of money which was to be brought in through the raising of taxes, and succeeded in having Onias relieved of his office and himself installed as high priest. The change in the office of high priest was accomplished without any resistance on the part of the defeated party. Onias was murdered some years later in Antioch; his son of the same name fled to Egypt and, with the support of the Ptolemies, around 160 B.C. established a temple in Leontopolis, where a sacrificial cult modeled after that of the temple in Jerusalem was adopted and continued until A.D. 73. Nevertheless the significance of this sanctuary remained slight, since even the Egyptian Jews continued to adhere to the temple in Jerusalem. In Jerusalem, it is true, Jason enforced the performance of the temple cult in accordance with the prescriptions of the Law, but he vigorously advanced the process of hellenization. A gymnasium was built, where young men played sports unclothed; and even priests took part in this activity. Jewish participants under these circumstances became ashamed of their circumcision, which the Greeks ridiculed; hence many of them underwent an operation to undo their circumcision (I Macc. 1:15) —a practice which still occurred frequently among Jews even in Paul's time (cf. I Cor. 7:18). When Jason had been in office three years, a certain *Menelaus* offered the Syrian king an even larger sum of money for the position of high priest than Jason had once paid, and thereupon was given Jason's place. The office of high priest had become a political entity which could be bought and sold.

The Romans, who after their victorious struggle against Hannibal had also made their military and political influence felt in the Orient, intervened in favor of the Ptolemies who were ruling in Egypt and against the party of Antiochus of Syria. Antiochus had made war against Egypt, but was forced to interrupt his undertaking when the Romans commanded him to stop. After the abortive Egyptian campaign, the rumor spread in Jerusalem that Antiochus had lost his life. Jason, who had been expelled from his office, sought to use this opportunity to drive out Menelaus by armed force and once again succeeded in taking upon himself both the office of the high priest and the rule over Jerusalem. When Antiochus learned of these events, enraged, he intervened and restored Menelaus to the office of high priest. Yet the latter could preserve his position only with the support of the Syrians and therefore offered no resistance to them when in 169 B.C. Antiochus replenished his own treasury, which had been emptied in the war, by plundering the Jerusalem temple: the precious furnishings of the temple, the altar of incense, the seven-branched lampstand, and the table of the shewbread were removed to Antioch (I Macc. 1:20-24).

This first offensive against the holy place was soon followed by a second, still harsher attack. The hellenization of Jerusalem and Judea, which in fact had encountered some resistance but for the most part had made significant progress, was to be completed with force; and thereby the Jewish community's indigenous way of life was to be abolished. The walls of Jerusalem were torn down, and a fortress was built on the hill of the ancient city of David (the Acra). The Jews were forbidden, on pain of death, to keep the sabbath and to circumcise their children. The king's inspectors traveled throughout the country in order to supervise the fulfillment of these decrees. In Jerusalem a pagan altar was erected on the site of the altar of burnt offering, and sacrifices were offered there to the supreme God, the Olympian Zeus (167 B.C.). Even swine were offered as sacrificial animals. Greeks were able to interpret this change as an expression of the view that in all cults ultimately the one God was worshiped, and that it was a matter of arbitrary choice whether his name was Yahweh, Baal of heaven, or Zeus; but for the Jews, the profanation of the holy place signified the abomination of desolation (cf. Dan. 11:31; 12:11). People saw in this event a sign of the last times and even later always spoke of the abomination of desolation as a phenomenon which was to occur shortly before the end of this age (Mark 13:14 par.). These events brought an extremely dangerous crisis for Judaism, whose end appeared to be imminent. But the believing community did not passively let itself be detached from the faith of the fathers. The book of Daniel was composed as a writ of consolation for the oppressed community; persecution and suffering were understood as signs of the last times, soon to be brought to an end by an act of God. Pious Jews preferred to accept suffering and death rather than to renounce their obedience to the Law (II Macc. 7).

In contrast to the city residents who opened themselves to the influences of the Hellenistic culture and civilization, the people of the countryside held stubbornly to the faith of their fathers. Within their circles resistance to Syrian policy increased and, as a result of an incident which occurred in the little village of Modein, not far from Lydda, escalated to outright rebellion against the alien rule. When the king's inspectors came to this place to compel the Jews to offer pagan sacrifices, the old priest *Mattathias*—the head of a family which was called, after its ancestor, the Hasmoneans—killed a Jew who was ready to offer a sacrifice on the altar, and also slew the royal official who had demanded that the sacrifices be made. This act created a great sensation. Mattathias and his sons had to flee and to withdraw into the hills of the wilderness of Judea (I Macc. 1:15-28), where a host of Jews ready for battle soon gathered around them. From this base, they at first carried out small forays here and there to destroy pagan temples which had been erected throughout the countryside or to punish apostate Jews. When the old priest Mattathias died soon thereafter, his son *Judas* took over the leadership of the warriors. He acquired the surname "the Maccabean," which probably means "the hammer-like one" (from the Aramaic *makkaba,* meaning "the hammer"), was regarded by his friends as an able warrior, and was feared by his adversaries. Judas was soon not content with small-scale guerrilla activities and attacks, and ventured to undertake large-scale attacks on the Syrians. Hence the Syrians were compelled to show resistance. The king, Antiochus, who was fighting the Parthians in the East, sent his commander Lysias to Palestine. Judas continued to be successful against him, defeated the Syrians in several battles, marched in triumph to Jerusalem, occupied the desecrated holy place, and reestablished the worship of the God of Israel prescribed by the Law. On the twenty-fifth of Kislev (i.e., in December) of the year 164 B.C., the altar was consecrated anew; and with an eight-day feast, worship in accordance with the Law was begun again. Ever since, Judaism has annually commemorated this event in the Feast of Dedication (Hebrew *Hanukkah*) (cf. John 10:22), during which lamps are lighted as a sign that shadows and darkness must inevitably give way to the light.

Notwithstanding these victories, the Syrians still occupied the fortress in Jerusalem. After a few smaller military undertakings, Judas began to besiege the fortress, and thereby provoked a counteraction from the Syrians. In place of King Antiochus, who had died during a campaign against the Parthians, the general Lysias was ruling as guardian of the king's minor son and regent of the kingdom. He sent a well-equipped army, which defeated the Jews and encircled Jerusalem. In this cramped situation Judas and his army were aided by an outbreak of disputes over the Syrian throne. Another general sought to depose Lysias. In order to be free to deal with his opposition, Lysias made an agreement with the Jews: he allowed them free exercise of their religion in return for their acknowledgment of Syrian sovereignty. From then on this compromise remained in force. Despite continual confusion in Syria over the occupancy of the throne, no Syrian ruler ever called this treaty in question.

Large segments of the Jewish populace were satisfied with this outcome of the Maccabean struggle for freedom, especially since after some time the deserted office of the high priest could again be filled. Menelaus, who had thoroughly misused the office, had been removed by the Maccabean reform. Under the reign of the Syrian king Demetrius, who in 162 B.C. had seized power, Hellenistic sympathizers in Jerusalem presented petitions and registered complaints that they were being suppressed by Judas. The king listened to them and installed as high priest a man named Alkimus, who indeed was a friend of hellenization, but was also of the Aaronic family. Since the cult was again being performed in accordance with the prescriptions of the Law and a believing Jew could live unmolested, the devout ones (Hebrew *chasidim*) who had resisted the Syrian policy of tyranny saw their goal achieved. They were prepared to recognize the high priest who had been installed by the Syrians as the lawful holder of the office. But Judas and his friends distrusted the Syrians. What concerned them was not the reestablishment of proper worship; instead, they wished to take further steps—to achieve political independence—by which alone they felt effective protection against the Syrian-Hellenistic influence could be achieved.

Therefore Judas challenged the high priest Alkimus, who then called on the Syrians for help. There ensued a series of various military engagements, in the course of which Judas

was killed in 160 B.C. His followers were bloodily persecuted by the Syrians wherever they could be seized. The bands
of fighters withdrew into the wilderness, and in Judas' place,
his brother *Jonathan* became their leader. Although the rebel
force was only a small one and the situation was extremely
difficult, Jonathan succeeded in making an impact on his
enemies. Owing to his skill in exploiting the continuing
disputes over the throne in Syria, he was able to weaken the
contesting parties by fighting first on one side, then on the
other. He managed to secure concessions from every side and
in this way enlarged the area that lay under his influence: the
southern part of Samaria, whose inhabitants held to the
temple in Jerusalem, became subject to his jurisdiction. Since
the demise of Alkimus, who had died at the end of the year
160 B.C., the office of the high priest had remained unfilled.
Now Jonathan succeeded in securing the agreement of the
Syrians to allow him to assume this office (153 B.C.). Thus, a
man who had constantly stained himself in war, who indeed
came from a rural, priestly family but was not of Zadokite
origin, became high priest of Israel. The devout persons who
once had shared in the Maccabean revolt were deeply concerned over this development.

When Jonathan was murdered in 143 B.C. through the
treachery of the Syrians, *Simon*, the third of the brothers,
assumed the leadership of the struggle. He succeeded also in
gaining for himself the same position which Jonathan had
attained. He became not only military commander and
leader of Judaism, but its high priest as well. While Jonathan
was able to expand the territory governed by him, Simon
besieged and expelled the Syrian garrison in the fortress of
Jerusalem. Since Jerusalem was now completely free of foreign rule, Simon was able also to gain independence abroad.
He succeeded in persuading the Syrians to concede freedom
of taxation to the Jews (142 B.C.), and minted his own Jewish
coins. The office of high priest, field commander, and leader
of the Jews was confirmed upon him in 140 B.C. as hereditary,
and thus the dynasty of the Hasmoneans, which was
acknowledged even by the Romans, was founded. The Jewish
community had achieved far-reaching independence, and
under Simon's rule experienced peaceful relationships once

again. People breathed a sigh of relief; Simon's rule was praised as a time of peace and happiness:

> People could cultivate their land in peace, and the land gave its yield and the trees in the field, their fruit. The elders sat about the streets and conferred with each other about the common good, and the young men clothed themselves with the decoration of battle dress. He [Simon] provided the cities with food and equipped them with fortifications, so that his glorious name was sounded as far as the ends of the earth. He created peace in the land, and Israel rejoiced greatly. Everyone sat under his own vine and under his fig tree, and no one was afraid. No one any longer made war in the land, and in that time the kings were humbled. He aided all the wretched ones among his people; he was full of zeal for the Law and rooted out every apostate and evildoer. He made the sanctuary splendid and increased the furnishings of the sanctuary. (I Macc. 14:8-15)

In these words from I Maccabees the age of Simon is rapturously extolled, and the peaceful conditions are interpreted as a fulfillment of the divine promise: each one would sit under his vine and under his fig tree, and no one would make him afraid (Mic. 4:4). The wise rule of Simon, his compassion for the needy, and his zeal for the Law and the temple are described as having features like those attributed to the messiah in the eschatological expectation. Yet this portrayal was by no means convincing to all the Jews. Many priests and other devout people sharply disapproved of the rule of the Hasmoneans, who came neither from a high-priestly family nor from the family of David yet had combined the office of high priest with the capacity of ruler over Israel. Previously, and seemingly inevitably, under Jonathan such a merger had led to disputes between members of the devout groups on the one hand, and the high priest and his followers on the other; and these disputes led to the withdrawal of a group of strict law-observing Jews into the desert, to lead their lives on the shores of the Dead Sea in rigid obedience to the Law (cf. pp. 99–100). They would never have agreed with the praise voiced in I Maccabees concerning the government of Simon.

Simon's rule came to a sudden end when in 134 B.C. he fell

victim to a murderous attack plotted by a son-in-law of Ptolemy. Yet the murderer did not succeed in gaining Simon's place for himself. Instead, the rule fell to Simon's son, John Hyrcanus, in accordance with the designation of the people under Simon's rule.

4. The Hasmonean Kingdom

After one last attempt by the Syrians to gain influence in the affairs of Palestine was defeated (128 B.C.), *John Hyrcanus* acquired a free hand to govern the entire country. He undertook military campaigns in the vicinity of Judea; however, he did not carry out these campaigns with a people's army which fought for Israel's faith, but with a band of mercenaries whom he had purposely gathered and who willingly did whatever he commanded. Though Jonathan and Simon had already succeeded in expanding the Jewish sphere of power, Hyrcanus was concerned with extending his rule still further. In 128 B.C., the temple on Mount Gerizim was destroyed and thereby the Samaritans were deprived of their holy place. He made another thrust into Idumea, the territory of the ancient Edom, whereby the local populace was converted to Judaism by force and their land was brought under Jewish rule. A campaign against Samaria ended equally successfully: in 107 B.C. that hellenized city was conquered and destroyed.

Although Hyrcanus' policy in his military undertakings turned out well, he received little acclaim from the masses and outright rejection in the circles of the pious. The latter were concerned with shaping their lives according to the law of God, and therefore they disapproved of the Hasmoneans' drive for power as worldly action on the part of the rulers. The society of the Pharisees (cf. pp. 77–78) was an offshoot of the groups of law-observing Jews who had supported the Maccabean revolt. Although they had originally stood close to the Hasmoneans, a serious breach now occurred, so that Hyrcanus sought support, not among the Pharisees, but among those who conceived of politics from a realistic viewpoint and did not wish to isolate themselves even from Hellenism. At first Hyrcanus had proceeded in accordance

with the Pharisaic understanding of the Law, but he gradually turned away from this and drew closer to the Sadducees
(cf. pp. 74–77), who were sympathetic to his efforts. The tradition reports that a sudden break came between Hyrcanus
and the Pharisees. According to this account, when Hyrcanus
once asked a gathering of Pharisees to tell him plainly if they
believed that he was departing from the right way at any
point, no one at first uttered any criticism, and all were full
of praise. But then a Pharisee named Eleazar arose and
demanded of Hyrcanus that he lay aside the position of high
priest, because in the time of Antiochus Epiphanes, Hyrcanus'
mother had been in prison. It was possible for a woman to
have been violated while in prison; therefore, the son of such
a mother might not be fit for the office in which the highest
degree of priestly purity is required. Hyrcanus was so angered
by this assertion that he regarded it as an expression of the
opinion held by all the Pharisees, and thus broke with them.
The narrative stresses the fact that the Hasmonean rulers
did not, in the view of the pious, satisfy the prescription of
the Law concerning the purity of the high priest. To Hyrcanus
the post of field commander and ruler over the Jews was more
important than the cultic task of the high priest, although
the coins which he minted bore either the inscription "The
high priest John and the commonwealth of the Jews," or
"The high priest John, the head of the commonwealth of the
Jews."

After the death of Hyrcanus the son *Aristobulus* seized the
rule for himself. Hyrcanus had in fact decreed that after him
his wife should govern; but Aristobulus threw his mother
and three of his brothers into prison. He shared the rule only
with his brother Antigonus, until others planted suspicions
about the latter in his mind and caused him to order
Antigonus' assassination. Aristobulus conducted himself in
the manner of the kings of petty Oriental states and was the
first Jewish ruler to secure for himself the title of king. He
continued the military campaigns, won successes in Galilee,
and compelled the people of the conquered territories to
practice circumcision. Yet the forced conversion to Judaism
did not further religious aims, but served to subjugate persons
to the power of the king. Abroad he represented himself as a

friend of the Greeks, and in this respect, also followed the example of other Oriental rulers.

After a short reign Aristobulus died in 103 B.C. His wife Salome Alexandra freed the brothers of the deceased king from prison, handed over the rule to the eldest of these, and became his wife. The new ruler grecized his name from Jonathan to Jannaeus, and called himself *Alexander Jannaeus*. He too waged many wars and, like his predecessor, continued for the most part to be successful. After he had conquered the region on the coast of the Mediterranean Sea and had undertaken some thrusts into the country east of the Jordan, he was able, but only with difficulty, to assert himself in the dispute with the rising kingdom of the Nabataeans. By means of his campaigns he united an area the scope of which corresponded approximately to that of Israel and Judah in the time of King Solomon; but his kingdom was not solidly established. Since the inhabitants of the conquered portions were either expelled or forced to become Jews, there was constant unrest, and the king was obliged to hasten from one corner of his country to the other to suppress or prevent rebellion. Because the rule of the Hasmoneans could not sustain itself through a broad base of support among its own people, it remained insecurely established. The devout stood in open opposition to the policy of the ruler, who as the man of war he was, nevertheless, simultaneously had to fill the post of high priest. He did not shrink from enforcing his will with cruelty and ruthlessness or from suppressing the Pharisees and their adherents with violence. The tension rose so high that it led to armed conflict. It is told in the tradition that Jannaeus captured eight hundred rebels, brought them to Jerusalem, and had them crucified. In company with his women he arranged a banquet in front of the crosses and had the wives and children of the crucified men slain before their eyes. Since the cruel punishment of crucifixion had never before been employed in Israel, the frightful vengeance with which Alexander Jannaeus punished his opponents by "hanging men up alive" (4QpNah. I. 6–7) evoked horror and fear among the people (cf. p. 97). Jannaeus indeed destroyed the open resistance by means of the terror, but the inward rejection of the populace continued.

On his deathbed Alexander Jannaeus advised his wife *Salome Alexandra* to be reconciled again with the Pharisees. After the king's death she took over the government and directed it for nine years with prudence and wisdom (76–67 B.C.). Although she was indeed queen, she could not, as a woman, perform a priestly office; so her son *Hyrcanus II*, a weak and not very energetic man, was installed as high priest. Salome brought about an agreement with the Pharisees, granting them an influence upon the political destiny of the land. Scribes of the Pharisees' company became members of the Sanhedrin, to which only chief priests and elders had previously belonged, and here were able to make their opinions felt and often to put them into effect. Anyone who had fled from Jannaeus' tyrannical rule could return home. The company of the Sadducees, whose opinion had been determinative in the supreme council of the Jews, saw themselves put at a disadvantage. Alliances with them and with all who were dissatisfied with the queen's government were formed by her younger son Aristobulus II, who was vigorously striving to gain power. In view of these tensions, Salome used the reins of power with caution and avoided initiating any military undertakings. She sought instead to safeguard peace abroad, in order to achieve internal pacification of the country as well. Hence in the Pharisaic tradition her reign is glorified as a blessed and peaceful time. It is said that in the years of Simon ben Schatach, who was the most outstanding scribe in the time of Queen Salome Alexandra, the rain fell so abundantly that the grains of wheat grew as large as kidneys, the grains of barley as large as olive seeds, and the lentils as large as gold denarii.

When Salome Alexandra died in 67 B.C., her son Hyrcanus II legally should have succeeded her in the office of king, but his brother *Aristobulus II* contested the position with him. Armed conflict began, in which the soldiers of Aristobulus proved to be superior to those of Hyrcanus. Hyrcanus was abandoned by his people, who went over to the stronger side. Therefore, he was obliged to accept an agreement whereby the dignity of high priest and king passed over to Aristobulus. Yet even with this the conflict did not end. For now *Antipater*, whose father had been royal governor in Idumea under Alexander Jannaeus, took his position on the side of the supplanted Hyrcanus. He lured the Nabataean king Aretas to their side by promising him the return of the cities which Jannaeus had taken from him. Aretas and Antipater marched with their troops to Jerusalem and began to besiege the city. But before matters could come to a decisive stage, the superior power of Rome appeared on the scene. From that time onward, this power was to determine the fate of the Near East and thus of Palestine as well. When *Pompey* approached with his legions, the weak kingdom of the Seleucids collapsed and was incorporated into the Roman realm as the province of Syria. Both of the parties fighting over the power in Judea appealed to Pompey, in order to win him to their side. But the people let him know that he might abolish the kingship altogether and restore the ancient rule of the priests. The kingdom of the Hasmoneans had not only lost the visible means of power; it also no longer possessed any following among the Jewish public who could have sustained it. Hence its end had irrevocably come. Yet, as referee, Pompey was in no great haste to announce his decision, and at first adopted a policy of "wait and see," before he made his decision.

5. Palestine Under Roman Rule

Each of the two contending parties which opposed each other in Judea was concerned with gaining for itself the favor of Pompey. At first it appeared that Aristobulus had better prospects of success for his cause. But when Pompey postponed the decision about Palestine, Aristobulus lost patience and sought to assure the continuation of his rule by military arrangements. Then Pompey became suspicious and advanced on Jerusalem. The Nabataeans were withdrawn at a gesture from the Romans. Aristobulus and his followers entrenched themselves in the city, but after a three-month siege their resistance was broken. Pompey entered Jerusalem and went into the temple; he even inspected the Holy of Holies. Yet he did not seize anything from the sanctuary, and he gave command that worship might be resumed at once. The fact that a Gentile did not stop even at the Holy of Holies, to which only the high priest had access, appeared to the pious

Jews a frightful desecration of the temple, which could only be conceived as God's judgment on his guilty people. In the Psalms of Solomon, which soon thereafter arose in Pharisaic circles, it is said, with clear reference to the events which occurred upon Pompey's conquest of Jerusalem: "In his insolence the sinner knocked down strong walls with the ram, and thou didst not hinder it. Alien Gentiles ascended thine altar, insolently trod it with their shoes; because the sons of Jerusalem desecrated the sanctuary of the Lord, they defiled God's sacrifice in godlessness" (Ps. of Sol. 2:1-3). The lament was followed with the prayer: "Let it suffice, Lord, that thy hand falls upon Jerusalem in the onrush of the Gentiles" (2:22).

After the conquest of the city Pompey put matters in Palestine in order. Aristobulus, along with his two sons Alexander and Antigonus, was brought prisoner to Rome, and Hyrcanus was once again installed in the office of high priest. The boundaries were redrawn; the cities in the coastal region became independent; the Hellenistic cities in the land east of the Jordan River, which had become subject to the Hasmoneans, were combined into a free league of cities which extended from Damascus in the north to Philadelphia (the present-day Amman) in the south. This league of the so-called Decapolis—i.e., of ten cities—existed for a long time and is mentioned at various points in the New Testament (Mark 5:20; 7:31; Matt. 4:25). Samaria also was given its independence, so that the high priest had dominion only over the area which belonged immediately to the Jerusalem cultic community, Judea, the interior of Galilee, and Perea in the land east of the Jordan. Then in the year 57 B.C., the Roman provincial governor in Syria, Gabinius, divided Palestine into five administrative districts which were to be immediately under his control. Judea was divided into the districts of Jerusalem, Gazara, and Jericho; Galilee was apportioned to the district of Sepphoris, and Perea to the district of Amanthus. This arrangement was well thought-out and might have made possible peaceful domestic development if the civil unrest which still smoldered in the interior of the country and impulses from abroad had not produced new and grave disturbances. Aristobulus and his sons soon began to stir again, after they had escaped from Roman imprisonment and were able to return to Palestine. In Jerusalem there were many people who were dissatisfied with Hyrcanus' weak conduct of his office and therefore sympathized with Aristobulus. Still the power of Roman arms prevented him from being able to realize his aims in Palestine.

The grave disputes over rulership in the Roman realm also affected Palestine. In the struggle between Pompey and Caesar, Hyrcanus and his people supported Pompey, who held the eastern part of the realm in his hand. However, when Caesar continued to be victorious and Pompey was murdered in Egypt in 48 B.C., Hyrcanus and Antipater were able quickly and successfully to switch over to the stronger party. They sent auxiliary troops to *Caesar* in Egypt and won his favor. Caesar not only renewed the traditional rights of the cultic community of Jerusalem, but added other privileges to these as well: the city of Joppa was again added to the territory ruled by the high priest, Hyrcanus was confirmed in his office as high priest and named ethnarch and ally of the Romans, and Antipater received the rights of a hereditary Roman citizen and was installed as procurator of Judea. This meant that alongside the ancient traditional office of high priest was placed the office of governor, the purpose of which was to safeguard the interests of the Roman realm in the country. Judea was freed from the obligation to house Roman legions during the winter months. The unhindered practice of worship was assured, not only for the temple community, but also for the synagogue communities in the realm, so that from this time on, Judaism stood under the protection of the Roman state.

Through this arrangement, Antipater had gained a strong position. He arranged to share his power with his two sons by transferring to Phasael the administration of Judea, and to Herod that of Galilee. In Galilee *Herod* eliminated the nuisance of the so-called robbers, i.e., nationalistic Jewish partisans, and in that connection imposed some death penalties without first consulting the Sanhedrin in Jerusalem, with whom the supreme power in legal matters actually lay. When some called him to account for this in Jerusalem, he appeared before the Sanhedrin in the company of a bodyguard, so that no one dared to take action against him.

With the murder of Caesar, in 44 B.C., new confusion broke out in the Roman realm. Hyrcanus and Antipater first allied themselves with Caesar's murderers, but the rule of these latter did not last long. In 42 B.C., Octavian and Antony defeated them in battle at Philippi. After the victory, *Antony* assumed the government over the eastern part of the realm and lived with the Egyptian queen Cleopatra in Alexandria. Antipater fell victim to an assassin. Hyrcanus and the two sons of Antipater, Herod and Phasael, however, were confirmed in their offices by Antony. Hyrcanus continued as high priest, and Herod and Phasael ruled the country. Antony stayed constantly in Egypt, so he was not able to involve himself significantly with Syria and Palestine.

Then an attack came from the Parthians in the east, with whom *Antigonus*, the son of Aristobulus II, was allied. Previously he, like his father, had striven in vain to gain power; but this time he attained his goal. The Parthians took Hyrcanus and Phasael prisoners. Phasael killed himself, and Hyrcanus was handed over to Antigonus. The latter ordered his uncle's ears cut off, so that as a mutilated person he would be unfit for the office of high priest. Antigonus assumed this dignity in his place and was confirmed in it by the Parthians. For three years he was able with their help to rule as high priest and king of the Jews (40–37 B.C.). Hyrcanus and Phaesael were eliminated, and only Herod remained.

Herod did the most clever thing he could possibly have done in this situation: he fled to the Romans and sought protection and help from them against Antigonus and the Parthians. In 40 B.C. he came to Rome and there gained confidence and advancement from Antony and Octavian. Upon the official decision of the senate, he was named king of the Jews, though a king without a country; for in Palestine were his worst enemies, from whom he first had to wrest the country. From a base in Syria, where the Romans soon were able to drive out the Parthians, he pushed with Roman help toward Palestine, and in 37 B.C. was able to capture Jerusalem and take up his royal office. Antigonus was imprisoned and then executed. Therewith the last attempt of the Hasmoneans to gain power was shattered. Herod was in possession of the kingship and did not allow it to be disputed again.

Just as Herod had acquired his power with Roman support, so he succeeded in fortifying it with Roman help. He was crafty and ruthless, but also daring and capable when it was a matter of making decisions quickly and acting decisively. At first he was on the side of Antony, who in Egypt ruled over the eastern part of the realm, and submitted to his directions, even when they ran counter to his own interests. Thus he had to make the best of it when Antony gave to Cleopatra, at her request, the cities on the coast and Jericho. He was too clever not to realize that, under any circumstances, he had to keep the support of the Roman ruler in order to be able to assert his own position. When Antony later was defeated by Octavian, Herod was obliged to act as quickly as possible to establish a good relationship with the new ruler of the empire. He traveled to *Octavian,* who was staying on Rhodes, openly confessed to him that he had belonged up to that time to Antony's party, and as a sign of his submission laid down his crown. The word and gesture did not fail to have their effect. Octavian confirmed Herod as king of the Jews and restored to him the cities which Antony had transferred to Cleopatra. Thus Herod also gained the favor of Augustus (Octavian had assumed this surname) and was able skillfully to maintain it. The peace which came to the Roman Empire with the reign of Augustus favored Palestine also. At long last the land was free from the torment of war.

Herod purged the opponents of his regime and all those who could possibly have endangered his rule without regard for ties of friendship and family. Through his marriage with *Mariamne,* who came from the family of the Hasmoneans, he was related to the old royal family. Since he came from Idumea, he was constantly plagued with anxiety that people did not regard him as their equal. The old Hyrcanus was murdered by him, even though the mutilations he had suffered disqualified him from holding the office of high priest. Herod himself was not of priestly lineage and therefore could not become high priest. After he had at first installed a man who was obedient to him, he finally yielded to the insistence of his mother-in-law and of the circles close to the Hasmoneans and assigned the office to his young brother-in-law *Aristobu-*

lus. Yet he did not escape from the anxiety that the Hasmoneans could become dangerous to him and seek to supplant him. When Aristobulus was murdered in his bath a year later, it was no secret that the murderers were hired by Herod; yet to the public the king feigned grief over the death of the high priest. His jealousy of the Hasmoneans finally became so strong that he even killed his wife Mariamne and later had their sons Alexander and Aristobulus murdered. He kept his affection for his firstborn son, Antipater, but shortly before his own death, sentenced him to death, also, as a traitor and rebel. Suspicion governed Herod's actions; the New Testament narrative of the massacre of the infants is entirely in harmony with this picture of his character (Matt. 2:16). Herod was constantly on guard against threats to his rule from any side and did not hesitate to take vigorous, harsh, and ruthless action to eliminate them. Neither did he shrink from having anyone murdered who might possibly become a personal danger to him as an opponent of his kingship.

Herod's kingdom included not only Jews, but also Gentiles, who dwelt predominantly in the regions which had come under his rule through the generosity of Octavian. Herod did not continue the Hasmonean policy of converting Gentiles to Judaism by force, but placed Greeks and Jews side by side with equal rights, and desired as king to be a Jew to the Jews and a Greek to the Greeks. He surrounded himself with a circle of educated Hellenists and furthered the building activities in the Greek cities; baths, gymnasia, theaters, and temples were erected. The devout Jews were indignant that the Jewish king showed favor to the Greeks. Yet he also sought to conciliate the Jews by having the temple enlarged and rebuilt, so that it again took the form which it had had in the time of King Solomon. In the extensive work of building, the king took care that things were done exactly in accordance with the Law. The sanctuary was kept carefully covered, so that no one could look in. In the Diaspora also, Herod appeared as a protector of Judaism and encouraged the development of the distinctive life of the synagogue communities. In spite of this he did not succeed in gaining the approval of the devout Jews. Because of his harsh regime and the terror with which he suppressed every impulse of opposition, he remained an object of hatred for the great majority of the people.

Among the Hellenistic populace, Herod found more gratitude than among the Jews. On the site of the destroyed city of Samaria was erected a new city, which in honor of Augustus received the name of Sebaste (from the Greek *sebastos*, meaning, as did the Latin *augustus*, "the exalted one"). On the coast a harbor was built, which was protected against filling with sand by means of moles which were built out into the sea. The city there was adorned with rich edifices and also received the name of its exalted patron: Caesarea. Strong fortifications were placed throughout the country. In Jerusalem there arose the citadel Antonia, located directly on the temple square; from here Herod could keep a constant watch over the events which took place in and at the sanctuary. The strongest fortress he built on the western shore of the Dead Sea; there the stronghold Masada stood almost impregnable on the top of the mountain. In Jericho Herod had a palace built for himself, for use in the winter. Testimonies to this building activity are still to be seen in the country today: the so-called Wailing Wall has remained from the Herodian temple structure, and the foundations of the citadel Antonia are still preserved. Excavations in Jericho, Caesarea, Masada, and other places have for the first time brought to light the full scope of the huge works. While the fortification buildings served to make his rule secure, Herod sought to enhance his reputation by giving donations to foreign cities, to have buildings erected there in his honor. In doing this he did not hesitate also to promote pagan cults, thereby following the example of Hellenistic kings who sought to make a visible display of their generosity.

Although this king did much for the country, he remained an alien to the Jews. The people did have to obey him, but the strongest influence upon the thought and behavior of the populace was exerted by the Pharisees, who nourished the hope of a change to be brought about by God, but yet did not advocate any violent revolt. Toward the end of Herod's years John the Baptist and Jesus of Nazareth were born (Matt. 2:1; Luke 1:5). Having managed by skill and cunning to assert his dominion during a long period of rule, Herod sought before his death to determine the succession to his throne. He had arranged the murder of three of his sons who otherwise would have had claims to the inheritance. In the will which the king made shortly before his death, his kingdom was divided among his three sons *Archelaus, Herod Antipas,* and *Philip:* Archelaus was to become king and was to rule over Judea, Samaria, and Idumea; Antipas was to receive Galilee and Perea, which lay east of the Jordan; and Philip was to have the region east of the Jordan in the northern part of the kingdom. But this disposition could become legally effective only when the necessary confirmation had been granted in Rome. Hence after the death of Herod (4 B.C.) the three sons made the journey to the world capital, each of them with the intention of gaining as much profit as possible for himself. But the people of Jerusalem sent an embassy to Rome to petition that the rule of the Herodians be abolished and the independence of the Jerusalem cultic community be restored. Reference is made to these events in the parable in Luke 19:12, 14: "A prominent man went to a distant land to receive the royal crown for himself and then to return home. . . . But his citizens hated him and sent an embassy after him and said, 'We do not want this man to be king over us!'" Augustus did not accede to these wishes but, in essence, acted in accordance with Herod's will. Antipas and Philip were named tetrarchs, i.e., minor princes; Archelaus did not receive the title of king, but was given only the lesser one of ethnarch. Yet these distinctions in title meant nothing to the people; to them the rulers were kings, so that both Archelaus (Matt. 2:22) and Herod Antipas (Mark 6:14, 26; Matt. 14:9) are mentioned as kings in the New Testament. While the three sons of Herod were tarrying in Rome, unrest broke out in the land. Roman troops, under the command of Quintilius Varus, the governor in Syria, intervened and restored quiet and order. Nevertheless the anti-Roman attitude of the people became more intense because of the harshness and strictness of the measures taken. After the withdrawal of the troops the three princes took possession of the inheritance that had been promised to them.

Most hated by the people was *Archelaus,* who ruled so arbitrarily and with such brutal harshness (cf. Matt. 2:22) that the enslaved subjects once more sent an embassy to Augustus and so effectively lamented their plight that they gained a hearing. In A.D. 6 Archelaus was relieved of his office and exiled to Gaul. His territory was placed under the jurisdiction of a Roman governor, who ordered and had carried out a general census of the people in Syria and Palestine (cf. pp. 83, 211). Hence in Jesus' time Galilee and the northern part of the land east of the Jordan were under the rule of Jewish princes, while Samaria, Judea, and Idumea were ruled by the Roman governor (Luke 3:1).

The governor resided in Caesarea and went up to Jerusalem only occasionally, mostly on the high feast days of the Jews, since at those times numerous Jews came to the city as pilgrims and the probability of rebellious movements developing quickly among the assembled throngs thereby increased. In such cases it was advantageous for the governor to be physically present. The distinctive life of the cultic community and the activity of the priesthood and of the Sanhedrin were not tampered with. No images of Caesar were set up in the temple, and the Roman troops marched into the city without their banners. Since the supreme legal power was placed in the hands of the governor, the Sanhedrin could indeed regulate the affairs of the Jerusalem cultic community but could not pronounce and inflict the death penalty (John 18:31). In the citadel Antonia there was stationed only a small detachment of Roman soldiers, which was augmented at the time of the great feasts or when there was danger of disorder. Soldiers were recruited from the non-Jewish population of the country. Thus Acts 10:1 mentions a Gentile centurion, Cornelius, who served in Caesarea, the governor's seat. Paul also was taken there for examination of his case, after he had been arrested in Jerusalem (Acts 23:23, 33).

In the time of Jesus, *Pontius Pilate* held office as the Roman governor (A.D. 26–36). Philo of Alexandria reports that the conduct of his office was marked by "corruption, violence, depradations, ill treatment, offenses, numerous illegal executions, and incessant, unbearable cruelty" (*Legatio ad Gaium* 302). He had no regard for the religious sensitivity of the Jews and one night caused Roman banners bearing pictures of the emperor to be brought into Jerusalem. Only when the Jews declared that they would rather die than tolerate a violation of the Law did he finally give command to remove the banners from the city. Great unrest ensued when Pilate took money from the temple treasury in order to finance an aqueduct to Jerusalem. But Pilate suppressed rising resistance with force at its first manifestation. When a Samaritan prophet had proclaimed that sacred utensils from the time of Moses were buried on Mount Gerizim and a large throng had gathered on the mountain, Pilate commanded his soldiers to deploy and arbitrarily to attack the people. Many were killed, others imprisoned, and the rest fled. The indignation of the Samaritans was so great that they turned to Vitellius, the legate in Syria, and lodged complaints about Pilate with him. They succeeded in having Pilate recalled to Rome there to account for his conduct.

The description given of Pontius Pilate in the contemporary accounts is confirmed by the New Testament. When Galilean pilgrims once wished to offer sacrifices in Jerusalem, he incited a bloodbath among them (Luke 13:1). He ordered persons suspected of revolution arrested and killed (Mark 15:7 par.; 27 par.). So hard and ruthless was he, that it is not surprising that he condemned to death on the cross, after a brief hearing, a Jew whom the Sanhedrin had handed over to him as a politically suspect person. Thus Jesus of Nazareth died outside the gates of Jerusalem, subjected by the Roman governor to the most shameful punishment known to the ancient world.

In Galilee *Herod Antipas* ruled from 4 B.C. to A.D. 39. On the Sea of Gennesaret he built himself a residence which, in honor of the reigning emperor, he named Tiberias (cf. John 6:1, 23; 21:1). Since the city was built on the land of a former cemetery and therefore was regarded by the Law as unclean, the law-observing Jews refused to live there. Herod Antipas did not trouble himself about this, but conducted himself instead, according to his own pleasure and desire. He was first married to a daughter of the Nabataean king, but later took as his wife Herodias, who had been the wife of his half-brother—a Herod of whom nothing is otherwise known. In so doing he came into conflict with the Law, which permitted divorce (Deut. 24:1-4), but forbade taking one's brother's wife (Lev. 18:16; 20:21). Herodias was a granddaughter of King Herod and Mariamne, the daughter of Aristobulus, who, like his mother, had been put to death by Herod. The ambitious and vain Herodias became the wife of Herod Antipas, who divorced his first wife and sent her back to her father in the Nabataean kingdom. The new marriage produced the daughter Salome. Reference is made to these events in Mark 6:17-29 par., though there Philip is erroneously named as Herodias' first husband. Mark recounts that John the Baptist had held the ruler's wrongdoing plainly before his eyes, was cast into prison, further persecuted by Herodias' intense enmity, and finally murdered.

The marriage with Herodias brought misfortune to Herod Antipas. The indignant king of the Nabataeans waged war on his former son-in-law and inflicted on him a painful defeat. Josephus relates these events and says that many Jews regarded the defeat of Herod's army as a divine dispensation; for God had required just punishment of Herod for his treatment of John the Baptist. The account continues:

> Herod had had him executed, though he was a righteous man and had exhorted the Jews . . . to be baptized; baptism would be acceptable to God if it were applied, not to eliminate certain delinquencies, but to sanctify the body, since the soul is already purified by a righteous life. Since people now streamed to John the Baptist from all directions, because they felt themselves uplifted by such discourse, Herod began to fear that the influence of such a man, by whose counsel all were letting themselves be guided, could produce an uprising, and therefore he believed it to be better to render him harmless before the outbreak of such a danger than later to regret his indecisiveness if his power should be threatened. On this suspicion John was put in chains, sent to the fortress Machaerus . . . and there beheaded. (*Jewish Antiquities* XVIII, 116–19)

In this presentation, it is true, the Baptist's proclamation is described in the sense of a Hellenistic sermon on virtue (cf. p. 144), but the stimulating and impressive effect of his proclamation still is strikingly maintained.

Herod Antipas was the ruler of Jesus' country. When he learned of Jesus' appearance, he thought that John the Baptist, whom he had executed, had risen from the dead (Mark 6:14-16 par.). He expressed the wish to see the miracle man himself (Luke 9:9). But Jesus called him a fox (Luke 13:32) and made his way to Jerusalem. Only in Luke's Gospel is it reported that after a preliminary hearing Pilate sent Jesus to Herod Antipas, who also had come to Jerusalem for the Passover feast, so that he too might pass judgment (Luke 23: 6-16). This enlargement of the Passion narrative, however, represents a legendary expansion of the originally very brief story of Jesus' trial before the Roman governor. Just as according to Psalm 2:1-2 the kings of the earth rebel and the rulers take counsel together against Yahweh and his anointed one, so according to the Lukan portrayal, the Roman ruler and the Jewish prince stand in judgment over Jesus while the raging people demand his condemnation.

In the end it became Herod Antipas' fate that his wife, Herodias, suggest that he try to persuade Caligula to bestow upon him the title of king. The prince's efforts misfired. Caligula became suspicious and had Herod Antipas exiled to Gaul (A.D. 39).

In northern Transjordania *Philip* ruled. He built himself a new residence, which he called Caesarea Philippi (cf. Mark 8:27 par.). The Sea of Gennesaret formed the boundary between his territory and that of Herod Antipas, a boundary which then ran northward along the Jordan River. In Capernaum there was a small border and customs station, in which there was a detachment of Antipas' men, whose commander is mentioned in Matt. 8:5-13 (and par. in Luke 7:1-10). Philip was the first Jewish ruler to have coins minted bearing the likeness of the Roman emperor. Since the populace which he governed was Jewish only in a small part, he did not need to take any account of the Jews' reluctance to produce any human likeness. Philip died in A.D. 34 without leaving behind any descendants.

For a short time Palestine once more came under the rule of a Jewish king. *Agrippa*, a grandson of King Herod, had stayed in Rome, and there had been able to gain the favor of Caligula. In A.D. 37 Caligula gave him the territory which Philip had ruled, and two years later assigned to him the land of the exiled Herod Antipas. In A.D. 41 he was also given the rule over Judea, Samaria, and Idumea, so that under his scepter the entire kingdom which his grandfather had ruled was once more united. During this period a sharp conflict threatened to break out. When Caligula demanded that his statue be erected in the temple in Jerusalem, great excitement broke out among the Jews. People already envisioned the abomination of desolation set up in the holy place (cf. Mark 13:14 par.). Then in A.D. 41 Caligula was murdered; and his successor, Claudius, did not insist that divine reverence be paid to him in the temple of the Jews.

Herod Agrippa represented himself as a devout Jew concerned with exact observance of the Law. For this reason he was warmly praised by the scribes and Pharisees. But he displayed this attitude only among the Jews; toward the Hellenistic population of his kingdom he appeared in a different light. Here he behaved as a Hellenistic prince, who, following the example of his grandfather, sought to enhance his reputation by erecting numerous buildings. Moreover, at the same time that he humored the Pharisees, persecuted the Christian community in Jerusalem, had James the son of Zebedee executed, and had Peter thrown in prison (Acts 12:1-3), he had himself hailed in the Hellenistic environment as a divinely sent prince and accepted the divine veneration shown to the ruler (Acts 12:21-23). When he died, the rule was not given to his son. Instead the entire country was annexed to the province of Syria and was governed by Roman procurators, who were subordinate to the governor in Syria and once again took up their official seat in Caesarea.

Some years later Agrippa II received the territory which Philip had once ruled. He was also given the right to oversee the temple in Jerusalem. He made use of this right by making appointments to the office of the high priest as it suited him, and thereby aroused the displeasure of the people of Jerusalem. He also caused offense by keeping his sister Berenice constantly with him (Acts 25:13). It was told that the brother and sister lived in an incestuous relationship.

Throughout the country hatred against the Romans grew, and it repeatedly reached the point of erupting into disorder. The band of Zealots wanted to throw off the foreign rule by the use of force, and they found growing support among the people who saw themselves as being repeatedly tormented by the thoughtless or even malicious conduct of the Romans. Of the series of Roman procurators who were to govern Palestine in this period, two are mentioned by name in the New Testament. Beginning in A.D. 52, *Felix* occupied the office of governor. As a freedman he had climbed his way to this high position, which he had received through the favor of the Emperor Claudius. Tacitus says of him that he "maintained the royal law with a servile disposition by means of all sorts of cruelty and greed" *(History* V. 9). The second of his wives was the Jewish princess Drusilla, the daughter of Agrippa I, whom he had wrested from her husband. As Acts 24:24 reports, Paul had to make his defense before Felix and Drusilla during his imprisonment in Caesarea. Felix was replaced—probably in the year A.D. 60, but possibly earlier— by *Porcius Festus.* Although, in contrast to his predecessors, he was a man who thought and acted in accordance with the Law, he did not succeed in reducing tensions between Jews and Romans. His time in office, which ended with his death in A.D. 62, includes the last part of the imprisonment of Paul, whose trial was to be decided in Rome (Acts 24:27–26:32).

6. The Jewish War
and the Revolt Under Bar Cochba

The brutal conduct of the Roman occupation forces brought the Jewish people's hatred to a climax. When anti-Jewish demonstrations arose in Caesarea among the Hellenistic inhabitants, the Jews sought protection from the Romans, paid money, yet gained no assistance. Their anger over the behavior of the Romans continued. The greed of the procurator *Gessius Florus* was so boundless that in A.D. 66 he stole seventeen talents from the temple treasury. Indignant Jews derided the governor by going about in Jerusalem begging for money for the poor procurator. Gessius Florus became enraged over this and allowed his soldiers to plunder the city. He advanced two more cohorts from Caesarea and demanded that the Jews welcome the troops with ceremony. Prudent persons, especially the high priest and his followers, advised the people to yield and not to reject this demand. Thus the people were ready to submit to this profound humiliation. But when the people, following the directive, greeted the Roman soldiers, they, at the direction of the procurator, remained silent and did not return the Jews' greetings. At this there was no more restraint; the wrath of the humiliated people burst forth. The temple area was quickly occupied, and the governor had to retreat from the rebels to Caesarea. Only one cohort remained behind in Jerusalem in the strongly fortified citadel Antonia. Other than this the entire city was in the hands of the rebels.

What would happen now? Agrippa sought to persuade the Jews that armed resistance to Rome was sheer madness. The high priest, the priestly circles, and even the Pharisees urged moderation. But the raging fire could no longer be extinguished. The sacrifice which was offered daily for the Roman emperor was discontinued, and this was the signal for open revolt. Even the citadel Antonia could not withstand the onslaught of the uprising. It was seized, and so the entire city was in the hands of the Jews. The first success swept along many who at first had hesitated. Others who behaved in a suspect manner were either slain or compelled by force to join the movement. The high priest, who had attempted in vain to prevent the calamity, was murdered.

The Romans, who were taken by surprise by the rapid developments, were no longer masters of the situation. Cestius, the Roman governor in Syria, marched down with his troops. But he did not succeed in taking Jerusalem. He had to break off the campaign, and on the return march to Syria suffered a painful defeat. The jubilation of the Jews was great; the Romans had been driven from the land, and the yoke of foreign domination had been thrown off. Since a counter-blow was bound to be forthcoming, people hastily prepared to defend themselves. A strike force was to be formed of partisans, and in Galilee fortifications were built. Josephus, a young priest, was sent from Jerusalem to Galilee to direct the measures which were to be taken in the northern part of the country.

The Emperor Nero commissioned *Vespasian*, his ablest general, to conduct the war against the Jews. Vespasian went, with his son Titus, to the East. He advanced from Antioch with strong forces, and Titus brought troops from Egypt. The Romans' attack was directed first against Galilee. As the powerful army advanced, the Jews were seized with fear and retreated into the fortresses, so that the open country fell into the hands of the Romans without a struggle. Josephus entrenched himself along with his people in Jotapata, but could not hold out. When after a forty-seven-day siege the Jews' resistance collapsed, the Zealots demanded that all the rebels commit suicide. Josephus rejected this demand and was able to save himself by surrendering to Vespasian and predicting to him that he would gain the imperial crown. Vespasian spared Josephus' life, and from that time on, Josephus remained in the Roman headquarters. Thus he became an eyewitness and later a writer of the history of the entire Jewish War (cf. p. 141). John of Gischala, the leader of the Zealots, escaped with his small band to Jerusalem. In A.D. 67 all Galilee once again found itself in the hands of the Romans.

The decision had to be made in Jerusalem, and the radical groups in the city won the upper hand. The Zealots under John of Gischala seized the temple area, and the rest of the city was occupied by Simon bar Giora. The followers of the two commanders were hostile to each other and attacked each other; opponents of the war and those who were hesitant were subjected to harsh terrorism. About this time, the original Christian community, which did not participate in the uprising, must have left the city and migrated to Pella in the land beyond the Jordan. In the meantime, the Romans waited quietly for the situation in Jerusalem to develop. When in A.D. 69 Vespasian was called by his soldiers to become emperor, he traveled to Rome and handed the direction of the war over to his son Titus. During the Passover season in the year A.D. 70, when many pilgrims had come into the city once again, Titus marched on Jerusalem with four legions and strong auxiliary forces and surrounded the city with its inhabitants and the pilgrims. Since Jerusalem is situated on an elevation and an approach across level ground is possible only from the north, the attack was launched against the city from this side. In the face of the fearful threat, the fraternal conflict which had raged in the city up to that time was broken off in order to offer a common front of resistance to the Romans. However, against the greatly superior Roman military tactics the defenders' courage in battle and gallantry could not long hold out. Reference is made to this hopeless situation in the version of Jesus' discourse on judgment which is given in the gospel of Luke: "But when you see Jerusalem surrounded by armies, then you will know that its desolation is near" (Luke 21:20). "For the days shall come upon you [i.e., Jerusalem], when your enemies will cast up a bank about you and surround you, and hem you in on every side, and dash you to the ground, you and your children within you, and they will not leave one stone upon another in you" (Luke 19:43-44). Jewish resistance fighters who were captured were nailed by the Romans to crosses which were set up on the banks around the city, in order thereby to terrify its defenders. In the city, however, the Zealots held the reins in their hands with inexorable strictness and compelled the populace to stand fast. People indulged in the hope that in the last hour God would intervene and rescue his people. Even if the outer court of the temple should be seized by the Gentiles and the city and the forecourt should be trampled underfoot by them, still God would not abandon to them the holy place (Rev. 11:1-2).

Yet effort and hope were in vain. The Romans broke through all three surrounding walls which encircled the city and continued to press forward against the bitter resistance of the defenders. In the final battles the temple went up in flames. Titus was just able to push his way into the Holy of Holies before it collapsed. The seven-branched candlestick and the table of shewbread were seized as trophies, to be carried later in the triumphal procession which is still commemorated by a relief on the arch of Titus in Rome. The Gospel of Matthew, in its account of the parable of the royal wedding feast, mentions the destruction of Jerusalem by fire: the king was enraged by the fact that his invitation had been rejected and his servants shamefully slain, and he "sent his army, killed the murderers, and burned their city" (Matt. 22:7). The last groups of rebels who still tried to offer resistance were tracked down; John of Gischala and Simon bar Giora were captured and were taken along to Rome for the victory celebration. With the fall of the temple and the city, Judaism had lost its visible center.

Here and there resistance persisted; small groups of rebels had managed to withdraw into some fortified places. Those who held the fortress of Masada held out longest. The Romans surrounded the fortress, which is situated on a high, inaccessible mountain on the shore of the Dead Sea. Traces of the Roman siege and the outline of the Jewish fortification, which is a construction of King Herod, were recently uncovered by painstaking excavations by Israeli archaeologists. When the Jewish freedom fighters saw that their situation had become hopeless, they determined to commit suicide. The Romans, who shortly thereafter entered the fortress, found only dead bodies. Only two women, who had hid themselves along with five children in an underground water conduit, survived the end of the Jewish defense. With the fall of Masada, which occurred in A.D. 73—or perhaps not until 74—the last resistance was broken. After the victory, Vespasian ordered that Judea be separated from Syria and made into an imperial province. Its governor again held his office in Caesarea. The tenth Roman legion, which set up its camp in Jerusalem, was stationed in the country.

Judaism was able to survive the frightful catastrophe, because within it resided strong forces which made possible a new beginning. The Pharisees had stood in sharp opposition to the priesthood, which was predominantly of a Sadducean inclination. But in the destruction of Jerusalem the Sadducees were killed. The Pharisaic movement, led by scribes, was instrumental in stimulating the reconstruction of the Jewish communities which had gathered themselves together after the catastrophe, and conferred upon these communities their distinctive mark. Along with the temple, the sacrificial cultus also had fallen. The worship of Israel's God, however, could continue in the synagogues, into whose services parts of the temple liturgy now were also incorporated (cf. p. 160). In *Jabne* (Jamnia) a new Sanhedrin came together, this one composed not of priests and elders, but only of scribes. The Romans did not attack the rights which had been originally conceded to Judaism, so the synagogues continued to be under the protection of the civil authorities and the life of the communities was able to develop anew. The temple tax, which had been collected from every Jew in Palestine and in the Diaspora to defray the expenses of the cultus in Jerusalem, continued to be collected, but now had to be paid as a tax to the Romans.

In the second century A.D., Palestinian Judaism once more undertook to throw off the Roman yoke (A.D. 132–135). No connected account has been preserved of the events which occurred during the rebellion under the leadership of *Bar Cochba* (or *Bar Cosiba*, as his name appears in recently discovered texts). This second Jewish revolt had no historian. Isolated and brief references which are noted in ancient literary passages have been corroborated by discoveries which have been made in archaeological explorations in Palestine. Traces of the rebels, including letters and written records, have been discovered, so that the course of events can be reconstructed with some certainty.

Under the reign of the Emperor Hadrian (A.D. 117–138) there came a sudden uprising of the Jews. It probably was prompted by two decrees which Hadrian had issued. During a tour which he undertook through the Orient in A.D. 130/131, the emperor gave instructions for erecting new buildings. In that connection he ordered a shrine for Jupiter Capitolinus to be erected on the ruins of the temple in Jerusalem. Then, in a decree, Hadrian ordered a general prohibition of castration, with which at the same time circumcision also was forbidden. That a pagan temple should be erected in the holy place and that Israel should be deprived of its sign of the covenant evoked great resentment among the Jews. As a result, the rebels undertook, through a surprise attack, to bring Judea and Jerusalem under their control. They were successful, and the offering of sacrifices was resumed, coins were minted as a sign of the newly gained independence, and people began to date events in a new era, beginning with the first year of the revolt. The leader of the rebels was hailed by Rabbi Akiba, the most highly regarded biblical scholar of that time, as the promised "son of a star" of Numbers 24:17. The messianic age appeared to be dawning. Since the Jewish Christians who lived in Palestine could not agree with the messianic claim of Bar Cochba, they were bloodily persecuted by him and his followers. Anyone who refused to renounce Jesus as the Messiah was arrested; many were executed (cf. Justin, *Apology* I. 31).

The Romans proceeded slowly against the rebels, who did not offer pitched battles; they were compelled to seek them in the hiding places where they had taken refuge, to surround them, starve them out, and force them to surrender. The Jewish warriors' powers of resistance began gradually to disappear. In Wadi Murabba'at several documents from the time of Bar Cochba were found, among them a letter which was written by several leaders of the rebels to Jeschua ben Gilgola, a commander at the Dead Sea fortress. In this letter it is said that the Gentiles were attacking and therefore they could not come to him. And in a document which Simon bar Cochba addresses to the same recipient, he threatens him with having his feet bound in fetters if he does not break off relations with the Galileans. Perhaps those Galileans had not been willing to take part in the uprising, or the reference pertains to some unreliable people. In any case, however, the leader of the rebels was obliged to push with full energy for unconditional obedience to his commands. In place of the rejoicing with which at first many Jews proclaimed the uprising as Israel's liberation, there appeared ever increasing disillusionment.

When the Romans little by little closed in on the rebels, Bar Cochba entrenched himself with his faithful followers in Beth-Ter in Judea. Yet this fortress was conquered by the Romans, and Bar Cochba was slain in the battle. Therewith, the hope that he, as the Messiah, would usher in the time of salvation, was shattered. Because the unhappy turn of events unmistakably proved that Bar Cochba was not God's Anointed One, rabbinical Judaism later only rarely mentioned his name. But the charge was not made that he had blasphemed God. This accusation is not applied in Judaism to a false Messiah, but only when in the Jewish view the uniqueness of God is attacked (cf. John 5:18; 10:36).

On the ruins of Jerusalem a Roman colony was established, which received the name of Colonia Aelia Capitolina. There a temple was erected to Jupiter. The new city was inhabited only by non-Jews; the Jews were forbidden to set foot in it.

Filled with profound grief, the Jews annually commemorated, on the ninth day of the month Ab (this is at the end of July, or the first of August), the devastation of Jerusalem and the destruction of the temple. Beginning in the fourth century A.D., they were allowed on this day of grief to enter the city and to raise their prayers of lamentation at the wall which had been left standing from the Herodian temple.

Judaism once again had suffered the gravest losses; many scribes who had supported the rebellion were killed. Legend tells that Rabbi Akiba was frightfully tortured and his flesh raked with iron combs. But when the hour came in which the Jew is to utter the prayer "Hear, O Israel, the Lord our God is One" (Deut. 6:4), as an expression of his confession of faith, Akiba is said to have held the word "One" very long— as is required in prayer which is meritorious—and to have expired with this word on his lips. Thus he maintained loyalty to the Law to the very last moment of his life. The firmness with which the suffering and dying people held to the Law also strengthened the living and helped the severely smitten communities to bind themselves again to the Law and to cling to the faith of their fathers.

CHAPTER 2
Religious Movements
and Intellectual Currents in Judaism
in the Time of the New Testament

1. Apocalyptic

a. The Basic Structure of Apocalyptic

In the course of a history marked by so many vicissitudes,
wars, and distresses, Judaism found the question ever more
and more urgent as to when God would make his promises
come true. Because the divine assurances of deliverance stood
in sharp contrast to the present, which was filled with sorrow
and disturbance, the hope of the pious was oriented not to
events within history, but to the future turning point of the
world, by which all would be transformed. This expectation
is treated in the apocalyptic literature that appeared in the
beginning of the second century B.C. and lasted to the beginning of the second century A.D. The designation "apocalyptic"
is related to the first words in the book of Revelation and
uses the Greek word *apokalypsis* (meaning revelation) to
refer to the apocalyptic literature as well as to the ideas
which are expressed in it. No such comprehensive concept
is found in the literary documents of apocalyptic Judaism. It
is true, however, that in the various books which arose in this
period there is expressed and set forth a hope which is oriented to the end, a hope in which a particular basic structure
is consistently discernible in spite of many variations in the
specific formulation.

Apocalyptic thought does not anticipate that the course of
history will take a turn for the better; instead, it expects that
this world will come to an end amid frightful terrors. But

salvation will begin with the new world which God will bring forth, and it will be bestowed upon the pious in never ending glory. This world is subject to death and corruption, but that world will know no need and will bring the return of the conditions of paradise. "The Most High has created not one eon but two" (IV Ezra 7:50). "He has weighed the eon on the scales, he has measured the hours with the measure, and has numbered the times by number" (IV Ezra 4:36-37). By God's intervention, the course of history is brought to an end and his eternal rule begins. Thus Daniel beholds an immense figure with the head of fine gold, the breast and arms of silver, the belly and loins of brass, the thighs of iron, and the feet partly of iron, partly of clay. Then a stone, set in motion not by human hands, rolls against the statue, strikes its feet, knocks it over, and shatters it, so that iron, clay, brass, silver, and gold scatter and nothing remains (Dan. 2:31-35). This image is interpreted to mean that the various metals represent the successive rise and decline of world empires from the time of the Neo-Babylonians to Alexander the Great and the age of Hellenism. By their combination into a single figure, perspective is given to the whole of world history. The succession of rising and falling great empires is transformed into a unity to which God puts an end in order to establish his royal kingdom which shall never pass away, shall shatter all the kingdoms of this earth, but itself shall remain forever (Dan. 2:44).

The problem as to why this world has fallen into decline has always concerned the apocalyptists. In the painful events of history they discern God's punitive action being applied not just to the guilt of living men, but also to that of past generations. The more they reflect upon this question, the more comprehensive does the answer which they seek to give become. At last they see the ultimate and deepest reason for judgment being imposed upon this eon in the deed of Adam, who transgressed a commandment of God which was given to him. But the consequences of his deed have affected all his descendants, and the evil seed which sprang up in Adam's heart has borne its fruit (IV Ezra 4:30). For from this time on, all men must die. Thus through his disobedience Adam has brought death into the world and shortened the years of those who are descended from him (Syriac Baruch 23.4). Nevertheless, the fate of death has not only become the inescapable fate of humanity, but "if Adam first sinned and brought premature death upon all, still every one of those who descended from him has incurred future torment upon himself" (Syriac Baruch 54.15). As a consequence of the fall, Satan and his host were able to gain power over this world. Existence is miserable for this eon because the powers of darkness exercise their rule in it. The evil angels, the offspring of the fallen heavenly beings (Gen. 6:1-4), are demons which lead men astray into idolatry and wicked deeds. The dark hosts, which work mischief wherever they can, are in the command of God's adversary, who is characterized as Satan, the dragon, the angel of darkness, or Belial (or Beliar). He is striving for mastery over the world and is leading his army to battle against the pious in order to move them, through the troubles into which he plunges them, to apostatize. Ultimately he will mount the final and most dangerous attack against the holy city.

Because Adam himself has precipitated this fate and Satan with demonic forces practices his mischief in this world, this world must come to an end. To be sure, it continues to be God's creation; for God has made both eons: the present one, which must pass away, and the one to come. But sinful men and devilish forces have brought corruption upon this world, so that the judgment is irrevocably approaching. In the last time, men will fail in strength, dreadful sicknesses will rage among them and weaken them. Children will be born with the white hair of old men, miscarriages will increase, and women will cease to give birth at all. The earth will fail to bring forth fruit, seeds will be sown in the fields in vain, no more rain will fall, so that the land will dry up and vegetation will die off. One nation will rise up against another, wars will tear mankind to pieces; within families fathers will oppose and quarrel with sons, and brothers with brothers, so that there is no longer any peace anywhere, and everything is devastated and destroyed. When at last even the cosmic order disintegrates, the stars will no longer follow their regular courses and in the heavens dreadful signs will be visible. These catastrophes which follow quickly, one upon the other, are understood by the pious to be the woes through which the coming of God's new world is being announced. God is fighting victoriously against the evil forces, however dreadfully they may rage, and at the end he will triumph over Satan and his minions.

The certainty of the pious that the coming world will appear to replace the eon that is passing away is unshakable; for God has informed them about the times, so that they know what must yet happen before the end arrives. Therefore, numbers play a major role in apocalyptic. The course of the world is unfolding in individual eras, which sometimes are calculated in terms of a great world-week: after six thousand years will follow a sabbath of a thousand years. The oppression, on the other hand, is limited to a short period, as is indicated, for example, by the half of the number seven—three and one-half years (Dan. 7:25; 12:7). In Babylonia people knew of seven heavenly bodies. These were worshiped as deities and were thought to rule the course of the cosmos. The number seven therefore served the ancient world as the number signifying comprehensive fullness. The number four also is frequently mentioned: four seasons, four corners of the earth, four directions defining the order of the course of the world. The number twelve also is connected with the heavenly bodies: in twelve months the year traverses its course, so that the number twelve serves as a symbol of perfection or completeness. While the content of the meaning of the numbers was already provided by the tradition that came to Judaism from its Oriental environment, still apocalyptic now added meaning to the numbers through its expectation of the end-time. God alone knows its terms; he has determined how long the distress is to continue and how many pious ones must suffer and die before the end comes. His hand, therefore, directs the course of all that happens; he will shorten the final terrors in order to save the elect ones.

When the distress has reached its climax,

then God's rule over all his creation will appear; then will the devil come to an end and sorrow will be taken away. . . . The

Heavenly One will rise up from his throne and come forth from his holy dwelling in wrath and indignation because of his children. Then the earth will tremble, shaken to its very ends, high mountains will be shaken and brought low, and valleys will sink in. The sun will no longer give light and will be turned into darkness; the horns of the moon will be broken, and it will be wholly turned to blood, and the course of the stars will fall into confusion. The sea will recede into the abyss, and the springs of water will fail and the streams will congeal; for the most high God will arouse himself, he who alone is eternal, and will come forth openly to punish the heathen and to destroy all their idols. Then you, O Israel, will be happy. . . . And God will exalt you and cause you to stand in the starry heavens, at the place of your dwelling. Then you will look down from above and see your enemies upon earth and recognize them and rejoice and give thanks and confess your Creator. (*Ascension of Moses* 1. 1–10)

When with the Day of the Lord the end of the time of distresses has come, the Most High will take his seat upon the throne of judgment, the heavenly court of judgment will gather around him, and tens of thousands of angels will appear. Books will be brought forth in which all the deeds of men are inscribed, from which it can be seen what everyone has done, whether good or evil, and in which it is noted who is destined for life and who for death and corruption, so that judgment then can be pronounced and carried out without delay. All men must appear before God's bar of judgment—not only Jews, but also Gentiles; not only the living, but the dead as well.

From the beginning of the second century B.C., the *resurrection of the dead* was discussed in plain words in Judaism. At first it was said that only the righteous who had died before the dawning of deliverance would rise and participate in the future glory (cf. Luke 14:14: resurrection of the righteous). But with the growing anticipation of the world-judgment, the idea of the resurrection was soon expanded (cf. pp. 194–95), so that now people thought that not only would the righteous rise to blessedness, but all men would be raised from the dead in order to appear before God's judgment seat. In the interim, the souls of the dead are preserved in a heavenly place, but their bodies rest in their graves. On the last day, "the storerooms in which the souls of the righteous have been preserved will be opened, and they will go forth, and the many souls will become manifest all at once, as an assembly of a single mind" (Syriac Baruch 30. 2). However, the dead will first arise in the form in which they once lived upon the earth. In this way the identity of the resurrected man with the one who once lived is preserved, since he must account for his deeds. Only after the judge's sentence has been pronounced will the transformation take place: the righteous will be radiant with celestial brilliance, but the godless must go down into the underworld (Syriac Baruch 49–52).

In many cases the scene of the judgment is depicted in such a way that God alone sits on the throne and pronounces judgment. According to the apocalyptic conception, it is not necessary, in the course of eschatological events, that a messianic figure appear; for it is God and none other who holds judgment and brings in the new world. However, more than once there also appears in apocalyptic descriptions a messianic savior-figure; though his features, to be sure, clearly differ from the vision, expressed primarily among the Pharisees, of an eschatological ruler, not unlike David, who will appear as a king of Israel (cf. pp. 189–90). The divine emissary will issue from heaven to bring in the new eon, to drive away distress, illness, and death, to conquer Satan, and to restore paradise.

The figure of the heavenly *son of man* is first mentioned in Dan. 7:13-14. After the "Ancient of Days" has taken his place on his throne to pronounce his irrevocable judgment, there appears on the clouds of heaven one like a "son of man," who is brought before the Ancient of Days. The latter bestows upon him power, honor, and glory, that all peoples, nations, and tongues should serve him. Then at the end of the chapter the son of man is interpreted to mean the nation of the saints of the "Most High," to whom the kingdom, the glory, and the power are given (Dan. 7:27). In contrast to the beasts which, according to Dan. 7:4-8, represent the successively arising world-empire, the son of man symbolizes the people of God at the future time of salvation, who will not pass away as do all the nations and powers of this present age.

In the Similitudes of the Ethiopic apocalypse of Enoch (37-71), the son of man is set over and against the people of God and is described as the savior and judge who will appear in heaven. In a vision the seer beholds the divine judge on the throne, who has the head of an old man, white as wool. "And there was another with him, whose face was like the appearance of a man, and his face was full of grace like one of the holy angels" (Eth. Enoch 46:1). In response to the seer's question as to who this is, the angel who is showing him all mysteries answers: "This is the Son of man, who has righteousness, with whom righteousness dwells, and who reveals all the treasures of that which is hidden; for the Lord of Spirits has chosen him, and through uprightness, his lot has surpassed all others before the Lord of Spirits forever. This son of man whom you have seen will remove the kings and the mighty from their seats and the powerful from their thrones; he will loosen the reins of the strong and will break the teeth of the sinners" (Eth. Enoch 46:3-4). He will exercise his office as judge and will topple the kings of the earthly kingdoms from their thrones, take away from them the rule, and hold judgment over all the godless ones. But he will act as savior to redeem the righteous, to lead the community of the chosen ones to freedom, to celebrate the messianic banquet with his people (Eth. Enoch 62:13-16), and to rule as the new king of paradise (Eth. Enoch 69:26-29).

The *sentence of judgment* which is pronounced at the Last Day is final and irrevocable. No more opportunity will be afforded the godless and sinners to be converted and to abandon their evil ways. They are handed over to eternal damnation from which there is no more escape, and in the darkness and eternal torment into which they are cast must remain in utter alienation from God. But the righteous will enter into eternal fellowship with God and will enjoy the unending joy of paradise. God himself will dwell above them, the celestial glory is opened to them, there will be no more pain and sickness, no sin and no evil. In undisturbed peace the meadows will be green and the fields will bear superabundant fruit. The pious will live in the inexpressible joy which comes with God's new world.

The *end of the old world* is occasionally described in terms of a destruction by an immense conflagration. In the place of that world appear the new heaven and the new earth, which are already spoken of at the end of the book of Isaiah (Isa. 65:17; 66:22). The dawning of the new world is sometimes thought of in these terms: Jerusalem, Zion, and the Holy Land are transformed, so that they become the garden of paradise. Alternatively, some imagined that the new world already exists in readiness in heaven and at the end of time will come down to earth. The new Jerusalem is already present with God, preexistent, and it will then appear in marvelous brilliance in the place of the old city. God had already constructed the heavenly city, when he determined to create paradise. Adam was permitted to behold it before the fall, and Abraham and Moses were allowed to glimpse a picture of it (Syr. Bar. 4. 2–6). The city, constructed of precious building materials, adorned with jewels, and fortified with immense walls and towers, will occupy a much greater area than the Jerusalem that is fallen in ruins, and at God's command will extend so far that it will provide a place for all who are permitted to belong to the Israel of the time of salvation and to live in the place of the blessed in glorious splendor.

The basic structure of apocalyptic, which in spite of its great diversity of pictures and expressions is everywhere recognizable in the individual writings, is marked by *dualism:* this world is passing away—another world is coming. Because the turning point is already being announced in the tribulations of the present time, it cannot be long until the suffering comes to an end and bliss becomes the lot of the righteous. Whatever terror may yet befall the community of the pious cannot affect the certainty that redemption is near.

This basic dualistic structure of apocalyptic cannot be explained solely in terms of the continuation of Old Testament, Jewish tradition. It is true that *Old Testament* tradition in abundant measure is incorporated and employed in apocalyptic, to give expression to the hope that is oriented to the end. In the prophetic writings, particularly in those

which arose in the period after the exile, discussions of judgment and redemption, the new heaven and the new earth
are included. The apocalyptists, who see themselves as heirs
of the Old Testament prophets, refer to these ideas. But
beyond this, the eschatological expectation which they pro-
pound is furnished with various features which are not taken
from the Old Testament. The judgment is not only passed
upon the heathen nations who dwell on Israel's borders, and
it not only affects the Jews, but it is held as a world-judgment
upon the living and the dead. The dead will arise from their
graves, then to go either into eternal damnation or into
eternal joy. The change from the old to the new eon has
cosmic proportions; everything, both heaven and earth, will
be affected by this event.

In the Persian Empire, Jews and followers of the *Iranian
religion* lived side by side in peaceful neighborliness, so that
many contacts between them could develop. The Iranian religion is marked by a sharp dualism: the good God stands
over against the evil God, and the two are in conflict with
each other. The contest between these two powers, which
runs through all the history of the world, is gradually leading to the superiority of the good over the evil. At the end of
the world the dead will be awakened to life. A fire will fall
from heaven and will destroy the old world, but all mankind
must pass through the fire. For some it will be like a bath in
warm milk, but for others it will bring dreadful torments,
which nevertheless will have a purifying effect, so that ultimately all men will be saved. At the end, however, the
powers of evil will be conquered and disarmed.

Judaism developed the basic dualistic structure of apocalyptic by adopting Iranian conceptions and combining them
with the confession of the God of Israel as Lord of the world:
that eon stands over against this eon. A hard struggle against
the satanic power must be endured. The dead will be awakened, and then will follow the judgment and the redemption
of the end-time. The appropriation of eschatological conceptions from Iranian religion was made possible by the fact
that in Judaism the preconditions existed for giving expression in a new way to the old faith with the help of the perspectives which came from Iran. For the Jews, Yahweh was

not only the Lord of his people, but the Lord of the history of all peoples, of the entire world. Nevertheless, the Iranian ideas did not remain unaltered, but were remolded, as to their content, from the perspective of the belief in Yahweh to which they were made serviceable. Judaism could not speak of an evil God who stands over against the good God as a counterpart of equal rank. While Satan is regarded as a fallen angel, far less powerful than God, God is and remains the Creator, who has allowed to the evil powers a definite time in which they may practice their mischief. In his hand lies the rule of the world that is passing away and of the world that is to come. This picture of the eschatological event which is formed in apocalyptic expands the earlier view, which was restricted to the boundaries of Israel, so that the horizon is enlarged at the same time that Israel's self-understanding is altered. For by Israel's confessing its God to be Lord of all the world, it no longer understood itself primarily as a fellowship of a people, but preeminently as the community of the elect which stands under the lordship of God, whose rule will become manifest to all the world.

The *eschatological expectation of the first Christians* frequently made use of apocalyptic concepts and ideas which Judaism had developed. Jesus preaches the imminent coming of the kingdom of God (Mark 1:15 par.), but very decisively rejects the demand for a calculation of the times and seasons (Luke 17:20-21). His preaching, therefore, in contrast to apocalyptic, is free of any and all legalism and announces the dawning of the kingdom of God as the great good news. The primitive Christian communities expected in the near future the appearance of the Lord to liberate his people and to judge the whole world. This eon is passing away (I Cor. 7:31), but the coming of the Son of man is announced amid war and distress, oppression, and cosmic upheavals (Mark 13:1-27 par.). Just as in Jewish apocalyptic either God alone is represented as the judge or the Son of man is described as the one commissioned by God to execute judgment, so also in the eschatological expectation of primitive Christianity the judgment seat of God is sometimes spoken of (Rom. 14:10), and other times the judgment seat of Christ (II Cor. 5:10), without any difference in meaning intended thereby. For the Son of man/Messiah acts by virtue of divine authority and exercises his office at the direction of the Most High. Because no one knows the day and hour of the end (Mark 13:32 par.), all must be constantly ready and watchful. Indeed, with Christ the new creation has already dawned; for anyone who is in Christ is already—here and now—a new creature (II Cor. 5:17). Hence he may no longer allow himself to be molded by the shaping force of this eon (Rom. 12:2) and may not follow the wisdom of this world, to which the word of the cross appears as folly (I Cor. 1:20); for Christ has given himself for our sins in order to snatch us from the present evil eon (Gal. 1:4). While in Jewish apocalyptic the change from the old eon to the new can be represented without the involvement of a messianic figure, the eschatological hope of the Christians cannot. Their faith in the crucified and resurrected Messiah, whom they expect as the Coming One, is absolutely determinative and crucial. Hence when apocalyptic conceptions were absorbed into the Christian communities, they were filled with new content from Christology, in order now to serve the purpose of unfolding and developing the Christian proclamation.

The Christians not only referred to various ideas from Jewish apocalyptic, but also read apocalyptic writings and interpreted the promises expressed therein to refer to the salvation that had become manifest in Christ. In order clearly to distinguish itself from the Christian faith, rabbinical Judaism, which after the two unsuccessful revolts once again gathered together the synagogue communities, dissociated itself from the apocalyptic books and rejected them. This distinction was so sharply drawn that the apocalyptic books in the synagogues were destroyed and only a very few apocalyptic texts have been preserved in the original Hebrew language. Most of the writings are handed down in translations, in which they have been read and handed on by Christians.

b. Apocalyptic Literature

The knowledge about the coming exchange of the eons and the plan which God has for the world has been imparted to the apocalyptists by means of secret revelations. In dreams, ecstatic raptures, and visions the future event is viewed. Whereas the Old Testament prophets received God's message primarily in words and handed it on through proclamation, apocalyptic avails itself of picture and parable, gives them a thoroughgoing interpretation, and proceeds to communicate the divine instruction. Where once the prophets preached directly to the men of their time, the apocalyptists compose literary works. They conceal their message in the veil of mystery to give it a particularly magnetic appeal, and they issue their apocalyptic books under the name of a great pious figure of the past. Behind the names of Enoch, Abraham, Jacob and his sons, Moses, Baruch, Daniel, Ezra, and others are concealed the anonymous authors of Jewish apocalypses. They let these men of God speak and predict the course of history. The previous history, from the days of the Old Testament prophets to the time of the writing of the apocalyptic book, is described as though the man of God had seen its course in detail in advance. As this prophetic vision heretofore has been precisely fulfilled *(vaticinia ex eventu),* so also will be the further predictions having to do with the events of the end. The occurrences which precede the end of this world are illustrated by diverse visions, richly imagined. The presentation of the interchange of the eons and of the new creation forms the conclusion of the variegated succession of scenes.

The pious ones of the Old Testament who according to the portrayal of the apocalyptic books were granted such visions have closed and sealed their writings, intending that in years to come, in the time of distress, they should be opened and read. Because the present moment in which the apocalyptists are writing stands in immediate anticipation of the end, the content of the apocalyptic writings now is being communicated to the community, in order to comfort it in its affliction. For it now knows about the coming end and the promised glory.

Apocalyptic sections are already found in some of the later Old Testament writings, as in the book of Zechariah and in chapters 24–27 of Isaiah, the latest part of the entire book of Isaiah. The earliest apocalyptic writing is handed down under the name of *Daniel.* In its first part it takes up stories in which we are told of the conduct of Daniel and his friends who are faithful to the Law in the Babylonian court (chaps. 1–6) ; in the second part (chaps. 7–12) , the prophetic visions beheld by Daniel of the events of the last time are described. The succession of the four great world empires, which are represented by four terrible beasts, develops into the rule of the *diadochi* and the godless tyranny of the Syrian King Antiochus IV, whose measures against Judaism are mentioned in the context of the prophetic utterances: "His armies will come and desecrate the holy place and the fortress, and put an end to the daily sacrifice and set up the abomination of desolation" (Dan. 11:31) . The historical events which preceded the Maccabean revolt are portrayed in precise detail and are set in the context of cosmic events. Until Daniel 11:39 the historical process is merely clothed in the aura of prediction, but then begins the genuinely predictive section: Antiochus will die in the campaign against Egypt (Dan. 11:40–45) . Actually, however, the Syrian king did not die in Egypt, but in the Orient, in 164 B.C. Hence the book of Daniel must have been written in the time between 167 and 164 B.C. to say to the community that the time of distress will not last long, and then God will intervene and put an end to the oppression. In dreams and visions the seer is told what will happen in the last time: "In the first year of Belshazzar, the king of Babylon, Daniel had a dream and a vision as he lay upon his bed; and he wrote down the dream" (Dan. 7:1) . The seer is not immediately able to grasp the meaning of what he has seen, so a clarifying explanation is required: "I, Daniel, was disturbed, and this vision frightened me. And I went to one of those who stood there and asked him to tell me more precisely about all this. And he spoke with me and told me what it meant" (Dan. 7:15-16) . The portrayal of what is to come develops into the challenge to stand firm in the appointed time of distress: "Blessed is he who holds fast" till the time of the end (Dan. 12:12) . While the book of Daniel has been accepted, as one of the latest writings, into the group of the canonical books of the Old Testament, no other book from among the multiplicity of apocalypses which soon thereafter emerged gained canonical recognition. Yet these books, in which secret knowledge is imparted to the pious, found wide distribution within Judaism.

Two books have been handed down under the name of Enoch, one of them in the Ethiopic language (Eth. Enoch) and the other in Slavonic (Slav. Enoch). The *Ethiopic book of Enoch,* which goes back to a Hebrew or Aramaic original, belongs to the Old Testament canon of the Ethiopic church and has been handed down in that church. The book contains quite diverse materials and can be characterized as a small library in which several writings are combined. An introductory exhortation (chaps. 1–5) is followed by a broader context in which an account is given of the fall of the angels (Gen. 6:1–4) and their fate, as well as an account of a journey of Enoch through the world and the underworld (chaps. 6–36). The so-called Similitudes (chaps. 37–71) represent an independent unit; they provide a glimpse into the imminent events of the end. Transported by clouds and winds to the end of the heavens, Enoch sees the dwelling places of the righteous and beholds the Son of man, whom the Lord of Spirits has destined to be judge in the world-judgment and to be savior of the elect. The meaning of the visions is from time to time explained to Enoch by an angel. Chapters 72–105 are astronomical passages that include commentary on the course of the stars, visions of the future, and hortatory statements. Chapters 106–8 conclude the entire book, whose various sections certainly were not all written at the same time. While some parts of the Similitudes stem from the Maccabean era, the latest parts could only have arisen under Roman rule. It cannot be determined with certainty when the Similitudes were composed. Nevertheless, the fact that none of the Similitudes was included among the fragments of the book of Enoch found among the writings of the Qumran community is not enough to warrant the inference that the portrayal of the Son of man was first sketched in Christian times. Rather, the materials which are used in the Similitudes may be clearly identified, in terms of the history of the tradition, as pre-Christian in origin. The final redaction of the entire book, however, which combines cosmological and astronomical traditions of non-Jewish origin with genuinely Jewish traditions, can hardly have taken place earlier than about the time of the birth of Christ. The fact that the book enjoyed great favor not only in Judaism but also in early Christianity is proved also by a quotation from the Enoch apocalypse in Jude 14–15: "But it was also about them (i.e., the godless heretics) that Enoch, the seventh from Adam, prophesied and said: 'Behold, the Lord comes with many thousands of saints, to hold judgment upon all and to punish all the godless ones for all the works of their ungodly conduct with which they have been ungodly, and for all the insolence which the ungodly sinners have uttered against him' " (cf. Enoch 1:9).

Slavonic Enoch, which goes back to a lost original in the Greek language, exhibits, as far as contents are concerned, many connections with Ethiopic Enoch, is certainly dependent upon the latter, and thus arose somewhat later. Enoch travels through the seven heavens and is given information by God about the process of creation. The descriptions in the book range from the creation of man to the threat of imminent judgment and then again develop into an exhortation to faithfulness and steadfastness. The fact that the original language was Greek indicates that the book was composed in the Diaspora, presumably in Egypt, about the middle of the first century A.D.

Under the title of *Ascension of Moses* is preserved in the Latin language the fragment of an apocalypse which was originally composed in Hebrew or Aramaic. It reproduces an address which Moses delivers, before his departure, to his successor Joshua, entrusting to him his legacy and predicting the course of Israel's history from the taking of the land onward. When the outline of history turns into the announcement that an impudent and ungodly king will rule for thirty-four years, and the end will come shortly thereafter, reference clearly is made to the just completed reign of King Herod. A man named Taxo (probably meaning "One who puts [Israel] in order") will appear, who will come from the tribe of Levi and with his seven sons will suffer martyrdom; then the great turning point will be immediately imminent. The fragment concludes with the admonition addressed to Joshua to preserve the foregoing discourse. The ascension of Moses must have been related in the last part of the work, which has been lost. A clause from this no longer extant section is cited in the epistle of Jude, where in verse 9 it speaks of the struggle of Michael with Satan over the body of Moses.

An apocalyptic writing which was composed under the name of Ezra seeks to answer the tormenting question of why Jerusalem was abandoned and destroyed. The Latin church, which has handed down a translation of this book written originally in Hebrew, identifies it as IV Ezra. This numbering comes about because the Old Testament writings of Ezra and Nehemiah are counted as I and II Ezra, and an apocryphal writing which, making use of pieces of Ezra and Nehemiah, describes the history of the cultus in Jerusalem, is counted as III Ezra. The seer of IV Ezra, who is supposed to have received his revelation in the thirtieth year after the destruction of Jerusalem by the Babylonians—thus in 557 B.C.— relates: "In the thirtieth year after the fall of the city, I, Salathiel (who am also called Ezra), was sojourning in Babylon, and as I once lay upon my bed, I fell into disquiet, and my heart was engaged with my thoughts, because I saw Zion devastated, but Babylon's inhabitants in abundant wealth. Then my spirit was greatly stirred, and in my distress I began to speak" (IV Ezra 3:1-3). The grave consequences of Adam's fall have finally been worked out in the fate of Jerusalem. But why has God smitten his people so hard, and why does he let things go so well for the heathen and the ungodly? The creation has grown old and is moving toward the time of the end. Just as a shower of rain passes by, leaving isolated raindrops falling in its wake, so also is the measure of the past far greater than the time yet remaining, which is comparable to the last few drops (IV Ezra 4:49-50). The harvest is ripe, and the judgment is coming (IV Ezra 5:56-6:6). After the end, however, the new world will appear, the reason for joy and hope. But first the judgment awaits, which even the pious fear. "What good will it be for us then that eternity is promised to us, if we have done the works of death?" (IV Ezra 7:119). "For alas! while we lived, when we sinned we did not consider the woes which await us after death!" (IV Ezra 7:126). "Truly, there is no one born of woman who does not sin, no one living who has

not gone astray" (IV Ezra 8:35). Therefore God has every
right to intervene with severity and to punish men. For since
the fall of Adam there is not one among them who is righteous, not one who deserves salvation.

The *Syriac apocalypse of Baruch* refers to the ideas of IV
Ezra, which arose some time after A.D. 70. This writing also
was originally composed in Hebrew, but it is preserved only
in a Syriac translation. First, the destruction of Jerusalem is
foretold to Baruch, the helper of the prophet Jeremiah; later,
on the ruins of the city Baruch laments over its fall. The
imminence of the future judgment, which will also break in
upon the heathen, is announced to him. As in IV Ezra, the
fate of death to which all men have fallen victim is traced
back to Adam's fall, the evil consequences of which have
affected the whole of humanity. But with the imminent end
the glory of the returning age of paradise also will begin.
Since the Syriac apocalypse of Baruch presupposes IV Ezra,
the time of its appearance is to be placed somewhere about
the end of the first or the beginning of the second century
A.D.

Alongside the Syriac book, there is also a *Greek apocalypse
of Baruch,* which is to be dated the second century A.D. Baruch
is troubled over the destruction of Jerusalem, he is comforted
and introduced to God's secrets. Led by the hand of an angel,
he travels through the five heavens, is permitted to see the
place of the blessed and the place of the damned, and receives
the promise that God will take him unto Himself.

In many Jewish writings which appeared in the time from
the second pre-Christian century to the beginning of the
second century A.D., one finds shorter and longer sections in
which apocalyptic material has been used. In the *Testaments
of the Twelve Patriarchs,* didactic and admonitory sections
are interwoven with passages having an apocalyptic content.
Each of the sons of Jacob delivers, before his death, a discourse in which he gives to his descendants instructions for
the future. The various traditions which underlie this writing
are loosely tied together by editors who provided a framework for the whole, and then in the Christian Era these
traditions underwent still another revision, whereby in isolated

71

passages, promises which relate to the future and which have christological allusions are supplied. The history of this scripture indicates that the Christian church took over the apocalyptic books of Judaism and gave them a new Christian interpretation by inserting references to the message of Christ wherever points of possible contact were found. This, for example, in the Testament of Benjamin it is said that Jacob cried out: " 'O child Joseph, you have overcome the heart of your father Jacob.' And he embraced him and kissed him for two hours, saying: 'In you will be fulfilled a promise of heaven [concerning the Lamb of God and the Savior of the world], that an innocent one shall be delivered up for godless men and a sinless one shall die for sinners [in the blood of the covenant, for the salvation of the Gentiles and of Israel, and that he will destroy Beliar and his servants]' " (Test. Benj. 3:8). The words enclosed in brackets are missing in a shorter version of the text which is preserved in an Armenian translation, and they clearly are linked to the hand of a Christian editor who later inserted them. In imitation of Greco-Roman books of the Sibylline Oracles, there developed Jewish collections of Sibylline sayings which later were expanded in Christian versions. In that process, along with many other materials, apocalyptic traditions were also employed—especially in the third and fourth books—to describe the events of the end-time (cf. p. 124).

Finally, the belief and thought of the *Qumran* community also was strongly influenced by apocalyptic conceptions (cf. pp. 99–110). In their writings, particularly in the so-called War Scroll, the battle is described which will take place in the last times between the sons of light and the sons of darkness. Michael and his angels fight against Belial and his host. In the writings of the Qumran community not only the present but also the past is considered in the context of this conflict, so that apocalyptic motifs found their way into the historical perspective, as it is given in the Damascus Document, and into the exposition of the Old Testament books of prophecy, which are related to the experiences of the community (cf. p. 95).

With respect to the question of the relationship of the

apocalyptic books to the canonical writings of the Old Testament, the legend which is recounted at the end of IV Ezra (14:18-48) provides information. Ezra laments the fact that with the destruction of Jerusalem the law of God has been burned up, so that now no one knows God's will and his deeds. He prays for the gift of the Holy Spirit, that he might be able, with the assistance of the Spirit, to write down what has happened since the beginning of the world and what was written in God's law, so that men might find the right way to eternal life. After Ezra has received the promise of divine assistance, he is able within forty days, with the help of five scribes, to write down ninety-four books. "Now when the forty days were ended, the Most High spoke to me, saying: 'You shall publish the twenty-four books which you have written first, for the worthy and the unworthy to read; but the last seventy you shall keep back and give only to the wise among your people. For in them flows the spring of understanding, the fountain of wisdom, the stream of knowledge'" (IV Ezra 14:45-47). Thus in the apocalyptic books there is to be unfolded what has been imparted to everyman in the canonical books as God's will and law, so that God's word and commandment is contained in the apocalyptic tradition just as it is in the Holy Scripture. But in the apocalypses it is the wise, who can comprehend, that are addressed, in order to communicate to them understanding, wisdom, and knowledge. Now anyone who has been counted worthy to gain insight into God's plan of history for the end-time is all the more under obligation to act according to the knowledge which is given to him, to receive the comfort of the divine promise, to turn from the wrong way, and to prepare himself for the approaching end by keeping God's commandment. Thus the apocalyptic writings constitute the admonition of the pious community and the summons to faithful steadfastness. To be obedient to this summons was the intention of the groups and communities which were formed in Judaism in the course of the second and first centuries B.C. and which were all the more solidly united by virtue of their constant inquiry into the proper understanding of the law and their striving to translate it into deeds.

2. Groups and Communities in Palestinian Judaism

a. The Sadducees

The Jewish historian Josephus describes for his Hellenistic readers the groups and communities which were present in Judaism at the beginning of the first century A.D., following the example of the Greek philosophical schools: "Among the Jews there are three kinds of philosophical school; one is formed by the Pharisees, a second by the Sadducees, and the third, which lives in accordance with particularly strict rules, by the so-called Essenes" (*The Jewish War II*, 119). The Sadducees were repeatedly compared by the rabbis with the Epicureans, whose philosophy was wholly oriented to this life (cf. p. 244). Since the Sadducees disappeared with the destruction of Jerusalem in A.D. 70, hardly any direct accounts of them have been preserved. Nevertheless, one can strongly affirm that the Sadducees were anything but a philosophical school whose views would be comparable to those of the Epicureans. But who were the adherents to that group who were called the Sadducees?

The label "Sadducees" certainly is to be connected with the name Zadok who, long ago under King Solomon, was installed as high priest (I Kings 2:35) and from whom, as their ancestor, the priests traced their lineage. In the sketch of the future of Israel, of the land, and of the sanctuary which is presented in Ezekiel 40–48, the priestly ministry is committed to the sons of Zadok (Ezek. 40:46; 43:19; 44:15; 48:11). Then in the construction of the postexilic community the Zadokites played a crucial role and as the legitimate priests in Jerusalem, took care of the temple service.

In the confusion under the rule of the Syrian King Antiochus IV the old Zadokite dynasty of high priests came to an inglorious end. Jason, who was friendly to the Greeks, supplanted his brother Onias and directed his actions toward the promotion of Hellenism. The Maccabean revolt presented a roadblock to the increasing influence of the hellenizing process. Then when the Hasmoneans for some time thereafter took over the high priest's office, although they were not of Zadokite origin, there still were sons of Zadok in the temple in Jerusalem who functioned as priests. In the long run, the

Hasmoneans could rule only if they established a compatible relationship with the priestly aristocracy in Jerusalem, who, in turn, could exert an influence on the political events only if they engaged in collaboration with the ruling house. Of course the entire priesthood was not prepared to do this. A group of priests who were faithful to the Law gathered around the Teacher of Righteousness and formed a company who insisted on a painstaking observance of the cultic provisions of the Law (cf. pp. 99–100). Thus came about the conflict with the high priest which led to the necessary withdrawal of this community from the temple and establishment of a settlement on the west bank of the Dead Sea, in which the community of the covenant gathered together under the leadership of "sons of Zadok, the priests who keep the covenant" (1QS V. 2.9). The priests who remained in Jerusalem continued to function in the temple and to approve accommodation to the Hasmoneans, thereby distinguishing themselves from these Zadokites.

From the circles of the Jerusalem aristocracy arose the company of the Sadducees, which was composed predominantly of holders of the high priestly offices and members of the influential Jerusalem families. Their heritage gave them a conservative stamp; the offices and positions which they held, however, committed them to practical action and to a realistic estimate of their situation. Therefore they found themselves ready to adjust to existing political realities. Under the rule of Queen Salome Alexandra their influence significantly declined (cf. p. 33). Since Pharisaic scribes had been admitted to the Sanhedrin, the Sadducees, though they continued to be in the majority, were compelled constantly to give attention to Pharisaic views.

The Sadducees held strictly to the literal wording of the Law and refused to admit to equal rank with the written letters the oral tradition which the Pharisees treasured. There were also some scribes, biblical scholars, among the Sadducees, who had to study and to decide questions on the interpretation of the Law. It was in keeping with their sober thought that they did not believe in angels and demons (Acts 23:8). Above all, they did not share in the expectation that at the last day the dead would be raised from the grave. By the question which, according to Mark 12:18-27 par., they posed to Jesus, they wanted to show that there can be no resurrection of the dead. A woman had seven husbands in succession; one after another they preceded her in death, and then finally she too died. Would the woman then have seven husbands at the last day? Jesus rejects this notion as absurd. For when they rise from the dead, they will neither marry nor be given in marriage; the life after death can in no way be compared with earthly relationships. But the hope of the resurrection of the dead is grounded in the Law of Moses: God is the God of Abraham, and the God of Isaac, and the God of Jacob (Exod. 3:6). Because God is not a God of the dead, but of the living, the names of the fathers whose God he is are a guarantee that the dead are raised.

The Sadducees were even more strictly concerned than the Pharisees that the sabbath be maintained with painstaking care, and they did not attempt to find some escape or another, by means of any calculated casuistry, to weaken the sabbath commandment or to avoid it. Penalties that were imposed had to correspond precisely to the prescriptions of the Law, so that a death penalty pronounced by a Jewish court always was to be executed by stoning.

Political prudence and skillful action, which the Sadducees had already displayed under the Hasmoneans, made it possible for them to occupy the highly regarded offices in Jerusalem under Herod and the Roman governors also. The high priests, whom the current holders of power placed in their office, were always chosen from their circles. As the Sadducees had always been concerned with linking their beliefs with an attitude of receptiveness to the world at large, they recognized the existing government and strove to moderate the hostility toward the Romans which was increasing among the people. They were opponents of the Zealots, who called for active resistance, but also of the Pharisees, who took a position of inward rejection of the Gentile authorities. Actually, however, the power and influence of the Sadducees was limited, as Josephus explicitly relates: "For whenever they gained office, they held firm—even though under compulsion and unwillingly—to what the Pharisees say, because otherwise the people would not tolerate them" (*Jewish Antiquities*

XVIII. 17). When the revolt against the Romans broke out, they attempted in vain to prevent the armed conflict. The fall of Jerusalem sealed their fate as well. With the death of the Sadducees in the destruction of the city and the temple, the reconstruction of the Jewish communities fell solely to the Pharisees, who had survived the catastrophe.

b. The Pharisees

The name Pharisee must be a derivation from the Hebrew *peruschim* or the Aramaic *perischaya* (meaning "the separated ones"). It is possible that this designation was first applied to them by outsiders, because they held themselves aloof from their environment, in order, as God's holy community, to avoid contact with any impurity. The name came to be used generally because in fact it correctly emphasized an essential feature of the Pharisaic movement. Hence the Pharisees were no more a philosophical school, as Josephus wished to describe them, than were the other groups which were formed in Judaism (*Jewish War* II. 119; *Jewish Antiquities* XVIII. 11).

The beginnings of the Pharisaic movement date to Maccabean times, when it was necessary to defend the Jewish faith against the infiltration of Hellenistic influence. In I Maccabees 2:42 there is mention of "a company of pious Jews, brave men from Israel, none but those who willingly submitted themselves to the law." Out of these circles of the *chasidim* i.e., "the pious ones", who supported the Maccabean rebellion, issued the Pharisees, a group of law-observing Jews who did not have political aims, but who were filled solely by zeal for the law by which Israel was supposed to lead its life (I Macc. 7:13). When proper worship and life in accordance with the law were restored, therefore, the Pharisees separated themselves from the Hasmoneans, who displayed a striving for political power. There arose not only an estrangement between them and the ruling house, but under Alexander Jannaeus, there even erupted a bloody conflict, in which the high priest gained the upper hand by means of terror and execution of the rebels (cf. pp. 30–31). From that time on, the Pharisees gave up striving for a change in the political circumstances by means of violence, and sought to prepare themselves, by means of pious living, prayer, and fasting, for the future change which God would bring about. Later, therefore, they also refused to make common cause with the Zealots, the latter having equipped themselves for a revolt against the Roman occupying forces in order to bring in the messianic age by force, by means of war against the Gentiles.

The Pharisees combined to form distinct societies in which they could follow the commandments of the Law exactly. It became the particular obligation of all members of the Pharisaic society to observe with the greatest care the prescriptions of cultic purity and the commandments concerning the tithe. The Old Testament commandments which describe the necessary priestly purity were to be maintained not only by priests and Levites, but by all Pharisees, even in everyday life. Anyone who had come into contact with anything unclean—such as a corpse or the body of a dead animal—or had a bodily discharge had thereby lost his cultic purity. In order to gain it back, he had to undergo a bath of purification and, in certain cases, also allow a waiting period to elapse before he could once again be regarded as clean. Hence the Pharisees washed their hands before every meal (Mark 7:3-4), in order to be able to lift up clean hands in prayer and thus to have the meal with each other. Yet they gave attention not only to the purity of the person but also to that of the vessels which they used. If, for example, a mouse ran across a plate or a bone fell into a cup, the vessel was thereby rendered unclean. Hence even cups and bowls had to be kept clean (Matt. 23:25-26 par.; Luke 11:39-40). The commandment to give a tenth of everything that was harvested and earned so that the tribe of Levi, which had not received a hereditary portion of the land, might live on it and the sacrificial service in the temple might be paid for (Lev. 27:30-33; Num. 18:21-24, *et passim*), was not being carefully observed by the Judaism of that time. Non-Jewish residents in the country naturally did not trouble themselves about it, and many Jews were glad when they could now and then avoid taxes and thereby gain something for themselves. Hence it was not certain whether wares which one bought from a Jewish merchant actually had been tithed by their producer. In order to be obedient even to the very letter of the Law, the Pharisees gave the tenth not only of the produce of their land, but also of all that they acquired by purchase. They subjected even spices and herbs to the tithe, and left out nothing that could be brought under this commandment (Matt. 23:23 par.; Luke 11:42).

Beyond these obligations, there were still other pious achievements, such as voluntary fasting, which was observed twice a week on Mondays and Thursdays, even in the heat of the day, to show penitence and to pray for Israel and its salvation. Hence the Pharisee mentioned in the parable was not boasting, but was simply reciting what he actually did: "I fast twice in the week, and give tithes of all that I acquire" (Luke 18:12). In the Talmud there is handed down a prayer, formulated in the first century A.D., which a pious Jew was to utter and which sounds altogether like the words of the Pharisee who viewed the tax collector in the temple:

> I thank thee, Lord, my God, that thou dost give me my portion with those who sit in the house of instruction and not with those who sit on the streetcorners; for I rise up early, and they rise up early; I rise up early to the words of the law, and they rise up early to vain things. I busy myself and receive a reward, and they busy themselves and receive no reward. I journey, and so do they; I am journeying to the life of the future world, and they are journeying to the grave of corruption. (Babylonian Talmud, Berachoth 28b)

Thus the Pharisee summarizes everything that he experiences and does in his life in a word of thanksgiving to God, by which, however, at the same time he sets himself apart from others who do not lead a life according to the Law as he does.

The Pharisaic societies included some priests, but were composed primarily of laymen, craftsmen, farmers, and merchants, who lived not only in the city but also in the country, in Judea and in Galilee. They came together for meals because they could so much the better maintain the commandment of purity (cf. Luke 7:36; 11:37-38, et passim). As much as possible, a Pharisee would buy only from a comrade, because then he could be certain that the goods had been tithed according to the requirements. According to Josephus' report, the fellowship of the Pharisees included "more than 6000" members (Jewish Antiquities XVIII. 42). Even though this number is not particularly high in proportion to the whole of the Jewish community, still the influence of the Pharisees was considerable. It was determined chiefly by the scribes (the leadership in the Pharisaic societies), who studied the Law of Moses, discussed its interpretation, knew the orally transmitted tradition, and understood how to bring the latter into a right relationship with the written law. By their conduct they set the example by which a student of the law was to be guided, and hence enjoyed high regard among the people. They honored the graves of the prophets and cared for the memorial shrines of the righteous (Matt. 23:29), and in this way combined popular piety with high esteem for tradition.

From the peoples who neither knew nor followed the Law, the Pharisees separated themselves. In fact, they avoided any contact with them. The Old Testament expression, "people of the land" (Jer. 1:18; 34:19; II Kings 11:14, 19; 15:5, *et passim*), was used as a scornful designation for "this people who know not the law" (John 7:49), and one kept one's distance from such people. Above all, this dissociation was practiced with respect to the tax collectors and sinners, and it was simply unheard of for a pious Jew to sit with such people at a table (Mark 2:14-17 par.; Luke 15:2). The tax collectors were, after all, in the service of the pagan occupying power, which awarded the tax collecting office to the highest bidder; they tried to profit as much as possible by their position and unhesitatingly went beyond the official prescriptions if it was to their advantage to do so. Since a sinner who wishes to be converted must make restitution for all the injustice which he has committed, the Pharisees were of the opinion that a tax collector could not repent, because he no longer knew how many people he had defrauded. They regarded as sinners not only those who with evil intent violate God's law, but also such people as practice a vocation whereby they necessarily come into conflict with the Law. This included prostitutes, fallen men, and tax collectors, who made common cause with the heathen.

The life and activity of the Pharisees were dedicated to following God's law, as befitted the true community of Israel. Of the canonical books of the Old Testament, the Law was for them by far the most important part. According to their conviction, however, its instructions were not only contained

in the written commandments, but also in the regulations
which had been handed down by word of mouth and incorporated into the written tradition, so that for the Pharisees,
the "tradition of the elders" (Mark 7:3) was as important and
valid a witness to the divine will as the Scriptures. The Pharisees sought, through skillful explanation, to adapt the understanding of the divine commandments to the present and
succeeded to the extent that practicable regulations for their
observance were discovered. Thus the effort was made to shape
the prescriptions concerning the sabbath into something realistic: where there was acute danger to life, an exception to the
rules might be made and the sabbath might, as an exception
to the rule, be desecrated in order to help a person who was
in distress. The area within which one might carry a burden
on the sabbath could also be expanded by explaining that
the court appertaining to several houses was all one common
area.

It is true that for the belief in the resurrection of the dead,
there was some support in the most recent sections of the Old
Testament (Isa. 24–27; Dan. 12:1-3); but the adherents of
resurrection claimed support for the belief from their interpretation of the entire Scripture, as that interpretation had
been expanded and developed to include the oral tradition.
That a dead person could be awakened again to life was not
held to be at all impossible at that time (cf. Mark 6:16 par.;
Luke 9:9). But the Pharisees developed the expectation of
the resurrection of the dead into a tightly formulated doctrine,
by which they distinguished themselves from the Sadducees
(Acts 23:8), and cultivated a strong messianic hope. Once the
people had prepared themselves in purity and holiness for
his coming, then the Messiah would appear as the Son of
David, gather the scattered tribes of Israel and reestablish
the kingdom. The more decisively the rule of the Hasmoneans
was rejected by the pious, the greater became their expectation
that the Anointed One from David's lineage would soon appear to cleanse Jerusalem of the heathen, to cast down all
the ungodly ones, and to take over the political rule (cf. pp.
189–90).

Because the Pharisees endeavored to orient their lives to
the coming messianic age and to fulfill the righteousness

which the Law demanded, they were constantly on guard against incurring the guilt attached to any transgression. They built a "fence around the law" in order not to commit an offense through oversight. Thus they even began their rest from labor some time in advance of sabbath eve, so that under any and all circumstances the seventh day might be properly sanctified to the God of Israel. In order to compensate for sins which even the pious now and then commit, the Pharisees attempted, through additional pious achievements, to assemble a surplus of good works, which later could be calculated to balance offenses, so that at the end, God's judgment would declare them righteous. People strove to act in prayer and deed in accordance with God's will and gave alms for the poor (Matt. 6:2) in order to lead a life well-pleasing to God.

The preaching and deeds of Jesus of Nazareth met with outright rejection among the Pharisees. How could Jesus, who in many respects stood close to the Pharisees (as in the expectation of the resurrection of the dead, and in the call to repentance and conversion) consort with tax collectors and sinners (Mark 2:15 par.; Luke 7:36-50; 15:1-2, *et passim*), set himself above the sabbath regulations (Mark 2:23-3:6 par.), and not bother himself about the commandment concerning purity (Mark 7:1-5)? Jesus charged the Pharisees with being hypocritical in their striving for righteousness: they were indeed intent on outward observance of the Law (Luke 11:39-43 par.; Matt. 23:23-26), but did not know the purity that is of the heart. Even though they carefully tithed everything, they were oblivious to the crucial demand that we give God our entire and undivided obedience. On the basis of their pious conduct, they appeared self-assured and scornful of the lost, and thought that they could make the claim before God that they were righteous (Luke 18:9–14). The Pharisees resolved to take action against Jesus, in fact to eliminate him because he transgressed the Law. This decision was activated when Jesus came to Jerusalem. In spite of the divergence of their views in other respects, here the intentions of the Pharisee and Sadducee members of the Sanhedrin were one— to accuse Jesus and hand him over to the Roman governor as a politically suspect prophet.

Until the destruction of Jerusalem the Pharisees enjoyed a

weighty influence in the Sanhedrin (Acts 5:34-40; 23:6-8). But when the hatred of the people for the Roman rule had become so intense that it sparked armed revolt, not even the Pharisees could prevent the disaster. Many of them joined the rebels; others held back. Although many Pharisees died in the war, many also survived the catastrophe, so that the Pharisaic movement was able to exert a decisive influence on the spiritual and intellectual character of the synagogues after A.D. 70 and to acquire wide recognition for its teachings.

c. The Zealots

When, in the year A.D. 6, the Jewish ruler Archelaus was relieved of his office and the Romans themselves took over the government of Judea, they ordered that the entire population of the new province be registered, in order to be able to assess future taxes in accordance with this calculation (cf. pp. 42, 211). In some Jewish circles this measure evoked indignation and determined resistance, especially within a group of Pharisees who had separated themselves from the Pharisaic society, which had renounced active political involvement, and, because of zeal for the Law, refused to obey the Romans. These "Zealots" (Greek *zelotai*) indeed continued to agree with the Pharisees' views in all matters of doctrine, but they strongly emphasized that "they cling to their liberty with great tenacity and will acknowledge none but God as their Lord and King" (Josephus, *Jewish Antiquities* XVIII. 23). According to the Zealots' views, anyone who acknowledged the emperor as lord and paid taxes to him transgressed the first commandment, which requires men to worship God alone.

The Zealots refused to submit to the rule of the Roman emperor and to call him *kyrios* ("lord"). They were not willing to wait patiently, as did the Pharisees, for the future messianic transformation, but wished to determine the course of history by their own active involvement. At the beginning of the first century A.D. their founder, Judas the Galilean, "led a great number of people to revolt" (Acts 5:37). Other messianic prophets like him also appeared (cf. Acts 5:36; 21:38), who led their followers into the desert, there to experience the miraculous onset of the end-time. The Zealots could not directly confront the superior military might of the Romans, but they established hiding places in the nearly inaccessible area on the eastern slope of the hill country of Judea, from which they could arbitrarily sally forth to make repeated attacks on the occupying forces. In the eyes of the Romans, they were robbers and bandits, against whom the former sought to proceed with all vigor and harshness. Nevertheless, since they distinguished themselves by their zeal for Law, they found a growing body of followers among the inhabitants of Palestine. They incited hostility against the Gentiles, repeatedly kindled unrest, finally called for rebellion, and were the driving force in the Jewish war. With the destruction of Jerusalem and the annihilation of the last resistance groups which had been able to subsist for a short time in the countryside, the Zealot movement then came to a frightful end.

According to Luke 6:15 and Acts 1:13, there was a former adherent of the Zealots in the circle of Jesus' disciples, Simon the Zealot. Yet Jesus' activity and preaching were clearly distinguishable from the efforts of a political messianism. For the rule of God will come without any human contribution, through God's act alone (Mark 4:26-29). When Jesus was asked whether it was right to pay taxes to Caesar, he did not answer from the viewpoint of the Zealots, but said that one should give to Caesar what is Caesar's, and to God what is God's (Mark 12:17 par.). Thus Jesus did not let himself be misled into attributing to the existing political circumstances the splendor of divine dignity, nor did he agree with the revolutionaries' desire to change conditions by the use of violence and to introduce the kingdom of God by force.

d. The Essenes

Along with the Sadducees and the Pharisees, Josephus names the Essenes as the third Jewish group, which he likewise represents as a philosophical school. While the New Testament frequently alludes to the Sadducees and Pharisees, no mention is made of the Essenes. Detailed accounts of the Essenes are handed down only by Philo of Alexandria (*Quod omnis probus liber sit,* 75–91) and Josephus (*Jewish War* II. 119-61; *Jewish Antiquities* XVIII. 18–22). However, because their presentations are obviously colored by the particular views of the authors, who wished to make the Essenes understandable to their Hellenistic readers, they must be read with some caution and must be subjected to critical evaluation.

In contrast to the Sadducees and the Pharisees, who strongly affected the political and religious life of the nation, the Essenes were an independent Jewish movement, who preferred to live in seclusion. Their name is probably derived from the Aramaic *chasajja* ("the pious ones"), a name which perhaps was first given to them by outsiders. Presumably the Essenes is also a reference to the origin of the movement; for the law-observing Jews who supported the Maccabean revolt were called the *chasidim*, because they were the pious ones "who willingly submitted to the law" (I Macc. 2:42). Thus the Essenes arose from the same circles as the Pharisees (cf. p. 77), from whom they were distinguished by still stricter obedience to the Law, which they would not weaken by any lightening or any concession to everyday practice. According to the accounts of Philo and Josephus they numbered 4000. They lived chiefly in villages in Palestine, some of them also in cities, and formed themselves into a community, in order to separate themselves from all uncleanness. Their members, all male, did not marry. Their avoidance of marriage was not due to ascetic tendencies, which are foreign to Judaism, but to a desire to prevent an association with women which might contaminate them with uncleanness. Nevertheless, there were groups of married Essenes, who would enter into marriage after a three-year testing period of the woman, and after it had also been ascertained that she could bear children. Marriages were contracted solely for the purpose of propagation; during the time of the woman's pregnancy sexual intercourse was prohibited. Thus all the Essenes were subject to the unconditional commandment to preserve the cultic purity of the entire community and of all its members.

The Essene community lived under the direction of leaders whose instructions were obligatory. Anyone who wished to enter the fellowship received, at the outset, a small hoe, an apron, and a white robe. These were symbols of the great significance attached to the commandment of purity. The hoe was used to bury excrement in a foot-deep hole. The apron served to cover the private parts, in order not to offend the emanation of God's brilliance, the sun. And the white robe was worn as the garment of the pure. The candidate who sought acceptance into the fellowship was obliged first to undergo a one-year probationary period. If his conduct was declared satisfactory, he was admitted to the washings, and thus began to participate in the purity of the community. Only after two more years was he admitted to full membership and permitted to partake in the common meals.

The members of the community transferred ownership of their personal property to the community, in which all goods were shared. Administrators chosen by the fellowship were given the task of determining how this would be done. The course of the day began early, before sunrise, with the offering of prayer. Then the members went to work in the fields. At midday they reassembled, washed in cold water, put on white robes, and partook of the common meal, at the beginning and end of which a priest offered the mealtime prayer. They then returned to the fields to work until evening when they once more gathered for fellowship at the table. The highly regulated daily schedule was rigidly enforced. Only enough food to satisfy hunger was eaten. When the company were together, silence ruled; speaking was occasionally allowed, but always separately and in a specified order.

A newly admitted member of the fellowship solemnly assumed the obligation of keeping the rules. Before he "was permitted to appear at the common meal, he must swear a solemn oath to the members of the fellowship that he would revere the Deity, fulfill his obligations toward other men, harm no one, either on his own initiative or at the behest of others, always hate the unrighteous and support the righteous, as well as practice fidelity toward everyone and especially toward those who were set over him" (Josephus *Jewish War* II. 139–40). The fellowship was divided into four strictly separate classes. A newer member would stand far enough behind an older member that he might not touch him. If contact was made, it resulted in contamination which could be removed only by cleansing. The sabbath commandment was also observed in strict obedience to the law. No work of any kind might be done on the seventh day; all foods were prepared in advance. One was not even allowed to relieve oneself on the sabbath, in order that the day might not be desecrated. If anyone let himself become guilty of an offense against the regulations, the observance of which was carefully guarded, it was stringently dealt with. Grave offenses were punished by exclusion of the guilty person from the community.

The members were not allowed to tell outsiders about the life, the regulations, and the books of the community. The accounts in Josephus and Philo do not specify what writings were involved here. As for their doctrine, relates Josephus, the Essenes believed that the immortal soul of man comes from heaven and its destiny is determined in advance, but the body is a fleshly prison house of the soul. After death it is liberated from the fetters of the body; the good souls then will ascend to heaven and reach the abode of the blessed, while the wicked will be brought to the place of punishment to receive their just recompense (*Jewish War* II. 154–58). Underlying this hellenistically-grounded description of the views of the Essenes is perceptible a doctrine which assumes fate to be the determinant of the way to be pursued by each individual. It is God's choice whether one man's life will lead him to salvation or to perdition. The flesh passes away, but life is opened to the spirit that is given by God. These basic features of the Essene teaching, which in Josephus are mentioned only vaguely, coincide in large measure with the doctrinal statements of the Qumran texts (cf. p. 109). The Essenes' life-style and beliefs are guided by a strong determination to be the pure community of Israel. It is in light of this determination that we are to understand their rigorous interpretation of the law as well as their painfully exact observance of the rules of purity.

According to the report of Pliny the Elder, the Essenes maintained the center of their fellowship on the shore of the Dead Sea (*Historia naturalis* V. 17). Although they rarely appeared in public, their manner of life, nevertheless, had the effect of setting an example. They attracted particular attention during the revolt against the Romans, in which many Essenes actively participated, some of them in leading positions. To the very end they courageously maintained unwavering loyalty to Israel's Law. Josephus extols their dedication when he emphasizes their scorn of death: "This attitude of theirs thus was evidenced in the war against the Romans. They were tortured and tormented, burned and torn in pieces; their way took them through all the torture chambers in the effort to make them blaspheme their Lawgiver or to eat forbidden foods. But they held firm yielding neither to the one nor to the other, neither addressing a pleading word to their tormentors nor shedding a tear. Smiling in their pain, they mocked their executioners, and joyfully surrendered their lives in the confidence that they would receive them back again" (*Jewish War* II, 152–53). In the suffering and terrors of the war the Essene community disappeared.

The picture of the Essenes which has been sketched here is derived from the accounts of Philo and Josephus. However, it is the extensive discoveries of the texts of Qumran that are responsible for the view, now advanced by many scholars, that the community of Qumran was the center of the Essene society. The hypothesis is in fact highly probable—and will be argued in more detail (cf. p. 109), although the name "Essenes" is nowhere to be found in the writings of the Qumran community.

c. The Therapeutae

Philo contrasts with the Essenes, who led an active life, the Therapeutae, a community which devoted itself to the contemplative life (*de vita contemplativa*). Even though Philo's portrayal is colored by his own beliefs, it surely contains a kernel of historical truth. The Therapeutae had a cloister-like establishment on the Mareotic Lake, not far from Alexandria. Their name means "servants" or "slaves" (viz., of God). They renounced private property and were committed to the simple life, each member living as a hermit in a small hut and spending his days in study of the Scriptures and in meditation. The modest daily meal was taken only after sunset. The sabbath was the one day on which members of the community assembled for worship. Every seventh sabbath was specially honored; on the eve of that day the community wore white robes to both the common worship service and fellowship at table, thus uniting the sacred night ceremonies. This community, too, intended to give undivided obedience to the Law and to live in accordance with its instructions. The Therapeutae probably are to be regarded as an offshoot of the Essene movement which independently underwent further development during the Egyptian Diaspora. The church fathers regarded Philo's history as a description of early Christian monks (Eusebius Church History II. 17) and although it is not impossible that there is continuity between such Jewish societies and the beginnings of Christian monasticism, certain essential documentation in support of this conjecture is lacking.

f. The Qumran Community

1) Survey of the texts from Qumran

The story of the various discoveries of previously unknown Jewish manuscripts begins in the year 1947 when some Bedouins stumbled upon a cave in the desert of Judea in which scrolls had been hidden in several large clay jars. In subsequent years, intensive explorations were conducted in the vicinity of the original discovery—in part by scholars, but in greatest number by Bedouins—and thousands of caves located in the slopes which descend from the desert of Judea to the Dead Sea were searched. As late as 1956, texts and text fragments were discovered in a total of eleven caves, the most extensive and most significant ones in Caves One and Four. In order to classify and to identify the great number of writings and sheets, it became customary in each case first to indicate the number of the cave in which the item in question was found: 1Q, 2Q, and so on; and then to add the initial letter in the title of the writing: for example, "S" stands for *Serek hayyachad* which means "Order of the Community;" "pHab" stands for *pesher Habakkuk* which means "commentary on Habakkuk"; and so on. Archaeological investigations which were conducted in the vicinity of the caves from 1951 to 1956 have produced information, sufficient to trace the general history of the community that produced, or at least read, the documents that were found.

a) The archaeological findings: In the vicinity of the cave that was discovered in 1947, not far from the shores of the Dead Sea, lay a small mound of ruins. It was possible, on the basis of their subsequent excavations to give an unequivocally affirmative answer to the question of whether there was a connection between this place, called Kirbet Qumran, and the manuscripts. A settlement was discovered which had been the nucleus of a Jewish community. A main house with a tower yielded measurements of thirty by thirty-seven meters. A large meeting room, which was also used for common meals, a sideboard, situated beside this room and stocked with earthenware for use in the dining room, a potter's workshop, a writing room, and other workplaces served the entire community. In the settlement there were several cisterns, for storing the rain water that flowed through a conduit from the hills. These installations were obviously important not only for providing drinking water, but also for providing water for ablutions and baths of purification. Since there were no living accommodations or sleeping quarters in this settlement, one may conjecture that the members of the community spent the nights in the caves, which exist in great number in the immediate vicinity, and by day occupied themselves in the workplaces or gathered in the assembly rooms. Presumably some of the caves in which manuscripts were found presumably were sleeping quarters for members of the community. However, the careful wrapping of the scrolls in Cave One, suggests that it was an intended hiding place; and the amazingly large number of texts and text-fragments in Cave Four indicates that it may have been the community's library.

Discovery of various coins in the settlement made possible a reliable estimate of the date in which it was founded. The oldest coins date from the time of John Hyrcanus (134–104 B.C.) ; thus the settlement was begun in the middle of the second century B.C. or shortly thereafter. According to the evidence of other discovered coins, it was used throughout an entire century. The disappearance of the coins after this period of time was probably due to an earthquake, dated according to ancient reports 31 B.C. (Josephus *Jewish War* I 370–71), which caused such severe damage that for some time the houses must have been uninhabitable. The coin finds begin again with the time of the reign of Archelaus (4 B.C.–A.D. 6) and continue to the time of the Jewish uprising against the Romans. Strong evidence of fire suggests that the establishment was destroyed by violence. It must have been occupied by the Romans in the year A.D. 68, when Vespasian with his troops marched along the Jordan valley all the way to the Dead Sea and once again brought the country under the rule of the Romans. It is likely that the news of the Romans' approach prompted the members of the community carefully to conceal in jars the large Scripture scrolls which were discovered in Cave One, in order to be able to bring them out again after the fighting had ended. This, however, did not come to pass, since the community disappeared in the course of the war. For some time after the war, a detachment of the Tenth Roman Legion was stationed in Qumran, and during the uprising under Bar Cochba, Jewish partisans once again established themselves there. Thus ends the history of the settlement, which from that time remained in ruins.

In the eastern part of the settlement lay a large cemetery in which more than a thousand of the deceased members of the community were buried. Investigations which have been conducted at the fresh water spring Ain Feschcha, located to the south, indicate that cattle were bred here, date palms were planted, and even crops were cultivated on a small scale, so that in this lonely setting the community could provide itself with a modest livelihood and exist independently of the outside world.

The archaeological findings clearly delimit the period in which the manuscripts which have been discovered were prepared: the community lived in Qumran from the middle of the second century B.C. to A.D. 68. Hence there can be no doubt that the Qumran texts had their origin in a Jewish community, the center of which during the time of Jesus and earliest Christianity was Qumran.

b) The biblical texts: Among the manuscripts and text fragments which were discovered in the caves of Qumran are numerous biblical texts. In Cave One, two large scrolls of the book of Isaiah were found, one of them in very good condition and containing almost the entire book ($1QIs^a$), the other severely damaged and briefer in content than the first roll ($1QIs^b$). These manuscripts are a full thousand years older than the oldest previously known manuscripts of the Hebrew Old Testament. It is true that in these two scrolls there are all sorts of variations both in the style of writing and in particular usage, differences by which the scrolls are distinguished from the version of the text that was later handed down by the Jewish scholars who were responsible for the reproduction of the biblical books (the so-called Masoretes) ; but on the whole the text of Isaiah in the two scrolls is not too far removed from the later Masoretic version. This is not the case, however, with other biblical manuscripts, as is shown by a Qumran version of the books of Samuel, which agrees to a large extent, not with the Masoretic text, but with the Greek translation in the Septuagint (cf. pp. 128–33), which occasionally diverges significantly (4QSam[a] and 4QSam[b]). Thus the Greek translation of this book did not take shape arbitrarily, but evolved from an earlier edition, which later was not recognized as the informing text. That some biblical manuscripts and fragments suggest an early stage of the later Masoretic text while others significantly differ from it in places implies that at the time of the Qumran community there was not yet a single textual version of the biblical writings. The establishment of a single, normative form of the text was first undertaken by the scribes, who after A.D. 70 gave to the communities a universally binding text of the Scriptures.

It is true that the question as to which books are to be canonically recognized was definitively settled by the rabbis only near the end of the first century A.D. (cf. pp. 167–69), but for the community of Qumran the circle of the canonical books of the Old Testament had already been established. Among the numerous biblical texts are found excerpts from all the books of the Old Testament Canon with a single exception: the book of Esther. Its absence may be accidental, but could also be traced to the fact that this book presents the festival ceremonies for the Feast of Purim, a feast that quite possibly was not approved by the Qumran community, and, therefore, purposely deleted.

As instructive as the biblical texts from Qumran are for our knowledge of the tradition of Old Testament writings and of the gradual definition of the limits of the Canon, still more significant are the nonbiblical texts which were discovered in the caves of Qumran; for through them we are exposed to the actual life of a Jewish community, the manner and method by which teachings about the right way to live were translated into deed.

c. The Jewish texts: Of the large number of texts found in Qumran, the most important will receive a brief description here in the hope that they may suggest a picture of the faith and life of the community. Unfortunately, many of the scrolls have been damaged, so that in the text some passages and individual letters are missing or display even larger gaps. However, it is still frequently possible to infer the missing portion from the context. In quotations from the Qumran texts, such restorations of the text are set in brackets.

The *Manual of Discipline* (1QS) —frequently identified as the sect rule—is preserved almost intact in a manuscript of eleven columns. In addition to those in Cave One, there were eleven more copies in Cave Four, of which, however, only small parts are to be found. The Manual, which is not a literary unity but is put together from various pieces, begins with liturgical instructions and regulations for the feast of the renewing of the covenant, which was to be celebrated annually (I. 1-III. 12). There follows an instructive passage about the two spirits that determine human life, the spirit of truth and that of mischief (III. 13–IV. 26). Then rules for the order of the community are given, as well as a number of penal regulations for transgressions against law and order (V. 1–IX. 25). At the end there are instructions about prayer and a psalm, in which the supplicant confesses God's righteousness, with praise and thanksgiving (IX. 26–XI. 22). This book— like almost all the other writings as well—is composed in pure Hebrew, which, as the language of the Law, was cultivated in the community. The various rules which are assembled in this manual are meant to show how the community leads its life in accordance with the Law. To this extent the writing affords an exemplary summary of instructions for the religious practice, doctrine, and life of the community.

Two briefer texts have been preserved as appendixes to this manual of discipline. In the *Community Rule* (1QSa) directions are given for the community of Israel at the end of time. Prescriptions for the training of community members are given, the method of summoning the entire assembly is treated, and finally the seating arrangement at the messianic banquet is described. In the *Benedictions* (1QSb) are found prescribed words of blessing for the believers, the high priest, the priests, and the rulers of the community. It is uncertain whether these blessings were ever used in worship services. Presumably they were meant to serve as liturgical outlines for the coming time of salvation.

The *Damascus Document* had already been discovered in the Ezra synagogue in Old Cairo in 1896. A title for the document is not given. Since the community calls itself the community of the new covenant in the land of Damascus (cf. Amos 5:27), the label of Damascus Document (CD) has become generally customary. This work involves a manuscript, A 1, composed of four leaves written on both sides (columns I-VIII) and a manuscript, A 2, written by another hand, of the same length (columns IX-XVI), as well as the manuscript B, whose text is on both sides of a single leaf (columns XIX-XX). Since a number of fragments of the Damascus Document were found in Caves Four, Five, and Six of Qumran, and they exhibit numerous parallels with the Manual of Discipline, the Damascus Document must have originated in the Qumran community. Columns I-VIII contain a long hortatory discourse, which incorporates the inception and the history of the community into a comprehensive interpretation of the history of Israel and argues for the strict interpretation of the Law by the community. This discourse, minus some beginning introductory passages, breaks off at the end of column VIII, but is continued in manuscript B, which at first runs parallel to a considerable extent with columns VII-VIII. Columns IX-XVI contain legal regulations in which the radical understanding of the Law is set forth in numerous detailed prescriptions. Since CD, in contrast to 1QS, mentions married members and presupposes private property in their possession, the regulations of 1QS and CD obviously do not apply to the same group. The company of which CD speaks live together in encampments in which the same strict ranking of priests, Levites, and Israelites as in 1Qs is maintained. It is not easy to determine the interrelationship between the writings 1QS and CD. The editing of CD probably was undertaken later than that of 1QS. But since in CD a distinction frequently is made between earlier and later prescriptions of the law, many of the sentences there could also very well represent an earlier stage than the corresponding parallels in 1QS.

The scroll of the *Hymns* (Hebrew *hodayoth*) (1QH) contains eighteen columns. In addition there are sixty-six fragments, mostly small ones, from Cave One, and still other pieces of other manuscripts of the same work from Cave Four. The form and content of the hymns are modeled after the Old Testament psalms. The person who is praying regularly begins with the words, "I praise thee, Lord," then pictures his distress and the forlorn condition from which God has redeemed him, praises the deliverance which has come to him, praises the true knowledge which is granted to the pious, and petitions God for gracious preservation and guidance. This collection likewise displays no literary unity. In some passages sorrowful experiences are mentioned and the claim is made that salvation can be attained through the teaching that is being transmitted, so that these can probably be traced to a particular personality, presumably the "Teacher of Righteousness" (cf. pp. 99–101; thus, for example, VII. 6–25). In other songs, however, echoes of Old Testament expressions and the formula-like utterances which portray typical situations of the one praying are heard in far greater measure. In these passages is expressed what any pious person who belongs to the community of the covenant can and should confess when giving thanks to God; therefore, by "I" here is meant the member of the community who prayed these psalms (thus, for example, XIII–XVI) as songs of thanksgiving and confessions and in so doing applied the expressions of the text to himself.

The struggle of the sons of light against the sons of darkness is set forth in the *War Scroll* (1QM). In Cave Four, along with the scroll of nineteen columns, smaller fragments of other manuscripts were discovered, which in part offer earlier versions of the text of Cave One's War Scroll. This finding verifies that the form of the War Scroll as it is found in 1QM is based upon earlier traditions and versions which, in the meanwhile, had been revised and developed further. The battle which must be endured in the last times is described mostly in Old Testament terminology into which have been incorporated motifs of the holy war, which had once again become a reality in the circles of the pious in the Maccabean period. The precise directions given for equipping and drawing up troops and for achieving the desired style of battle make it evident that the war is an actual battle, despite the apocalyptic context of events—Belial and his army standing on one side, and Michael and his angels on the other, the latter waiting for God to bring about the final victory. The portrayal of the war is repeatedly interrupted by liturgical texts, prayers of thanksgiving, hymns, and priestly addresses. In many passages we find striking repetitions, and even a lengthy hymn recurs in an almost verbatim doublet (XII. 7 ff.; XIX. 1 ff.) . From this it can be deduced that various traditions were loosely combined in order to relate the ancient tradition of Israel's holy war to the situation of a struggle in which the sons of light find themselves in the conflict with the sons of darkness.

In the Qumran community an intensive study of the Scripture was conducted, not only of the Law, but also of the prophetic books and the Psalms. In this study the effort was made to read the texts in such a way that their significance for the present and for the particular experiences of the community was shown. Difficult passages offered the opportunity of deducing hidden meanings and of setting forth connections with the history of the community. Thus the *Habakkuk Commentary* (1QpHab.) goes through the first and second chapters of the Old Testament book, verse by verse, and affixes at successive points an interpretation (Hebrew *pesher*) which undertakes to manifest the prophetic significance of the words. Thus the commentary does not propose to provide a contribution to the clarification of the historical situation in which the prophet and those whom he addressed once found themselves, but to explain the situation of the eschatological community in the light of the prophetic message. When the enemy nation of the Chaldeans, mentioned there, is interpreted to mean the Kittim, either the Seleucids or the Romans could be the intended meaning. Since it speaks of their making sacrifices to their insignia (VI. 3–4) , however, the Romans are suggested. Hence the author of the commentary first wrote in the days of Roman rule, and is looking back on the history of the community which has already run its course. The Teacher of Righteousness, to whom God has granted the gift of prophetic knowledge, has been persecuted, and his followers along with him. Consequently his flock are sent with him into exile. But in Jerusalem rules the sacrilegious priest, who immediately after assuming his office was called by the name of "truth," but later disregarded the commandments for the sake of gaining wealth (VIII. 8–11). By means of the thoroughgoing interpretation of the text, the understanding of the eschatological event in which the community has been placed will be revealed and, thereby, the meaning of the word of Scripture, which has been concealed up to that time, will be brought out.

Other biblical writings are similarly explicated and related to particular events of the times. In the commentaries on Psalm 37 and the prophetic books of Isaiah, Hosea, Micah, Nahum, and Zephaniah are sufficiently numerous and detailed references to events which the community has experienced to supply the dates of the community's emergence and to describe its history. Thus in 4QpNah. I. 6–7 is mentioned the lion of wrath that hanged men while alive, and this clearly refers to Alexander Jannaeus' cruel treatment of his opponents (cf. p. 32). In Psalm 37, in which the fate of the righteous is contrasted with that of the godless, the explanation is again made relevant to the community's own situation, and the words of the Scripture are interpreted as a reference to the oppression suffered by the Teacher of Righteousness and his community through the persecution by the godless priest.

The so-called Genesis-Apocryphon deals quite freely with its Old Testament counterpart, paraphrasing Genesis in Aramaic and in the process considerably expanding and developing several passages. Thus the birth of Noah and the marvelous appearance of the child is described in the context of a conversation between Lamech and his wife Bath-Enosh and included in a delightful story of the patriarch Abraham, is a lengthy description of Sarah's beauty. Lauded in succession are her face, her hair, her eyes, her nose, her radiance, her breasts, her arms, her hands, her palms, her fingers, her legs, her thighs, and her wisdom.

On a single leaf which was found in Cave Four there is a small collection of Old Testament texts which probably were compiled because of their relevance to the messianic expectation of the community (4Qtest.). Deuteronomy 5:28–29 and 18:18–19 are combined into a single quotation, followed by Numbers 24:15–17 and Deuteronomy 33:8–11; and Joshua 6:26 forms the conclusion. This document signifies that in the Judaism of that time sections of the Old Testament were assembled and integrated in such a way that they could be used for general reference or for instruction.

In concluding this survey, attention will be given to some especially peculiar texts. In Cave Three was found a *copper scroll* which contained a list of treasures and revealed their hiding places. The amount and value of the items, however— altogether some 200 tons of gold and silver—are so great that this could not be a registry of existing possessions, hidden or not. Perhaps it is a listing of priestly and royal treasures imagined by the people to have been in the possession of ancient Israel. In Cave Eleven was found a *psalm scroll* in which, along with forty-one biblical psalms, there are seven nonbiblical ones, and, in addition, a prose commenting on the psalmody of David, who is credited therein with having composed a total of 4050 psalms. The presented collection is intended as a sample of his art and therefore, does not observe the boundaries of the Canon. Finally, a small fragment, composed in code, was found in Cave Four, which advances the curious view that the sign of the zodiac under which a person is born determines his outward form—whether husky or frail—and is related to his share in the light and in the darkness (4Qcry.).

The multiplicity of texts indicates that the doctrine of the community may not be regarded as a homogeneous entity that was established from the outset. Instead, in the course of the community's history, it underwent alterations and expansions (as evidenced by the references to diverse strands of tradition and the compilation of various materials) to render the teachings appropriate for exposition of the Law. While at first the community was filled with the expectation that the end of time was imminent, the realization gradually prevailed that the last times had been protracted (1QpHab.

VII. 7). But thereby greater significance was placed upon reshaping the doctrine, for the community required a new interpretation of their changed historical situation. The impact of introducing new perspectives into the old texts must be taken into account when attempting to sketch a picture of the faith and teaching of the community from the artifacts at Qumran.

2) The belief and teaching of the Qumran community

The *emergence of the community* may be traced to the priestly circles in Jerusalem who pressed for careful observance of the law. In the social hierarchy of the community, priests were superior; even the messianic expectation is stamped with a priestly mark since it is oriented to the coming of a priestly anointed one who will stand at the side of the royal Messiah (cf. p. 108). In commentaries on the biblical writings repeated reference is made to the Teacher of Righteousness who founded the community. He was a priest upon whom God bestowed the gift of true knowledge and the authority to explicate the Scripture (1QpHab. II. 8–19; VII. 4–5). Around him was gathered a host of law-observing priests, Levites, and laymen who were concerned with the preservation and observance of the festal calendar which they regarded as the only valid one. The calendar in Jerusalem being calculated in terms of the moon's cycles, the followers of the Teacher of Righteousness wished to introduce a solar year which would have twelve months of thirty days each, as well as an additional day for each quarter. This made it possible for every year to begin on the same day of the week, a Wednesday; provided for all feast days to fall consistently on the same day of the week; and avoided a feast day ever coinciding with a sabbath. Nevertheless this group did not succeed in establishing their plan, which would have served to sanctify the sabbath even more stringently. Instead, there developed a sharp confrontation between the followers of the Teacher of Righteousness and the ruling high priests, who were accused of inadequately following the prescriptions of the Law. This conflict with the incumbent high priests, who thereafter were called sacrilegious priests, resulted in the forced departure from Jerusalem of the Teacher of Righteousness, who with his community retreated into the loneliness of the desert on the shores of the Dead Sea.

Of the *godless priest* it was said that in the conduct of his office he had been unfaithful to the commandments of God. When he took office, "he was called by name of truth. But when he had achieved dominion in Israel, his heart was exalted, and he forgot God and acted f[ai]thlessly toward the commandments for the sake of wealth. And he stole and gathered wealth from men of violence who had risen up against God. And he took wealth from the nations, so that he heaped upon himself the sin of indebtedness, and he went the ways of ab[om]inations in all sorts of vile uncleanness" (1QpHab. VIII. 9–13). The godless priest sought to oppose the Teacher of Righteousness with violence, in that he "appeared among them at the place of his exile and at the time of the festival of rest, on the day of atonement, to ensnare them and to cause them to fall on the day of the fast, the sabbath of their rest" (1QpHab. XI. 6–8). For his evil actions and his persecution of the Teacher of Righteousness, however, he received God's punishment, which was deliverance into the hands of his enemies, "to humble him by plague and destruction" (1QpHab. IX. 10–11). These references to the godless priest most readily recall the events which took place in the time of the Maccabean Jonathan (cf. p. 28). After Jonathan had taken over the leadership of the battle against the Syrians, following the death of his brother Judas, he had appropriated to himself, as the ruling Hasmonean, the position of the high priest, although he did not come from a Zadokite family. His violent political behavior contrasted sharply with the standards of purity traditionally expected of a priest, and continued to do so until his death at the hands of his enemies.

Nevertheless the name of the *Teacher of Righteousness* is unknown, for nowhere is it recorded. He led the community out into the desert and understood that this way had been foreshadowed in the challenge of the prophet in Isaiah 40:3: "Prepare the way of the Lord in the desert, make smooth in the wilderness a way for our God." This scriptural saying is quoted in 1QS VIII. 14 and then is interpreted as follows: "This [the way] is the study of the Law [which] he has commanded through Moses to be done, according to all that is revealed from time to time, and as the prophets have revealed through his spirit" (1QS VIII. 15–16). Hence the community is aware of having been called to prepare the way of the Lord by studying and living in obedience to the Law, and of having been made able by the Spirit of God to understand the prophetic words and from them to comprehend the times.

The *priestly community*, which was unable to continue the temple ministry and to offer sacrifices in Qumran, hoped that a cultus more observant of the Law would be restored in the coming time of salvation. Thus banishment from the temple by no means caused rejection of the cultus itself but only criticism of its current practice by the priests holding office in Jerusalem. Under the leadership of the priests, the community kept itself in constant readiness, to assume the role of victor in the battle designated for the last times and once again to institute the proper cultus. Their intention was to strive for and maintain priestly purity by avoiding any contamination and partaking in daily ablutions. Yet washing alone would not produce purity, if there were no conversion to proper obedience toward the Law. "They [those who had been contaminated] cannot be cleansed unless they are converted from their wickedness; for uncleanness clings to all who transgress his Word" (1QS V. 13–14). Repentance means turning away from the world of wickedness and falsehood and turning to God, "to seek [him with the whole heart and soul, to] do what is good and right in his eyes, as he has commanded through Moses and through all his servants, the prophets; and to love all that he has chosen, and to hate all that he has rejected, to keep oneself from all evil, but to cling to all good works; and to practice faithfulness, righteousness, and justice in the land" (1QS I. 1–6).

The community submitted to *strict regulation,* in order that they might be made fit to wage war against the sons of darkness. At the head stood the sons of Zadok, the priests; then came the Levites, and then the host of the men of the covenant, and finally those who had applied for admittance into the community. These first underwent two years of probation during which time they were not permitted to participate in the common meals. When the two years elapsed, "then he is

to be tested at the behest of the many [the whole assembly]"
(1QS VI. 21). "And when the vote is cast for him, to bring
him into the fellowship, then he is to be inscribed among his
brethren, in the order of his rank, for law and justice and
purity and the sharing of his possessions" (1QS VI. 21–22).
Then he must "obligate himself with a binding oath to turn
to the law of Moses in accordance with all that he [God] has
commanded, with the whole heart and soul, and to all that is
revealed by Him to the sons of Zadok, the priests, who keep
the covenant and search out his will, and to the host of the
men of their covenant, who in the fellowship have proven
themselves submissive to his truth and to walking in his will"
(1QS V. 8–10). At this time the new member had to transfer
ownership of his personal property to that of the entire
community, an activity administered by an overseer; and
afterwards he was admitted to the purity of the many, i.e., he
was permitted to participate in the ablutions of the community. The idea of priestly purity, which committed the
community to maintaining constant fitness for receiving and
enacting God's truth and will, shaped the entire life of its
members. [They abstained even from marriage, in order not to
be rendered unclean by intercourse with women.]

At *mealtimes* the priestly community gathered for worship
and for the study of the Scripture: "They are to eat together,
utter praises together, and take counsel together. And at every
place where there are ten men of the council of the fellowship, there must be a priest among them. And they shall sit
before him, each one according to his rank, and thus they
shall be asked for their counsel on every occasion. And when
they come to the table to eat, or to drink wine, the priest
shall first stretch out his hand to pronounce the blessing over
the first fruits of bread and wine. And at the place where
there are ten men, there must be among them one who
studies the Law day and night, constantly, one [day] after
another" (1QS VI. 2–7).

Strict discipline prevailed in the community; every member
was given a particular rank and was obliged to conduct himself accordingly. Anyone who committed an offense against
the order of the community expected harsh punishment. "If
a man is found among them who gives false information about

his possessions, while knowing otherwise, he is to be excluded from the purity of the many for a year, and he shall be punished by the withholding of one-fourth of his rations" (1QS VI. 24–25). Even minor offenses were harshly punished: "Anyone who utters a foolish word with his mouth, three months. And for one who interrupts while another is speaking, ten days. And anyone who lies down and sleeps during the session of the many, thirty days" (1QS VII. 9–10). "Anyone who laughs foolishly with a loud voice shall be punished with thirty days" (1QS VII. 14–15). To be excluded from the community meant a painful punishment. For the person who was excluded was no longer permitted to participate in the common meals; and furthermore, could not secure nourishment outside of the community since the risk of contamination by contact with the world of falsehood was too great. Hence he was compelled to search painfully for a wretched subsistence in the desert until the fellowship finally readmitted him.

While the Pharisees strove to interpret the Law in such a way that its prescriptions could be adapted to everyday living conditions, the Qumran community rejected compromise or softening of the rules. The whole of the Law was to be observed; all the demands of the Torah were to be fulfilled. This strict interpretation of the commandments contained in the Law was also responsible for the long list of *sabbath regulations* which are set forth in the Damascus Document (CD X. 14–XI. 18). The instructions "concerning the sabbath, that it is to be kept according to its [Damascus Document] direction" (CD X. 14) are introduced with the command that in the evening before the beginning of the day of rest, no more work is to be done after the time "when the disc of the sun is the distance of its diameter from the gate" (CD X. 15–16). On the sabbath no one may speak a foolish or an idle word (CD X. 17–18). "One may not go out of his city farther than a thousand paces" (CD X. 21), while according to the Pharisees' view the sabbath day's journey might equal two thousand paces. If a beast "falls into a well or a ditch, it may not be lifted out again on the sabbath" (CD XI. 13–14). According to Matt. 12:11 (and the parallel passage in Luke 14:5), however, Jesus takes it for granted that one may lift a sheep out of a ditch into which it has fallen on the sabbath, and then concludes further how much more worthy of help is a man in distress on the sabbath.

The covenant to which the community knows itself obliged to be faithful is the covenant of Moses or, as it is also called in the Damascus Document, the new covenant (CD VI. 19; VIII. 21; XIX. 34; XX. 12). However, this does not mean a second covenant that has taken the place of the first one. Rather, this new covenant is the covenant which God made with Israel at Sinai and which now, in the last times, has been reinstituted. A person who turns away from wickedness and falsehood and becomes a member of the community is converted to the Law of Moses (1QS V. 8) and thus has escaped the world of falsehood, to which have fallen victim not only the heathen, but also those among the Israelites who do not live according to the Law with an undivided heart. But truth and light guide the community of the elect, of which one becomes a member only by deliberate conversion.

The situation of conflict in which the community sees itself involved is described in terms of the *contrast between light and darkness*. Outside stand the sons of darkness, the army of Belial (i.e., the antagonist of the end-time), and the hosts of the Gentile nations of whom the Old Testament often spoke: Edom, Moab, Ammon, the Philistines, and the Chittim of Asshur (1QM I. 1–2). But the sons of light are supported by Michael, the guardian angel of the people of God, and his army. The harsh conflict which must be played out is traced back, in an illuminating instructional passage, to God's original intention. "All that is and happens comes from the God of knowledge" (1QS III. 15). "And he created man to rule over the earth and determined that there would be for him two spirits in which to walk until the predestined time of his visitation. These are the spirits of truth and of wickedness. The origin of truth is at the source of light, but from the source of darkness comes the origin of wickedness" (1QS III. 17–19). On the one side stands the prince of light, whose hand rules all the sons of righteousness who walk in the ways of light. But on the other side, the angel of darkness exercises his rule over all the sons of wickedness who walk in the ways of darkness. However, these two realms are not utterly separated from each other; indeed, the angel of darkness "causes the wandering astray of all the sons of righteousness, and all their sins, misdeeds, and guilt; and the offenses of their deeds come through his rule, in keeping with the secrets of God, until his time" (1QS III. 21–23). The evil powers "strive to cause the sons of light to fall. But the God of Israel and the angel of his truth give aid to all the sons of light" (1QS III. 24–25). By the manifestation of the works of men in one of these two realms one can recognize to which side they belong (1QS IV. 2–14). But not even in the course of doing good does a man escape conflict; he must struggle constantly against falsehood, wickedness, and darkness. Indeed—the instruction becoming more passionate—the two spirits, that of truth and that of darkness, struggle in the heart of man until the end of time (1QS IV. 23). Therefore no one can avoid the battle; even the pious must continue to fight. "According to a man's portion in truth and righteousness he hates the evil, and according to his portion in the lot of wickedness he conducts himself godlessly in it and abhors the truth" (1QS IV. 24–25). Thus the battle rages until God puts an end to it. "For God has placed them [the spirits] side by side until the appointed time, until the new creation" (1QS IV. 25).

The opposition of light and darkness is also repeatedly described in the Old Testament (cf. Gen. 1:3-5, 14-19; Amos 5:18; *et passim*); the tradition of the holy war in which the God of Israel fights for his people is well known since antiquity, and in the Maccabean age was again revived. However, the concept of two spirits that are in conflict with each other throughout history has no prototype in the Old Testament or in the Jewish tradition attached to it. It is true, however, that similar ideas are found in Iranian religion in which the world's course is interpreted as a struggle of good with evil, a struggle which has prevailed since the very beginning and will continue until, at last, the day arrives when the victory of the good God over the evil God is complete. Since the good spirit induces the practice of good, and the evil spirit, evil, it becomes evident through people's actions to which side they belong. Just as Iranian ideas have had an impact upon Jewish apocalyptic (cf. pp. 63–64), so also the dualistic doctrine of the battle between the spirit of truth and the spirit of evil must have been developed as a result of the adoption of Iranian views. Certainly there was not a direct impact of Iranian motifs upon the Qumran community, but rather an assimilation of Iranian ideas by virtue of some obscure contact during the Jewish Diaspora in Mesopotamia. These ideas did not remain unaltered; they were adapted to the belief in the God of Israel as the Creator and guide of history, who has made all things and therefore has predetermined the opposition of the two spirits, to which conflict he will one day put an end. Thus the Jewish dualistic teaching serves to give emphasis to God's omnipotence and at the same time to explain the conflict which the community must struggle with until the last day. In this teaching, the dualism consists of an opposition which on the one hand is established by God's pretemporal decision, but on the other hand is dealt with anew in the decision of every man each time he struggles with the two spirits.

In the teaching it is also said that God guides the way of man, that God's election decides for him; yet it is repeatedly emphasized that the Law demands the obedience of man, that he is to repent, walk the right way, and fulfill the commandments because he has been made to be fully and entirely responsible for his deeds. That man cannot stand by himself before God is plainly acknowledged by the pious and is expressed in prayer to God:

I belong to impious humanity, to the company of wicked flesh. My sins, my transgressions, and my iniquities, together with the perversity of my heart, belong to the company of worms and to those who walk in darkness. For no man determines his own way, and no man guides his own steps; but with God is righteousness, and from his hand comes the perfect walk, and all things have come about through his knowledge. All that is he guides according to his plan, and without him nothing happens. But as for me, if I stumble, God's mercies are my everlasting help. And if I stagger because of the wickedness of the flesh, my righteousness shall stand through the righteousness of God forever. (1QS XI. 9–12)

The acceptance of the lost man comes about *solely through God's grace*, by which he saves him and sets him on the right path:

> What is a creature of clay (i.e., a man), to do great marvels? He is in sin from his mother's womb, and down to old age he is in the guilt of faithlessness. And I confessed that there is no righteousness in man, and no perfect way in the children of men. With the most high God are all the works of righteousness, but the way of man is not established except by the spirit which God created for him, to make perfect the way of the children of men, that they all might recognize his works in the strength of his might and the abundance of his mercy toward all the sons of his good pleasure. (IQH IV. 29–33)

In these sentences is described the frailty of man, who is made of clay, falls victim as flesh to corruption, and therefore is weak and powerless. But at the same time that man is alienated from God because of his own guilt and lack of inherent righteousness; he has alienated himself by committing wickedness and acting in an ungodly manner. By God's grace he is saved and brought near; that is, he is introduced into the community of the covenant, which in turn gives him membership in the host of the saints. Thus the godless one is saved solely by God's mercy, and the *iustificatio impii* occurs *sola gratia*. Yet when he is justified, he is set on the right way and made competent to observe the Law and fulfill its demands. Thus the Qumran interpretation of the justification of the sinner does not intend to detract from the importance of the Law as a guide to salvation; Salvation is bestowed only on those who do the works which are commanded in the Law of Moses. The weak sinner is strengthened by God's grace and mercy, so that now he can keep the Law and prove true in obedience. Hence the verse, "The just shall live by his faithfulness" (Hab. 2:4), is interpreted as follows: "Its meaning refers to all those who observe the law in the house of Judah, whom God will deliver from the house of judgment, because of their suffering and their faithfulness to the Teacher of Righteousness" (1QpHab. VIII. 1–3). The Law, as the Teacher of Righteousness has expounded it, is kept by his community, in that the community follows its teacher and founder with unwavering loyalty and therein is certain of gaining the future salvation. However, nothing is said anywhere in the texts of Qumran about a resurrection of the dead. In this respect the teaching of the community is distinguished from the further development of the tradition by the Pharisees. But it anticipates so imminent a dawning of the Messianic Age that the interim period possesses hardly any significance of its own, and everything hinges on being constantly ready for the coming day.

The *eschatological hope* of the community is oriented to the coming of "the prophet and the messiahs of Aaron and Israel" (1QS IX. 11). Thus three figures are to appear at the end of time—first the prophet who will announce the Messianic age, then the two anointed ones. The priestly and the royal messiahs—the spiritual and worldly leaders of the community of salvation—will stand side by side, in fulfillment of the prophetic prediction of Zechariah 4, in which the prophet sees two olive trees, which then are interpreted as the anointed ones. While a king like David will appear and will govern the people, the priestly anointed one will minister to the purity of the eschatological community. The chief position is properly his, as the description of the messianic banquet in the rule of the community establishes.

No one may stretch out his hand over the firstfruits of the bread and the wine before the priest does so; for he shall pronounce the blessing over the firstfruits of the bread and the wine. And he shall first stretch out his hand over the bread, and and then shall the messiah of Israel stretch out his hand over · the bread. And then they shall pronounce the blessing, the entire company of the fellowship, each in keeping with his station. (1QSa II. 18–21)

The scriptural support for the two anointed ones is found in the speech of Balaam in Numbers 24:17: "A star shall arise out of Jacob and a scepter shall be raised out of Israel" (4Qtest. 12).

The *knowledge and insight of the pious* are imparted by means of divine revelation. As the worshiper says, "He [God] has disclosed his light from the source of his knowledge, so that my eye beheld his marvelous deeds and the light of my heart, the mystery of what has come to pass" (1QS XI. 3–4). "My eye has looked upon that which is eternal, the deep insight which is hidden from men, knowledge and clever thoughts, hidden from men" (1QS XI. 6–7). Therefore: "Blessed art thou, my God, who dost open up the heart of thy servant to knowledge" (1QS XI. 15–16). "Thou hast taught all knowledge" (1QS XI. 17–18). This knowledge, however, does not refer, as in gnosis, to cosmological relationships and mythological speculations about the heavenly home of man, who is exiled in the prison of matter (cf. pp. 254–62). The dualism of light and darkness is not understood as a physical-material opposition of spirit-substance and earthly shell; instead, it describes the struggle in which the community that is faithful to the Law is placed here in the world. Therefore every man must decide for himself whether to heed the call to repentance and conversion. If he does convert, if he turns to the Law of Moses, then he belongs to the realm of the light and by God's grace gains true insight. He recognizes that God is the creator and lord, understands God's will as it is contained in the Law, comprehends that man before God is lost, and discovers the gracious mercy of God. Because the manner of life of a man proves which spirit governs him, that of truth or wickedness, true knowledge must find expression in behavior; and all who belong to the community must "purify their knowledge through the truth of the commandments of God and commit their strength to the perfectness of his ways" (1QS I. 12–13).

When one considers the faith and teaching of the Qumran community, as evidenced by the various writings, it appears in fact to be highly probable that we are dealing with the *fellowship of the Essenes*. The settlement lies on the shores of the Dead Sea, which is attested as the site of the Essene community (cf. p. 87). The community was led by priests, and it performed daily ablutions, in order constantly to be in a state of readiness, of priestly purity. The people rigidly separated themselves from the rest of the nation, in order to actualize, as the community of the saints, the life that is in accordance with the Law. Anyone who wished to enter the community first had to undergo a period of probation before he was accepted, at which time, by means of a binding oath, he was admitted to the purity of the community and to their fellowship at table. No one owned property privately; instead, it was owned collectively by the community. The community was divided into distinctly separate classes. It maintained strict discipline and prohibited marriage in order to prevent possible contact with impurity. According to Josephus' report, however, in addition to the fellowship which lived in an unmarried state, there were also Essenes who were married (cf. p. 85) ; so also the Damascus Document persupposes a group which lived very close to the Qumran community, permitted marriage, and allowed its members to have certain possessions of their own. The fact that the name "Essenes" does not appear in the Qumran texts could be due to the fact that this designation was perhaps applied to the community by outsiders (cf. p. 85). The community referred to itself as the true Israel, which included the saints and the ones elected to learn the mysteries of God.

3) The Qumran texts and the New Testament

While in the New Testament there are repeated accounts of direct confrontation between Jesus and the first Christians on the one hand and between the Pharisees and Sadducees on the other, nothing is said of any confrontation with members of the Qumran community or the Essenes. Although the community lived in isolation on the shores of the Dead Sea, the example of their piety and their teaching must have had a certain influence, and it is likely that many ideas which had been developed in Qumran were disseminated beyond the boundaries of the community and assimilated into the Judaism of that time. Hence it is not surprising that echoes of the concepts and ideas of the Qumran texts are perceptible not only in various apocalyptic writings, but in the written proclamations and descriptions of the life of earliest Christianity. These connections cannot be traced to an influence of Christian ideas upon the Qumran community but just the opposite. Many passages in the New Testament illustrate the use of conceptual material from Qumran, whether it be for the purpose of support or refutation.

It was not far from Qumran, on the banks of the Jordan, that *John the Baptist* appeared, preached, and administered

the baptism of repentance (cf. Mark 1:4 par.). Even in Qumran people knew that the external washing could not alone
engender purity, but that conversion was required in order
for cleanliness to be received with a penitent heart (1QS III.
4–9; V. 13–14). The biblical saying of Isaiah 40:3 played an
important role in Qumran (cf. pp. 100–101) and it is central,
as well, in the preaching of the Baptist: thus the community
of salvation chose the desert as its gathering place (1QS VIII.
13–16; IX. 19–20; Mark 1:3 par.) But while in Qumran this
community gathered around the Law in a specified and strict
fashion and isolated itself from other people, John did not
seek to found a community which would live according to a
precisely stated legal set of rules, but called upon all to be
converted and to prepare themselves for the arrival of the
Coming One. Because his activity was entirely oriented to
the announcement of the one who is mightier than himself,
he does not call for repeated washings; instead, the single
bath of baptism is considered sufficient cleansing and preparation for the messianic transformation.

Jesus calls, in his preaching, for repentance and teaches a
radical version of the divine commandment, whose unconditional demand man cannot avoid (cf. Matt. 5:21-48 par.).
In Jesus' preaching repentance and conversion are understood
altogether differently from the view in Qumran: because the
kingdom of God is drawing near, because God's imperative
will and at the same time his generous mercy affect men
directly, it is necessary for men to repent and to believe (cf.
Mark 1:15; Luke 11:32 par.; 13:1-5; 15:7,10, *et passim*). God's
radically interpreted commandment is matched by his unprecedented mercy, which is bestowed upon man in the
forgiveness of sins in order to lead man to obey God's
commandment. Because the last meal Jesus took with his
disciples before his death is described as a Passover meal
only by the Synoptic Gospels (Mark 14:12-25 par.), and
because the account in John's Gospel places the event a day
earlier (John 18:28; 19:14, 36), some have conjectured that
Jesus could have been observing the festival with his disciples
according to the rite of the Qumran community. Nevertheless
it is simply inconceivable that in Jerusalem, where the paschal
lamb had to be slain at the temple, anyone could have ob-

served the festival according to the calendar of the Qumran community. In Jerusalem people acted only in accordance with the official calendar—that established by the temple priesthood. Jesus did not go to Qumran, but to Jerusalem, and obviously did not trouble himself about the intricacies of the calendar which so greatly concerned many Jewish circles. He did not practice, like the pious persons in Qumran, an involved casuistry of the Law which develops precise prescriptions for dealing with every problem that might arise (as, for example, in the detailed commandments about the sabbath in CD X. 14–XI. 18); instead, he proclaimed God's will as a blessing which is to set man free to love and should, therefore, be accepted by him in gratitude (cf. the words about the sabbath in Mark 2:27; 3:4 par.; Matt. 12:11-12 par.; Luke 14:5). Since Jesus does not teach a casuistic organization of the Law, neither does he embrace the dichotomy of the sons of light and sons of darkness, or advocate dissociation from other people or the world in general. Instead, he devotes himself to all and becomes a companion of tax collectors and sinners. While it is said in Qumran that all the sons of light are to be loved, but all the sons of darkness, hated (1QS I. 9-10), Jesus instructs his disciples to love even their enemies and to pray for their persecutors (cf. Matt. 5:43-44 par.); for God's mercy and love know no boundaries.

Like the Qumran community, *the first Christians* thought of themselves as the people of the end-time to whom the promises of the Scriptures applied—the poor, the saints, the ones chosen by God. They called themselves "the elect ones of [God's] good pleasure" (1QS VIII. 6), "the sons of thy good pleasure" (1QH XI. 9), the "sons of his [God's] good pleasure" (1QH IV. 32–33), and "the men of [God's] good pleasure" (Luke 2:14). Because it is the last time, the real meaning of what God endeavored to say to his people through the words of the prophets can now be understood (cf. 1QHab. VII. 1–2; I Cor. 10:11). Yet salvation is no longer a future expectation, as it is in Qumran, but an event already manifested in the sending of Christ. The Christian community, which confessed Jesus of Nazareth as the crucified and risen Messiah, transferred to him the various honorific titles which Judaism had coined as an expression of its hope of the time of messianic salvation. While in Qumran people expected appearance of a prophet, a messianic king, and a messianic high priest (cf. 1QS IX. 11; 1QSa II. 11–21, *et passim*), for the Christians there is only the one Anointed One of God, who is not only the Messiah-King, but also the prophet of God and the priest of his people. He had not appeared in glory and cultic purity, but as a despised and condemned person who had been nailed to the cross of shame and had died an accursed death—for our sins (cf. I Cor. 15:3-5). The Lord's Supper of the Christian community is not celebrated as an action led by priests (cf. 1QS VI. 2–5; 1QSa II. 17–21), but as a continuation of the table-fellowship with Jesus. The Christian community recalls the death of Christ, confesses him as the risen Lord, and receives from him the forgiveness of sins (cf. I Cor. 11:23-26; Mark 14:22-25 par.) In order to regulate the life of the community, in several respects the Palestinian church followed the example which the Qumran community afforded. The church appears to have had, for a time, a voluntary community of goods (cf. Acts 2:44-45; 4:34-35; 5:1-11) and, like the Qumran community, reproved erring brethren with strict punishment. Anyone who was not willing to heed an admonition was to be called into account in the presence of witnesses and ultimately before the entire community (cf. Matt. 18:15-17; 1QS V. 25-VI. 1). The Christian community, however, did not withdraw from the world to practice a stringent legalism; instead, they very soon carried the gospel into the world.

The apostle *Paul* expressed himself in metaphors which had originated in Qumran to say that the life of the believers can be lived only in warfare against Satan and the powers of darkness. The weapons of righteousness must be taken up (cf. Rom. 6:12-13; 13:12-14). The battle which must be fought is not directed only against the enemy who attacks from without: flesh and spirit contend with each other within man, and the flesh desires to assume dominion in place of the spirit (cf. Gal. 5:16-24). According to the teaching of the Qumran community, the two spirits, that of truth and that of wickedness, fight against each other, and man must decide which side he will choose and by which spirit he will let himself be guided (1QS IV. 23–25). Man is flesh, and in his frailty is constantly under assault. In Paul's thought, it is not two spirits that stand in opposition to each other, but flesh and spirit. Respectively, these are manifested by the man who trusts in himself and the man who lives solely by God's deed. Yet the basic structure of this contest, as it is set forth in the texts from Qumran and by Paul, exhibits quite similar features. For in both cases, two spheres of human existence are set in opposition to each other and a man is defined by the power which rules over him. He finds himself on the right side only when he accepts the judgment which God pronounces upon him and lives out of the righteousness which God bestows upon those who place their trust solely in him. In Qumran as in Paul, justification by grace alone is taught. But while in the understanding of the pious Jews this justification first puts man in a position to recognize and then to perform God's law, according to Paul, justification liberates man from the Law and makes him a servant of Jesus Christ. According to the Qumran texts, justification by grace obligates man to keep the entire Law, rather than bits of it. A *sola lege,* therefore, corresponds to the *sola gratia* because apart from the Law there can be no right relationship to God and no salvation. Paul, on the other hand, sees in the cross of Christ the end of the Law (Rom. 10:4). Therefore God's righteousness can only be received in faith, which obediently affirms God's act and is the way in which he places us in a right relationship to himself, so that the *sola fide* necessarily belongs together with the *sola gratia* (cf. the differing interpretation of Hab. 2:4 in Qumran and in Paul: 1QpHab. VIII. 1–3; Rom. 1:17; 3:21–31; Gal. 3:6).

Finally, many expressions of the Qumran texts appear in the *Gospel of John* and in the Johannine Epistles. In both contexts the issue is the decision between light and darkness, truth and falsehood. The truth is not only the object of knowledge, but is to be practiced. Anyone who clings to God is a son of light. But while in Qumran these are the members of the covenant-community, who strive for truth through strict obedience to the Law, according to the Fourth Gospel they are simply the believers, who as sons of light stand on the side of truth (cf. John 12:35-36). For the light of the world, the truth, is none other than Christ alone (cf. John

8:12; 9:5; 14:6). Nothing is said anywhere in the teaching of the Qumran community of an emissary of God who has descended from heaven.

The texts from Qumran illumine conceptions and views in which pious and law-observing Jews in the days of Jesus and the apostles thought, believed, and hoped. Jesus and the first Christians many times made use of the expressions and concepts that were coined by them to show that the proclamation of the gospel gave the valid answer (which to be sure in more than one respect was different from what was expected) to the questions being posed by the groups of pious people awaiting the time of salvation. Thus the texts from Qumran illumine the background from which, in contrast, the primitive Christian preaching clearly and plainly emerges.

g. *The Scribes*

The history of Judaism in the Hellenistic period was linked critically to the *profession of the scribes;* for the scribes, in effect, determined the various groups which were developed in the second century B.C.—the Sadducees, the Pharisees, the Essenes, and the Qumran community. The beginnings of scribal work, however, go farther back. Originally it had been the task of the priest to communicate and teach the word of God. Ezra, who established postexilic Judaism upon the Law, was a priest and a scribe (Ezra 7:11). He was a priest by virtue of his origins, but the title of scribe was given to someone who was able to practice the art of writing and who served as a royal official. With the express approval of the great Persian king, Ezra had obligated the Jesusalem community to keep the Law, so that in the tradition he was characterized as "a scribe, skilled in the Law of Moses which the Lord, the God of Israel, had given" (Ezra 7:6). From him and the men of the Great Synagogue, which Ezra is said to have founded, evolved the unbroken line of scribes (Mishnah Aboth I. 1; cf. pp. 169–70). It is said that the men of the Great Synagogue handed down the Law and bridged the gap between the prophets and the scribes. References to individual scribes, however, appear in the tradition only from the second century B.C. onward, the first ones being made to a man with a Greek name, Antigonus of Sokho (Aboth I. 3).

Simon ben Schatach served during the rule of Alexander Jannaeus and of Queen Salome Alexandra (cf. pp. 32–33). Then beginning with the time of Jesus and the first Christians names of a whole series of esteemed scholars are recorded.

The development of a scribal profession must have taken place in the encounter and conflict with Hellenism. When people desired to maintain, in the face of the strong influence of the Greek spirit, the independent instruction in the Law, the old priestly teaching no longer sufficed. They were obliged, instead, to make use of the methods and the intellectual equipment of the Greeks in order to study and properly expound the Scripture, and they learned from the Greeks how to conduct a didactic conversation of questions and counter-questions such that teacher and learner would simultaneously derive answers to the problem at hand. Just as the Greeks appealed to the authority of the teachers and preserved the lineage of their names in the philosophical schools, the Jewish scribes also began reciting the list of names deserving of honor, those supposedly associated with Ezra and the men of the Great Synagogue.

Because the scribes were skilled in the preservation of tradition and in the interpretation and application of the Scripture, they were also called wise men, teachers of the Law, and masters. Because the law of God regulates all areas of life, they had to decide not only theological questions, but legal ones as well: for example, the exact extent to which labor should be prohibited on the sabbath, the proper method of formalizing a marriage contract or effecting a divorce, or how to certify the purchase of a field or a house. The lofty task which the scribes had to perform was matched by the universally high esteem which they received from the people. A man gained entrance into the circle of the scribes, not by birth or ancestry, but by knowledge and ability. Among them were priests and members of prominent families, but also people from all strata of the populace, merchants, craftsmen, and even proselytes. Every scholar was responsible for providing for his livelihood through the work of his own hands. Thus even the apostle Paul worked as a tentmaker, in order to remain independent of the churches (cf. I Thess. 2:9; II Thess. 3:8; I Cor. 4:12; 9:6-23, *et passim*).

Anyone who wished to become a scribe had to undergo a long and *thorough course of study*. A group of pupils would gather around a famous teacher. Then, when a pupil applied for acceptance into the school of a teacher, the teacher would examine him and decide whether to accept or reject him. If accepted the pupil entered into a lifetime association with the teacher. He accompanied him on his journeys, listened to how he approached and solved problems, and questioned the teacher in order to glean his knowledge. The teacher delivered his teaching while seated (cf. Matt. 5:1) ; the pupil sat at his feet (cf. Acts 22:3) and had to assimilate the abundance of material that had been handed down in order to become familiar enough with the wealth of tradition to be able to apply it. The course of study consisted in large measure of remembering and repeating what was set forth.. Within the framework of the teaching conversation the pupil questioned the teacher, then by means of counter-questioning by the teacher he was instilled with the proper method of meditation and reflection. In response to a first question (cf., e.g., Luke 10:25), the teacher suggests: "What do you read, what do you find in the Scripture?" (Luke 10:26). When the pupil brings forward what he knows that he can cite from the Scripture (Luke 10:27), the teacher answers that he has spoken correctly (Luke 10:28). By means of further inquiry by the pupil, then, a detailed exposition by the teacher is evoked. The discussion is finally resolved by the presentation of a question which furnishes the pupil with the insight to recognize the inescapable conclusion (Luke 10:37). Jesus, in his instructional discourse, also converses with his disciples or with other men who come to him in various forms of questioning. But Jesus' relationship to the disciples differed, from the very outset, from that of a scholar to his pupils because the disciples did not apply for admission to a circle of pupils, but were called by Jesus to follow him and were taught, in contrast to the scribes, with unprecedented authority (cf. Mark 1:22 par.; Matt. 7:29, *et passim*).

When the pupil had completed his course of study, he was declared a scholar by his teacher, who laid his hands upon him and ordained him. Thereby, he was incorporated into the chain of tradition which was traceable to Moses and was given the authority to answer questions and discuss the Law independently, as a teacher. As a master he was addressed with the title of respect "rabbi" (Matt. 23:7-8), and might now wear the long robe of the scholar (Mark 12:38 par.). In the synagogue the place of honor on the cathedra of Moses belonged to him (Mark 12:39 par.). People greeted him with respect (Mark 12:38 par.) and were ready to follow his word. It is told that in the second century A.D., R. Me'ir ("R." standing for "rabbi") once visited a Jewish community in Asia Minor when the time of the Feast of Purim was approaching. Since it was customary to read the scroll of Esther on this day, and the Jewish community did not possess a copy of that scroll, the rabbi sat down, transcribed the book of Esther from memory, and read the scroll aloud (Babylonian Talmud, Megillah 18b). Such ability was hailed and admired by the people.

In the time of Jesus, *Hillel* and *Shammai* were the two prominent heads of schools among the scribes. Hillel had come to Palestine from the Babylonian Diaspora and had earned his bread as a poor day laborer in order to be able to study. Once on a cold winter day when he had been unable to secure the money for admittance to the house of instruction, he had climbed in through a window in order from there to follow the lecture, had grown stiff from the cold and been found in this state by other students. This indicates how zealously he pursued his studies. As a teacher he participated, with his school, in intensive discussion with Shammai and his pupils. In that discussion, the decisions reached by Hillel were usually milder than those of Shammai. While the latter declared divorce allowable only if the wife had acted contrary to morality and honor, Hillel taught that the husband might send his wife away whenever he found anything about her warranting reproof—even if it were that she was a poor cook; for the only thing that mattered was that the letter of divorce be legally framed (cf. p. 149). Hillel also succeeded in finding a rule for a previously unsolved problem. Because in the sabbath-year, according to Old Testament prescription, all debts were dissolved (cf. Deut. 15:9), for some time prior to the sabbath-year it was almost impossible to find anyone who was willing to lend money. Here Hillel pointed out an alternative for a creditor. He could declare in writing to the judges of his locality that he exempted his loan from the regulation concerning the sabbath-year. By means of this rule, the stipulation of the Law was simply being circumvented, but an opportunity had been provided for keeping financial matters in order. People praised Hillel because his procedure, known as the *prosbol,* had showed concern for the general welfare.

The school of Hillel produced Rabbi *Gamaliel,* whose counsel, according to Acts 5:34-39, enjoyed high esteem in the Sanhedrin. According to Acts 22:3 he is supposed to have been the teacher of Paul, and he is venerated in Jewish tradition as one of the most pious teachers. The reconstruction of the Jewish communities was given normative structure by R. *Jochanan b. Zakkai.* He was a meek and humble man, of whom the tradition says that never in his life did he engage in an idle conversation, never in his life had he gone the distance of four ells without the Torah and prayercords, never in his life had anyone else been earlier than he at the house of instruction, never in his life had he fallen asleep in the house of instruction, never had anyone else been later in leaving the house of instruction, never had anyone found him sitting in idleness, but only studying, never had anyone but himself opened the door for his pupils, never did he say anything that he had not heard from his teacher, and never did he say that it was time to leave the house of instruction (Babylonian Talmud, Sukka 28*a*). When Jerusalem was besieged by the Romans, he escaped from the city by having two of his pupils carry him out as a corpse. After having passed the guards without their noticing that the teacher was not dead, he was received by the Romans and given permission to found a new school in Jabne (Jamnia). The teaching of the Law was carried forth into the synagogue communities, and here a Sanhedrin, now consisting entirely of scribes, gathered again to rule on all matters affecting the Jewish population. In this process the attitude of Hillel on the part of the scribes was instrumental in determining the orientation which Judaism was to assume following the destruction of Jerusalem, toward continuing and expanding the Pharisaic tradition.

The most important teacher at the beginning of the second

century was R. *Akiba,* around whom a large group of pupils gathered with whom he studied the interpretation of the Scripture. When Bar Cochba began the revolt against the Romans, he was hailed by R. Akiba as the promised "son of a star." After the revolution collapsed, the famous teacher was executed, along with many others, by the victorious Romans (cf. p. 54). Although he had been mistaken in the opinion that Bar Cochba was the messiah, his memory continued to be revered in later Judaism. Other men who were learned in the Scripture also died, like Akiba, at the hands of the Romans—among them the famous R. *Ishmael,* who was also the head of a large school and had developed rules for the explication of biblical text that attained fundamental importance for further exegetical labors (cf. p. 171). Although the schools of the scribes suffered grievous losses in the time of Bar Cochba, Judaism survived even this catastrophe. Now people began to collect, to arrange, and to integrate in the tractates of the Mishnah the abundant material of the tradition (cf. p. 174). R. Judah, who because of the great authority which he enjoyed was also simply called "Rabbi", vigorously advanced this work, so that by the end of the second century it was completed, and there stood, alongside the letter of the Scripture, an exposition of the Law, whose definitions gained normative significance for the life of the community.

3. Judaism in the Diaspora

a. The Jewish Diaspora in the Hellenistic World

Jerusalem was and always remained the center of Jewish life. Here stood the temple, here the daily sacrifice was offered, and here were held the great pilgrim festivals, for which innumerable pilgrims streamed into the holy city. In the land which is Israel's, therefore, a Jew finds himself in the homeland granted to him by God; but outside the land of Israel he is a foreigner, in an unclean land (cf. I Sam. 26:19-20; Amos 7:17), one of the dispersed among the nations. Nevertheless, in the time of Jesus and the first Christians, far more Jews lived in the Diaspora than in the land of Israel. So numerous were the causes of their banishment into other countries that Jewish communities could be found all around the Mediterranean basin. Many Jews had adapted to a wandering life, following the great highways of commerce and settling in centers of trade or in port cities. Many had been driven out of their homeland by bitter poverty, because the wars which raged in Palestine in the second and first centuries B.C. brought with them want and misery. Oppressive taxes were extracted from the peasant population by the ruling power. Thus under the Syrian rule one-third of the grain harvest, and one-half of the wine and oil harvest, had to be given to the kings (I Macc. 10:30), and the Romans later demanded one-fourth of the grain harvest (Josephus *Jewish Antiquities* XIV. 203). As a result of these oppressive burdens poverty so increased that many Jews preferred to leave the country and seek their fortune elsewhere. Many people were thrown this way and that by the wars, and were taken away to distant lands as prisoners of war. Even in the early period Jews had come to Egypt in this way—some of them as mercenaries, and some as prisoners. When the Romans brought the Near East under their dominion, Jewish prisoners were taken also to Italy and to Rome. When they were later released, many remained in the foreign land. But Judaism in the Diaspora also grew by virtue of the fact that many non-Jews joined it; moreover, the Jews increased in number more rapidly than the rest of the population because large families were considered a blessing, and it was strictly forbidden to the Jews to expose their children.

Since the time of the exile, a strong Jewish community had lived in Babylon, and many Jews had taken up residence in Syria for reasons of trade and commerce. They were found also in Asia Minor and North Africa. In Egypt the number of Jews came to one million (Philo *In Flaccum* XLIII), a large part of whom lived in Alexandria. But there were Jewish communities in smaller localities also; even in the Roman military colony of Philippi there was a Jewish place of prayer (Acts 16:13). Josephus proudly writes: "One can hardly find a place anywhere in the world that has not sheltered this people and is not in their possession. Thus it is that Egypt and Cyrenia, which have fallen into their hands, and many other cities imitate their customs, are devoted to the great host of Jews in a very special way, and grow powerful along with them, by living according to the ancient and traditional customs of the Jews. In Egypt they have the rights of citizenship, and even a large section of Alexandria is specially allotted to them; they have their own ethnarch, who attends to their causes, arbitrates for them in business matters, and enforces their contracts and agreements as if he were an independent ruler" (*Jewish Antiquities* XIV. 115–117). The number of Jews who lived in the Roman Empire in the time of Caesar Augustus may be estimated at four and a half million—a half to three quarters of a million of them in Palestine —which amounts to about seven percent of the entire population of the empire. Thus the number of Jews in the Diaspora far exceeded that of the Jews who lived in the homeland.

The rights which Caesar had granted to the Jewish population throughout the entire Roman Empire (cf. pp. 35–36) favored the existence and expansion of Judaism. The Jews were free from military service, they did not have to appear before authorities and the courts on the sabbath, and the communities could take responsibility for regulating their affairs. Every Jew made his contribution to the temple by paying at least a half-shekel every year as a temple-tax (equal to a double drachma—a sum equivalent to two days' wages for a daylaborer; cf. Matt. 17:24-27; 20:2, 9). A person who could afford to do so would voluntarily pay a larger amount. At the time of the pilgrim festivals, many Jews made the journey to Jerusalem, so that even in the Diaspora the tie to the homeland and the holy city was preserved. Conversely, people in Jerusalem sought to cultivate ties with the Jewish communities in the Diaspora (cf. Acts 9:2; 28:21).

The Jewish people who lived *in the Hellenistic world* had to adjust to the foreignness of their environment. Since the time of Alexander the Great, Hellenism had gained considerable influence even in Palestine. This had stimulated the Jews to learn from the Greeks, but also to define the limits of their relationship to them, to assert the distinctiveness of their life in accordance with the Law. In the Diaspora, however, the Jewish people came into much greater contact with Greek culture and civilization. Not only did they build synagogues in the Greek style and adopt the Greek customs of going to the theater and participating in athletic contests, but they soon lost even their native Hebrew or Aramaic tongue, and thereafter used only the language of the Greeks. Where it was possible, the Jews secured the rights of citizens in the Hellenistic cities (cf. Acts 21:39) in which they resided, or strove to secure the rights of Roman citizenship. According to Acts 16:37 and 22:25-29, Paul, a Diaspora Jew who came from Tarsus in Cilicia, could boast of having been born a Roman citizen. In order to conform to the Greek-speaking society, the Jews adopted Greek or Latin names, preferably ones which sounded like their Hebrew or Aramaic names. A person who was named Joshua/Jesus would call himself Jason (cf. Rom. 16:21; Acts 17:5-7, 9) ; Silas became Silvanus (cf. Acts 15:22, 27, 32 et passim; I Thess. 1:1; II Thess. 1:1; II Cor. 1:19; I Peter 5:12) ; and Saul became Paul (cf. Acts 13:9) .

The Jewish Diaspora was much more receptive to the Greek spirit than were the Jews in Palestine. Many Jews accepted the idea that someday Jews and Greeks would constitute a single community in which the unity of mankind under the one God would be realized. Yet the events of the Maccabean era, which caused the Jewish people to defend their life according to the Law against alien Hellenistic control, had the effect, not only for the Jews in Palestine but also for the entire Diaspora, of reminding them anew of their own way of life and the necessity, for the sake of preserving the Law, of more clearly distinguishing themselves from their non-Jewish environment. When the Jews made use of the philosophical concepts of the Greeks and, with the help of these, sought to make the faith of Israel comprehensible even to the non-Jewish environment, they also intended to make sure that even in the Diaspora they would well understand the reasons for holding fast to the legacy of their fathers. The God of Israel is the creator of the whole world, whose Logos governs the universe and whose works of creation—thus it was stated, in the mode of Stoic thought—point to his omnipotence, so that from a consideration of nature one could infer that God is above it and in it (cf. Rom. 1:20) . Because in him men live, move, and have their being (Acts 17:28) , one must through rational perception arrive at the insight that God is above all and in all. It is his will that men lead a rational life, and he has given the most profound expression

to this demand in the Law of Moses, whose prescriptions
were understood and expounded by the Jewish Diaspora
primarily as ethical instructions. In this connection the effort
was made to align the divine commandments with the Greek
philosophical approach to the moral obligation of man.

Judaism's susceptibility in the Diaspora to the influence of
the Greek language and the Greek spirit inevitably meant
that the faith and life of the Jews would not remain unaltered.
While in Palestine the eschatological hope was oriented to
the resurrection of the dead, in the Diaspora people embraced
the contemporary Greek idea of the immortality of the soul.
In the Diaspora, eschatology and, in particular, the messianic
expectation receded into the background; for how was it
possible for people in foreign lands to think of the appearance
of a messiah who would restore the brilliance of the people of
Israel? In the teaching in the synagogue, ethics, which provided the individual with instructions for acting and living
responsibly, predominated. The cultic and ritual prescriptions
of the Law were frequently reinterpreted with the help of
allegorical methods of exposition and restated as moral commandments (cf. pp. 134–35), so that the Law of Israel was
fashioned into a summary of ethical rules. The attempt was
made to emphasize that in the final analysis the philosophers
are to be understood as pupils of Moses, by whom they have
all been enlightened (cf. pp. 136–37). Jewish propaganda
therefore manufactured many statements and attributed them
to Greek authors in order to add weight to that contention.
Jews read the oracles of the Sibyl, which were widely disseminated in the ancient world, and inserted Jewish theses into
the collections of mysterious sayings. The Sibyl predicts the
fate of the world from its very beginning to the present, but
at the end utters threats and promises for the immediate
future, reprimands the heathen nations for their sinfulness,
and demands their repentance and conversion. Thus, by
means of this new version of the oracles, the Sibyl becomes a
prophet of Jewish teaching. Jewish proverbial wisdom was also
set in verse, so that in hexameters it would sound familiar to
a Greek. By inserting moral instruction, as it was set forth in
Judaism, in a didactic poem and attributing it to Phocylides,
a poet of the sixth century B.C., the attempt was made to

persuade those living in the Hellenistic environment that the wisdom of the Greeks and the wisdom of Israel were of one and the same root.

The life and worship of the Jewish communities drew attention in the non-Jewish environment. Many non-Jews percevied the gatherings in the synagogue, in which the Scriptures were read, prayers and psalms recited, and sermons often delivered, as philosophical forums in which were discussed the ultimate issues of life. Besides, the faith of the Jews was distinguished by a mystery-enshrouded origin in the history of the people of Israel and an honorable tradition. Thus there occasionally gathered around the synagogue an impressive circle of persons who wished to hear the teaching of the Law. The demand for circumcision, however, discouraged many of them from converting to Judaism, becoming *proselytes,* and obligating themselves to keep the whole Law including the ritual prescriptions. The effort was made to accommodate Gentiles by requiring them to observe only the most essential and basic commandments—particularly the sabbath and dietary rules and the ethical stipulations—and to confess the one God. A person who accepted these obligations was regarded as a God-fearer (cf. Acts 13:43, 50; 16:14; 17:4, *et passim).* Although he remained legally a Gentile, he belonged to the synagogue in a loose relationship. Often then the next generation would decide upon full conversion to Judaism. In the course of the first century A.D. it became customary to precede the admission of a proselyte not only with circumcision, but also with immersion, by which the taint of cultic impurity attached to the Gentile was washed away. This proselyte baptism was understood to be a legal act, the conversion to Judaism requiring the presence of witnesses, and qualified the proselyte as a Jew in every respect. Thus the Jewish communities in the Diaspora grew in many places through additions from the non-Jewish population. Judaism exercised a strong influence upon its environment through its strict monotheism, refutation of the idolatry practiced by the Gentiles (which had already become questionable for many people), and the moral force of its life lived in accordance with the Law. There was, however, little interest in missionary undertakings (but cf. Matt. 23:15);

Judaism gained renown in the ancient world through the life of the synagogue communities and through word of mouth reporting.

The magnetism exerted by Judaism, however, was often matched by the attitude of rejection with which it was greeted by many circles and which individual Jews were made to feel sharply. The Jew could not conform to the society surrounding him, so he often appeared as an alien. The customs and practices of the Jews, and particularly their observance of the sabbath, were regarded as peculiar and were sometimes ridiculed. They were accused of superstition and secret practices, and often slandered. The ridicule, which in many places was directed at the whole way of life of the Jews, sometimes led to bloody excesses against them. Thus during the reign of Caligula there occurred in Alexandria some serious infringements upon the Jews' rights by the Gentile population, who undertook to avenge in the name of the emperor the Jews' refusal to venerate the emperor as a divine manifestation. The synagogues were plundered, fires were set, and Jews were murdered, without any intervention being offered by the Roman governor (cf. p. 134). The persecution ended only because of the sudden death of Caligula, at which time the Emperor Claudius restored the rights of the Jews (cf. p. 204). Thus the situation of Judaism in the Diaspora was not always a simple one. The people had to know all the intricacies of their alien environment, yet they could never really become a part of it and, therefore, feel secure in it. They wanted to be open to the Greek spirit, in order to take advantage of the intellectual tools it provided for justifying the traditional faith, but they could not and might not forget that the people of Israel belong to their God and are obliged to be faithful to Israel's destiny.

The tradition of the *Wisdom literature* acquired special significance for Judaism in the Diaspora, because on the one hand it transmitted the history of Jewish life and experience, which describes the proper conduct of the devout, and on the other hand created a link with philosophically grounded wisdom. Thus the collection of sayings of Jesus ben Sirach, composed in Jerusalem in the Hebrew language at the beginning of the second century B.C., was translated into Greek by the grandson of the author. Rules for proper conduct in home and family, for dealings with other people, and for conduct pleasing to God were also widely disseminated in the Diaspora. The title "Wisdom of Solomon" was given to a writing which appeared in Alexandria about the middle of the first century B.C. It likewise incorporates diverse traditions and seeks to show the Jews that the wisdom of Israel is superior to the religion and philosophy of the other nations.

A characteristic example of the combination of popular Greek philosophy with the traditions of Jewish life in accordance with the Law is afforded by *IV Maccabees,* which appeared about the time of the birth of Christ in the Jewish Diaspora—in Alexandria or in Syria/Asia Minor. The author proposes to deliver a discourse, such as may have been delivered now and then in the synagogues, and announces his intention to demonstrate that reason should rule the emotions. Thus he introduces his theme with these words: "Genuinely philosophical is the discourse which I propose to deliver on the question whether the pious reason governs the impulses. Therefore I may properly counsel you to give heed to this philosophy" (IV Macc. 1:1). First of all, therefore, some prefatory conceptual statements are provided: "Thus reason is understanding which with proper reflection elects the life of wisdom. Wisdom is knowledge of divine and human matters and of their foundations" (1:15–16). These general statements, however, are just the outline of the presentation which the author wishes to offer: "I could show you by many examples here and there that the pious reason governs the impulses. But I believe that it is best proved by the brave manliness of those who suffered death for the sake of virtue—Eleazar, the seven brothers, and their mother. For all these disregarded pain, even unto death, and thereby showed that reason has power over the impulses" (1:7–9). The steadfastness of the law-observing Jews who under Antiochus Epiphanes preferred to die rather than be unfaithful to the Law is then set forth in detail by means of the expansion of the earlier tradition as it is found in II Maccabees 6–7. The aged Eleazar is brought before the king, who disputes his claim to be a philosopher, for if he were, he would freely eat what nature offers him. Since he as a Jew does not want to touch unclean food, he is deemed foolish. Eleazar answers that he is and will remain obedient to the Law. "You ridicule our philosophy as though it were a lack of reasonable reflection for us to live in it. It teaches us discretion, so that we govern all our appetites and desires; it exercises us in manliness, so that we willingly suffer any pain; it trains us in righteousness, so that we act uniformly in all changing moods; it instructs us in piety, so that we worship only the God who is, with the glory that is his due. Therefore we eat nothing that is unclean" (5:22–25).

It may be clearly discerned from IV Maccabees how through the events of the Maccabean period even the Jewish Diaspora became reoriented to the fact that Israel is set apart from the nations and therefore might not be absorbed into the Greek environment, but was obliged at all times to remain obedient to the Law which God had given to her. It was precisely this obedience that the Jewish synagogue sought to render comprehensible to the non-Jewish environment, by explaining it with the help of philosophical concepts and thus by describing Judaism as true philosophy in which the ideals of virtue and constancy are not only taught, but also preserved and maintained in life.

b. The Septuagint

In order for the Jewish communities in the Hellenistic world to be able to hold to the Law, the word of God had to be translated from the Hebrew into the Greek language; for many Jews had lost their knowledge of Hebrew or Aramaic. It is likely that the Hebrew text was first translated orally in the synagogues, but that a written translation soon developed. The legend reports how the preparation of the translation was accompanied by marvelous events, and it seeks through its own narrative to establish the significance of these events. This legend is related in the so-called Letter of Aristeas, a writing from the end of the second century B.C., and is repeated later in the works of other Hellenistic-Jewish authors. It is said that King Ptolemy II Philadelphus (284–247 B.C.) was informed by his librarian Demetrius that his library lacked a Greek translation of the Law of the Jews, and that he immediately took measures to eliminate this serious gap. He sent a message to the high priest in Jerusalem and asked for seventy-two scholars, six from each of Israel's tribes, to undertake the task of translating the Law into Greek for his library. The high priest acceded to the king's wish; the seventy-two scholars were received in Alexandria with great honor, and set to work on the Island of Pharos, near Alexandria. Every day at evening each presented what he had translated, and through extensive comparison arrived at an agreement upon the proper wording of the text. After seventy-two days the work was completed: The Law was wholly translated into Greek and was read to the assembled Jewish community. There was great rejoicing, and unanimous admiration for the accuracy and exactness of the translation, so that it was declared by everyone: "Since the translation in its beautiful, devout, and utterly exact form is complete, it is right and proper that it should be preserved in this wording and not undergo any change" (Letter of Aristeas 310). The title of the Greek translation is derived from this story of the seventy-two scholars, the number seventy-two having been rounded off to seventy (Latin *septuaginta*).

The legendary nature of the account, which intentionally demonstrates the nobility of the Law by which the Jewish communities in the Hellenistic world live, is unmistakable. Even a heathen king is convinced of its loftiness and is very anxious to have a Greek version compiled and placed in his library. Yet once one discounts these features, some historically correct inferences can be drawn from this tradition. It is surely correct that the Jewish communities in Egypt urgently needed a Greek translation of the Law. In order to secure acceptance for this work in all the communities, contact must have been established with Jerusalem on the part of the Diaspora and help sought for the fulfillment of this intention. The time span referred by the legend—the first half of the third century B.C.—may also be approximately correct. The Jews of Egypt could without difficulty carry on relations with Jerusalem. No restrictions were placed upon the movement of emissaries during the time Palestine was under the rule of the Ptolemies (who were in power in Egypt), and the Jewish community enjoyed considerable self-government (cf. p. 22). Finally, it should be noted that the Letter of Aristeas speaks solely of the translation of the Law; the other parts of the Old Testament are not included. The Pentateuch was and still is for Judaism the most important part of the Scripture, from which all the other books are to be interpreted. Hence the five books of Moses would surely have been the first to be translated in the Hellenistic Diaspora of Egypt with the assistance of Palestinian scholars.

The remaining parts of the Old Testament were little by little translated into Greek. Word usage and style are by no means consistent throughout, and the same is true of the accuracy and reliability of the translations. While the Pentateuch was translated very carefully, the translations of some prophetic texts, as for example the book of Isaiah, were not as successful, and the Greek version of the book of Daniel is more a paraphrase than a translation. Since for Hellenistic Judaism a boundary for the Canon was not yet by any means clearly drawn, books which arose in the second and first centuries B.C. were accepted into the Septuagint, so that the group of writings in the Greek Old Testament is more extensive than the Hebrew Canon (cf. pp. 167–69). Altogether it contains nine more books than the Hebrew Bible: the books of Judith and Tobit, the four books of Maccabees, the book of Sirach (Ecclesiasticus), the Wisdom of Solomon, and the Psalms of Solomon. In addition, then, there are some revisions or expansions of Old Testament writings: the Greek Ezra, the Odes, the book of Baruch, the Epistle of Jeremiah, Susannah, Bel and the Dragon, and some expansions of the book of Esther. Parts of the writings are based on original Hebrew texts, but other parts were composed originally in Greek (IV Maccabees, for example). Then after the Greek and Roman churches decided to include in their Bible some books of the Septuagint which went beyond the Canon of the Hebrew Old Testament, the churches of the Reformation recognized as canonical only the writings which belonged to the Hebrew Bible. The books which the Septuagint offered in addition to these were labeled as Apocrypha, "that is, books which are not regarded as equal to the Holy Scripture and yet are good and useful for reading" (Martin Luther).

As a result of the translation of the Old Testament into the Greek language, many Greek words were infused with the meanings of the Hebrew expressions which corresponded to them. While the Greeks understood *doxa* as "appearance, meaning," under the influence of the Hebrew *qabod* the word *doxa* was employed in many passages to mean "splendor, glory." The Hebrew *panim* denotes "the side facing the viewer," so not only could the face of a person be called *panim,* but also the "face of the earth" or "the land" (Gen. 2:6 *et passim*) or the "face of the altar" (I Kings 8:22, 31 *et passim*). Thus, under the impact of Hebrew word usage the meaning of the Greek word *prosopon* was expanded and gained the figurative sense of referring to the side of objects offered to view. In the Hebrew language, adjectives are used far less than in Greek, and instead of adjectives people frequently made use of an appended substantive in the genitive case to indicate a more precise characterization. Since in the Septuagint this way of speaking is often preserved, there arise Hebraizing expressions such as "the paths of righteousness," meaning "the right path" (Ps. 23:3). In Hebrew, suffixes are frequently attached to substantives to indicate the relationship or connection; in the Greek of the Septuagint they usually are replaced by added personal pronouns such as "my," "your," "his," and so on. As a result of all this, expressions were formed which indeed were not impossible in Greek, but were not common. In the Hebrew sentence, as a rule, the verb stands at the beginning; the parts of the sentence are not constructed in artistic clauses, but are only strung together with "ands." In the Greek translation the form of the sentences usually remained unchanged; therefore very often the predicate is given at the beginning of the sentence and the separate individual expressions are only loosely joined by a connecting "and." This language, which became manifest in an oral form through the reading of biblical passages in the synagogue, was suited to an explicitly biblical context and also frequently influenced the informal narration and exposition of Old Testament stories. Since the New Testament authors almost always cite and interpret the Old Testament according to the Septuagint, the influence of the Greek Septuagint on the New Testament is also perceptible in many passages—not only in connection with Old Testament quotations, but also in longer passages in which biblical language is purposely used to give expression to the special character of the event that is being related (cf., for example, the infancy narrative of John the Baptist and of Jesus in Luke 1–2).

If on the one hand the Greek of the Septuagint is influenced by the prototype of the Hebrew Old Testament, on the other, the translators' effort to make use of a set of concepts by which they could render the biblical discourse comprehensible to Greek-speaking readers is unmistakable. Where possible, they sought to dissociate anthropomorphisms from God and to make use of a rational concept. Thus, instead of speaking of the hand of God, they spoke of his power (Josh. 4:24), and God's omnipotence was underscored by translating the term *Jahweh Sebaoth* as *Kyrios Pantokrator*. In his loftiness God is far removed from the affairs of men, so that not God but God's angel appears to Moses (Exod. 4:24). When Moses at the burning bush asks the name of God, the answer is: "I am that I am" (Exod. 3:14). In the Septuagint this designation of God is translated as "I am the one who is," and therewith God is described as the true and highest Being, as conceived by Greek thought. He is Creator and Lord over all the world, who by means of his word makes known his will and through his Law communicates his commandments to all men in order to lead them to ethical action. Whoever follows this Law will find the way to achieve virtue, happiness, and peace, the details of which prescriptions are set forth more explicitly in the sermons and teachings of the latest portions of the Septuagint (cf. IV Macc.; see above, pp. 127–28).

The language and message of the Septuagint prepared the way for early Christianity, the way by which it could advance upon the Hellenistic world. The Greek Old Testament was the Bible of the Christian communities which in rapid succession appeared in the cities of the Roman Empire. The one God, who is making his will and his commandment known to all the world through Israel, has revealed himself as the Father in Christ. The Christian message could be proclaimed, first in the synagogues and then among non-Jews, in the language which was formed by the Greek translation of the

Old Testament. Since the Christians used the Septuagint as their Bible and a source of scriptural proof for the truth of the gospel, the Jews more and more drew away from it. In the course of this process, new strength was gained for a movement whose first impetus had been felt in earlier times— namely an effort to secure a Greek translation of the Old Testament text which gave more precise and literal expression to the language and content of the Old Testament than did the Septuagint. The present Septuagint afforded the Christians a justification for their arguments at many points. For example, in the statement in Isaiah 7:14 that a young woman would conceive and bear a son, in Greek the word "virgin" is used, so that the Christians could derive from this a scriptural proof of the miraculous birth of Jesus (cf. Matt. 1:23). In order to be able to refute this interpretation, a new translation was prepared in Jewish circles which strove with slavish exactness to imitate in Greek every expression in the Hebrew, without paying any attention to the fact that thereby an extremely strange form of the Greek language emerged. This work, which was prepared by the proselyte *Aquila*—a pupil, according to the rabbinical tradition, of R. Akiba (cf. pp. 52–53)—about A.D. 130, received the explicit approval of the scholars in Palestine. In addition to the work of Aquila a translation was produced by *Theodotion*. Theodotion strove to use a more natural sounding Greek and revised the Septuagint by following the Hebrew text more closely. His translation was also used by Christians, and for the book of Daniel his text generally came to be preferred to the version in the Septuagint. Then about the end of the second century A.D. a man named *Symmachus* produced still another Greek translation of the Old Testament which clearly betrays the influence of the rabbinical exposition of the Scriptures. The history of the development of these translations verifies that in the second century A.D., the Jewish Diaspora in the Hellenistic world (insofar as it had not become Christian) came under the influence and guardianship of the rabbis, who thereafter determined how the word of the Scripture was to be understood and what should be taught in the synagogue.

c. Philo of Alexandria

The works of Philo of Alexandria bear witness to the intellectual power of this Jewish scholar. Few of the practical circumstances of his career are known. Born about 25 B.C., he led the life of a retiring sage in Alexandria, who nevertheless did not refuse when the Jews in Alexandria required his active assistance. When the Jews in Alexandria began being persecuted by the Gentile population with the tacit approval of the Roman governor Flaccus (cf. p. 126), the Jews decided to send an embassy to the Emperor Caligula. Philo then traveled to Rome as leader of this embassy and conducted the negotiations (A.D. 39/40). Philo himself has told about this journey (*Legatio ad Gaium*), but other than this no further particulars from his life are included in his writings.

Like the Hellenistic Jews, Philo too, in his thinking and activity, was concerned with establishing a rational basis for Judaism with the aid of philosophical reflections. The bulk of his writings are concerned with the explanation of the Law, particularly of the books of Genesis and Exodus, for which detailed explanations and reflections are offered. Philo did not create a systematic framework for his thoughts, but always developed his ideas in the immediate context of Old Testament texts. Nevertheless a unifying theme, whose basic ideas frequently recur, is discernible from the multiplicity of his pronouncements. For Philo the Law of Israel is the unassailable authority, but he is also aware of his profound commitment to the legacy of Greek philosophy and seeks, therefore, to bring this heritage into harmony with the Law of Moses. He speaks of the divine Plato and frequently refers to Platonic ideas; he knows the Greek tragedians and the popular Hellenistic philosophy and utilizes them in many passages. In the interpretation of the Pentateuch, Philo adheres to the Greek biblical text, and to a large extent he interprets it with the aid of the *allegorical method,* which had been developed primarily in Stoic philosophy and had already been used in Jewish biblical exegesis before Philo's time. The Stoics intended on the one hand to hold to the ancient myths and sagas of the gods, but on the other hand to offer a reasonable explanation of these stories in order to distill from the myth its soul, that is, to set forth its ethical meaning (cf. p. 245). The allegorical explanation proceeds from the presupposition that the actual content of the text is something other than what it appears at first to be saying, so that its rational meaning can be brought out only by means of an interpretation which lays bare the actual significance of the text. Thus Philo too proposes to distinguish the soul of the text from the outward form of its body.

Allegorical interpretation of the Old Testament was also occasionally employed by the authors of the New Testament writings in order thereby to establish continuity between the Old Testament and the Christian communities. Thus Paul refers to Deuteronomy 25:4—"You shall not muzzle the ox that grinds the grain"—to ask whether God is concerned for the oxen. No, the apostle answers, in truth this saying is not uttered for the sake of the animals, which are to get a little nourishment in the course of their work, but for our sake. From this, then, it is inferred that support must be provided by the community for the person who is in the service of the gospel (I Cor. 9:9–10). And in Galatians the apostle refers to the story of Abraham's two wives and then goes on to say that the story of Hagar and Sara and their two sons is to be interpreted allegorically: Hagar with her son is interpreted to mean slavery, but Sara with Isaac to mean the freedom to which the believers are called (Gal. 4:21–31). Where allegorical interpretation of the Scripture is proposed in the New Testament, use is being made of a method of exposition which was widely disseminated in Hellenistic Judaism and which Philo in particular used frequently.

The books of the Law are described by Philo, with the help of allegorical explanation, as excellent *moral teaching;* the people who are mentioned in Genesis serve to impart psychological and ethical instruction. Thus the creation narrative reveals that Adam symbolizes reason; the beasts of the field and the fowls of the air, the emotions; and Eve, standing in opposition to reason, sensuality. The serpent, as the symbol of appetite and love, unites Adam and Eve. When Abraham first begets a son by Hagar, before he has offspring by Sara, this means that one must first concern oneself with the propaedeutic disciplines before one can apply oneself to wisdom and can attain virtue as its finest fruit. The life of Joseph offers a political model and shows how the wise man must conduct himself in affairs of state, by giving an example of prudent action. Just as the narratives in Genesis are rationally explained in this manner, so also the prescriptions of the Law are allegorically interpreted and thus are made sensible in their ethical contents. The biblical requirement that a sacrificial animal must be without blemish means: "You will find that this examination of the animal that must be so very carefully conducted symbolically indicates your obligation to improve your own conduct; the Law indeed is not given for the benefit of unreasoning animals, but for beings who have reason and understanding. Therefore the concern is not for the sacrificial animals, that they show no visible defects, but for the ones offering the sacrifices, that they not be subject to passions" *(De specialibus legibus* I. 260).

Consequently the Law teaches what is fitting to the nature of man according to divine order. Just as the sabbath affords the opportunity to spend the day of rest in philosophical reflection, so also in each case the individual commandments correspond to nature's dictates. Therefore Moses taught nothing different from what the Greek philosophers taught, indeed, he is in fact their teacher, from whom all of them have learned. Therefore the Jew does not need to be ashamed when he lives in accordance with the Law in an environment which does not share his belief. For he is a cosmopolite in the truest sense of the word; he is obedient to the law of nature, which has been most clearly set forth by Moses. Since Moses prefixed to the Law an account of the creation of the world, it follows therefrom that the Law corresponds to nature and therefore offers instructions which in essence pertain to all men.

Philo also discovers Israel's confession of the one *God* in the teachings of the philosophers. In agreement with them he denounces the pagan polytheism and idolatry. The one God exists over against the world as the Highest Good. Man can speak of him only in negative terms, so that his nature cannot actually be described but only imagined by allusion. He is invisible, unchangeable, complete, and free from human faults. He is simply the Good and Beautiful; all conceivable perfection is with him. Thus Platonic ideas are employed by Philo in developing his doctrine of God:

> God alone in truth celebrates festivals; for he alone may rejoice, he alone may be joyous and gay, he alone has peace without strife; he is without sorrow or fear, perfectly free from evils, inferior to none, without pain, without weariness, full of pure blessedness, his nature is utterly perfect; nay, more, God himself is the summit, the goal, and the boundary of blessedness; he needs no other to heighten it, but rather grants to all individual creatures a share in the source of the good, in himself; for all that is good in the world would never have become so if it had not been formed in imitation of the truly good prototype, the uncreated, imperishable. (*De cherubin* 86)

God stands high above the world and communes with persons on earth through intermediate beings or hypostases. The kinship of the Platonic notion of ideas to the Jewish conception of angelic beings is apparent in Philo's claim that before the founding of the world God created the prototypes of all things. God remains active in the world through the powers that issued from him. These powers Philo names Wisdom, Spirit, Goodness, and Strength, but above all *Logos*. The latter is the Idea which contains within itself all other ideas. It is God's ambassador and deputy in the world, his instrument and revealer, through whom he created, sustains, and governs the world. However, the Logos is not only active as God's Power which comes to men, but as a high priest who represents men before God and intercedes for them. Thus the Logos is *the* intermediate being between God and man.

The creation came about by God's act of forming, through use of the Logos and the divine powers, the formless and featureless matter, which was lifeless and without order, in such a way that the prototype, which was already at hand, was actualized. Matter in its lifelessness is the absolute opposite of God; for it is dead and vain. Only through the divine Logos could the creation be formed out of it. In the creation of man, God first created the primal man, who as the reflection of his true being was made after God's likeness. While the statement in Genesis 1:26-27 refers to the primal man, that in Genesis 2:7 refers to the earthly man, who emerged as a reflection of the prototype. The heavenly man assumed God's likeness, but the earthly man was created. He was guilty of the fall and was expelled from Paradise, but the heavenly man, as the pure and perfect "idea" of man, dwells with God.

Man therefore stands between two worlds. His soul comes from God and belongs to the heavenly home, but his body is formed out of perishable matter, houses the soul as in a prison, and will again pass away. The body is the cause of all evils, sins, and weaknesses of man, but the soul is of divine origin and will return to God. Therefore man is given the task of purging his soul, denying the passions and lusts, achieving moral perfection. Of course he will not be able to reach this goal by his own power. But God's help supplements his efforts and strengthens him, so that he is able to lead a virtuous life.

The sense of belonging to God the believer knows is intensely experienced by the truly *wise man* because the truly wise man detaches himself from all that is earthly and experiences the immediate vision of God. According to Plato, the highest level attainable by the wise person is an intuitive vision, the inspiration which can also be described as intoxication and being filled with heavenly love. Philo follows these ideas and expresses them in connection with Genesis 12:1. God had commanded Abraham to depart from his fatherland, his kinsmen, and his father's house, to go to a land which he would show him. Of this passage Philo says:

> Therefore, O soul, when the yearning comes over you to become heir to the divine blessings, leave not only "land" (the body), and "kinsmen" (sensuality), and "father's house" (the logos), [here logos means the reason which is expressed in speech], but flee even from yourself, go out of yourself, enraptured like those who are possessed and delirious after the corybantic fashion, and divinely filled with prophetic inspiration. For this is the legacy of the soul which, divinely inspired, is no longer in itself, but is driven and inflamed by heavenly love, is led by the true Being and exalted to him, while the truth leads the way and removes whatever is in the path, so that the soul may walk on a smooth way. (*Quis rerum divinarum heres* 69–70)

Just as Philo utilizes concepts from the philosophical tradition to describe the wise man's inward relationship with God, he also borrows from the language of the mystery religions, for example, when he says:

> Receive these teachings as truly sacred mysteries into your souls, O you initiated ones who have clean ears, and do not divulge them to any of the uninitiated ones, but keep and guard them as a treasure chest, which does not contain silver and gold (perishable things), but the most precious of all possessions, the knowledge of the creator [of the universe], of virtue, and thirdly of the offshoot of the two. But when you meet an initiated person, cling to him and beg him that if he knows of a new and secret teaching, he will not hide it until you are fully taught concerning it. For even I, having been initiated into the great secret teachings by Moses, the friend of God, was not reluctant, when later I became acquainted with the prophet Jeremiah and recognized that he was not a mere initiate, but an important hierophant as well, to go to him for instruction. (De cherubin 48–49)

The language which Philo is speaking here must not be misunderstood. For he neither intends to defend esctatic experiences as such nor to portray Judaism as a mystery religion (pages 232–43). When he occasionally says that the person lifted up by divine inspiration experiences sacred mysteries and divine initiations, he is employing a mode of speech in current use in the Hellenistic world in order to apply it in a metaphorical sense. True initiation is experienced through the study of the Law and the prophets, and ecstatic experiences are granted to the person who comprehends the knowledge that is vouchsafed to him as God's gift.

Philo's piety has a decidedly individualistic character; for he conceives of Israel as a community of wise men. In the circle of the synagogues Philo remained a lonely thinker whose work did not exert a wide influence, since soon after his time even the Judaism of the Diaspora came under the influence of the rabbis (cf. p. 133). But Philo's ideas had a strong impact upon the early Christianity in Alexandria. The Christians made use of the concepts developed by Philo, and they were able in particular to use the idea of the Logos for the development of Christology. Thus Philo, for his part, became a forerunner of Christian theology, which preserved and handed down his writings. Without Philo the theology of Clement of Alexandria and of Origen is inconceivable; for the Christians learned from the great Jewish philosopher and theologian how biblical faith is to be given a philosophical foundation and made comprehensible as the fulfillment of all striving after wisdom and virtue.

d. Josephus

Josephus, whose origins were in Jewish Palestine but who later lived in the Diaspora, intended through his books to provide for his Hellenistic readers a vindication of Judaism and to propagandize the faith of Israel. In so doing, the Palestinian tradition is given expression (though even in this is evident the pervasiveness of the Hellenistic influence), and similarly there is offered, in Hellenistic concepts, an account of Judaism consistent with the self-understanding derived from the experience of a Jew living in an environment that did not share his faith. Josephus is a much less independent thinker than Philo of Alexandria. But for this reason his statements about contemporary Judaism are all the more reliable as an expression of the typical conceptions and views in the circles of the synagogues.

Josephus has described his career in an autobiography. Born the son of a priest in Jerusalem about A.D. 37, he became acquainted in succession with the groups of the Pharisees, the Sadducees, and the Essenes by becoming a member of each of them for a certain time. Then after he had lived for three years with a hermit named Bannus and had shared the latter's hard life, he returned to Jerusalem at the age of nineteen, joined the Pharisees, and began to be active in public life. When the Jews revolted against the Romans, Josephus indeed counseled moderation, but then joined the uprising and was sent as a commander to Galilee. After he was taken prisoner by the Romans in the conquest of Jotapata, he succeeded in winning the favor of Vespasian (cf. p. 49) so that he was able to witness the entire war in the company of the Roman field commanders and later to go to Rome, there to settle and use his literary talents to restore the honor of his defeated and despised people.

Soon after the end of the war Josephus wrote his history of the Jewish war, which describes the sequence of events from the time of Antiochus IV to the conquest and destruction of Jerusalem. The work was first written in the Aramaic language but later translated into Greek and in the late seventies was presented to Vespasian. It was intended to demonstrate that the absurd activities of the Zealots were the true cause of the misfortune of the Jews. In A.D. 93/94 Josephus published a history of Israel, the *Jewish Antiquities*. The first ten books, like the Old Testament writings, relate the history of Israel from the Creation to the Babylonian Exile. Josephus had access to only a few sources for the period following, so the postexilic period is presented quite briefly. The account becomes detailed once again for the time of the Maccabees, for which the books of the Maccabees afforded abundant material. The reign of Herod is portrayed with particular detail in books 15–17; the last three books then guide the reader to the outbreak of the Jewish war. In these histories Josephus is most valuable as a witness for the events in Palestine in the first century B.C. and the first century A.D. Their detailed rendering—to be sure not always reliable—offers abundant information about the Judaism of the time of Jesus and the first Christians. Finally, the apologetic tendency of Josephus' literary style, also shapes his book *Contra Apionem* ("Against Apion"). In it Josephus refutes the widespread suspicion of the Jews and the accusations that were made against them by calling attention to the great antiquity and noble ethics of the Jews, whose state was neither a monarchy, oligarchy, nor democracy, but a theocracy, in which God alone was believed Lord of all areas of human life (*Contra Apionem* II. 16–17).

Josephus wrote like a Hellenistic man of letters and wished to be recognized as a historian in the Greek-speaking world. Thus, in keeping with Greek custom, he begins his history of the Jewish war with a foreword in which he briefly describes his task, emphasizes the reliability of his account, and explicitly recommends his work:

Many have already described the war of the Jews against the Romans, the most significant war not only of our times but among all wars which, as we have heard, have broken out between cities or nations. Yet some of these were not even present at the events, but have collected foolish and contradictory accounts from rumors and reworked them in sophistical fashion. Some of them were present; yet in order to flatter the Romans, or out of hatred against the Jews, they have falsified the events. Hence their writings consist in part of base flattery, but they do not offer historical truth. Therefore I, Josephus, son of Matthias of Jerusalem, a priest, who myself fought against the Romans at the beginning of the war and was forced to attend the further course of it, determined to give to the people living under Roman rule an account in the Greek language of what I have already issued to the non-Greeks living in the interior. (*Jewish War* I. 1–3).

In what follows, then, Josephus gives a detailed exposition of the methodological principles of his labors, which he claims will do nothing other than portray things as they actually happened. At about the same time in history, the evangelist Luke also introduces his book with a foreword. In it he describes his task, his theme, and the sources of his presentation and emphasizes, in addition to his intention to portray the events in the time of Jesus and the beginnings of the church, his hope that the account might be favorably received by the reader (Luke 1:1-4). By means of such an introduction an author announced his claim to be presenting a literary work of equal rank with those of the leading authors of the Hellenistic world.

Josephus wanted to stimulate general understanding of Judaism by non-Jewish readers and particularly of Judaism as a rational way of life. When God, who is the creator of the entire world, is called Overseer, Father, and Source of all things, concepts are being used which are familiar to the Greeks. The loftiness of God can be described only in negative terms: he is without needs, unbegotten, unchangeable, indestructible. Because God's dwellingplace cannot be localized, the question of where God is is answered: "Everywhere you are in that which God is" (*Jewish Antiquities* V. 109). Hence also Josephus does not speak of an ascension of Enoch or

Elijah to heaven, but instead of a progression to deity and invisibility. As the Creator, God has awakened inanimate matter to life by contemplating it, and created the entire cosmos out of the four elements. Thus the Old Testament Jewish belief in the creation is reiterated in Greek pantheistic concepts in order to preserve the confession of the one God, the Lord of all things.

Through the hellenization of religious language, a rationalistic element is introduced into the narration of Old Testament stories. When, for example, it is said that because of the theft of the ark of the Covenant the Philistines fell victim to a series of plagues, Josephus suggests, by way of explanation of the events, "that no other cause of these can be considered than nature alone, which produces such changes in the course of time for bodies as well as for the earth and vegetation and everything that consists thereof" (*Jewish Antiquities* VI. 9). The reason for the famine which plagued Palestine could either be traced to the fact "that God was angry or that the misfortune came in the course of time" (*Jewish Antiquities* XV. 299). Although it is not decided how this question is to be answered, it is apparent that the Greeks chose to attribute the events of life to a variety of natural causes.

If Josephus was not a truly original philosopher and scholar, he still took great pains to represent himself to his readers as an educated and cultivated man. He classifies the groups of the Pharisees, Sadducees, and Essenes as philosophical schools (cf. pp. 77, 74, and 84) and remarks about the Pharisees, with whom he was permanently affiliated, that they were very closely akin to the philosophical school of the Stoics (*Vita* 12). In fact, however, one cannot speak of any such connections or similarities between them apart from the fact that the Stoics, like the Pharisees, placed great emphasis upon ethics and demanded of man a just and virtuous manner of life. Even the Jewish freedom party of the Zealots was designated a philosophical school (*Jewish Antiquities XVIII.* 23), although their political activity was far removed from philosophical reflection (cf. pp. 83–84).

To describe the future-oriented hope with the Greek conception of the immortality of the soul—as was frequently attempted in Hellenistic Judaism—left no room for a vital eschatological expectation. Therefore the report concerning the appearance of John the Baptist (cf. p. 44) had to be framed by Josephus in such a way that it no longer contained any statement about the announcement of the Coming One. Instead, John is called a noble man who taught the Jews "to strive after virtue, and to practice justice toward each other and piety toward God" (*Jewish Antiquities* XVIII. 117). If the Jews hoped to explain their faith to the Greeks without arousing suspicion among the Roman authorities, they could not speak of the messiah. Therefore, in place of an expectation for Israel's future, there appeared an expectation which pertained solely to the future destiny of the individual and his immortal soul.

Although Josephus could have known something of the beginning of the Christian church, or perhaps actually did know something of it, he wrote nothing about it. Only in connection with the account of the violent end of the Lord's brother James does he mention that this righteous man, who was highly regarded even by the Jews, was "the brother of Jesus, the so-called Christ" (*Jewish Antiquities* XX. 200). It is true that Christians who later handed down the writings of Josephus also inserted references to Jesus Christ in some other passages, but these statements can easily be recognized as such.

Judaism in the Hellenistic Diaspora knew how to be open and responsive to Greek thought without sacrificing fidelity to the Bible. Of course now and then small Jewish groups succumbed to the influence of the alien environment. Thus astrology and ideas of magic penetrated Jewish circles too, and in Asia Minor there was a group of sabbath observers who also worshiped the god Sabazios. Even though the influences of other religions were in evidence in the synagogues, still Judaism in the Diaspora as a whole demonstrated amazing internal strength and unanimity. It is true that there was an openness to the Greek culture and intellectual world, but participation in heathen cults was never a temptation for a Jew. Moreover, the Jews did not accept the rationalization that essentially one and the same God is worshiped in all religions. Instead, even in the Diaspora where they had accepted and adopted the Greek language, the Jews firmly held to the confession of the God of Israel. They were prepared even to suffer ridicule and persecution for this confession, for they knew that the truth was on their side. As Moses was the teacher of the philosophers, so Israel is the teacher of the nations, who must bear witness to them of the one God who is eternal and who utters his word through the Law which he has given to all the world through Israel.

CHAPTER 3
Jewish Life and Belief
in the Time of the New Testament

The picture afforded by the groups and movements within Judaism in the time of the New Testament is rich and diverse. No less evident than this variety, however, are certain features of the life and faith of the Jews which were common to all of them and which distinguished them from the non-Jewish environment. The confession of the one God who is lord of the world and king of his people was to become visible in their obedience to his will. The teaching of Judaism therefore insisted upon actualization in everyday life and was not unfolded in a speculative theological system, but in the application of the Law to all issues of life. Even though within Judaism there were differing views about how the Law was to be interpreted and followed in detail, still all Jews were united in the conviction that the Law, as God's holy will, is given to his people, who have been set apart from all other nations. In temple and synagogue his name was praised and his will proclaimed; both the belief in the one God who does not abandon his people and the hope in the coming redemption were shared by all Jews, whether they lived in Palestine or in the Diaspora, and whether they lived in security or in circumstances of oppression.

1. The Social Circumstances of the Jews in Palestine and in the Diaspora

It was in keeping with the Roman policy enacted in all the provinces of the empire that supreme jurisdiction was indeed placed in the hands of the Romans, but in no other way were existing political and legal circumstances altered. Thus a Jewish state continued to exist in Palestine under the rule of King Herod; and when in the year A.D. 6 a Roman governor replaced the Jewish ruler, the Sanhedrin was still able to exercise its office as the supreme Jewish authority (cf. p. 42). The highest judicial power now lay with the Roman governor, but the leading circles in Jerusalem still maintained their influence upon the temple cult and the character of Jewish life. The high priest and the chief priests continued to determine the course of the religious activities in the temple, and the old established families were still able to intervene in political affairs and to sustain an economically secure life. It was necessary only to avoid provoking the Roman authorities. For the masses of the people, however, the change in government had almost no impact on daily life.

The Jews in the Diaspora enjoyed the protection afforded by the privileges Caesar had granted them (cf. p. 36). They could, without hindrance, establish synagogue communities anywhere in the Roman Empire; conduct their worship; and, within the Jewish fellowship, insist upon the observance of the Law. Even though by their obedience to the Law the Jews were set apart from their environment, in terms of social behavior they were not. In the large Jewish populations of the major cities of Alexandria, Antioch, and Rome, almost all occupations were represented: from craftsmen and small merchants to actors and beggars.

The *economic circumstances* in which the Jews in the homeland lived were generally quite modest. Only the small groups of the upper stratum in Jerusalem and the major landowners in Galilee were well-to-do. Since large parts of the Galilean hill country were originally royal lands, even in the Hellenistic period many farms belonged to non-Jews who lived in other countries and managed their property through administrators. The Jewish population of the country earned their living by farming, handicraft, and small businesses. The land was cultivated primarily in the plains in the northern part of the country, and to a smaller extent in the vicinity of Jerusalem also. At that time a large part of Judea was desert, as it is today, so that the road from Jerusalem to Jericho descended through dry, uninhabited territory (cf. Luke 10: 27-35). The barren country of Judea allowed only livestock and pasture farming; fishing was the industry around the Sea of Genessaret; and in the Jordan valley vineyards and fig groves flourished. The peasant population could secure only a modest livelihood through hard labor. Things were not significantly better for the artisans who worked as weavers, fullers, tailors, smiths, scribes, or potters. Many occupations were despised, such as that of the tanner, because he constantly had to make himself unclean (cf. Acts 10:6), or that of the tax collector, because he was in the service of Gentile masters and dealt fraudulently (cf. p. 80). Many men found work in the great building enterprises which Herod undertook in Jerusalem and other places. Nevertheless there was unemployment, so that anyone who lost his position was necessarily fearful of his future (cf. Luke 16:1-8). Poverty and mendicancy were widespread. Since in Jerusalem there were markets for the various goods which were brought into the capital city, Jerusalem attained a certain degree of prosperity. To be sure, the inhabitants of Jerusalem were said to be reliable as far as the word of the Law is concerned, but not in the conduct of business and trade. The roads which traversed the countryside were sometimes made dangerous by robbers who attacked and plundered the tradesmen. The wretched circumstances in which many peasants, artisans, and tradesmen found themselves prompted many Jews to leave their homeland and to seek their fortune abroad (cf. p. 121).

The *Jewish family* lived in a small house which usually consisted of a single windowless room (cf. Luke 15:8). Only the storeroom could be locked (cf. Matt. 6:6). At night the entire family lay in one bed (cf. Luke 11:7). As head of the patriarchially ordered family, the father not only had to care for the physical well-being of all the family's members, but also had to instruct his sons in the Law. The children were required to show respect to him and to their mother. The position of the woman was not equal to that of the man. To marry was regarded in Judaism as a divine commandment, because the command given at creation to be fruitful and to subdue the earth (Gen. 1:28) was understood as the divine establishment of marriage. Therefore celibacy, as it was practiced in Qumran, was rare. As a rule, marriages were contracted in youth; men usually married between the ages of eighteen and twenty-four years, and the bride often was no more than twelve or fourteen years of age. Upon betrothal, which took place through a legal agreement with the father of the bride, the marriage was already valid. If the bridegroom died before the wedding, the bride who was left behind was regarded as a widow. The betrothal could be dissolved only by a letter of divorce. Before the wedding ceremony the bridegroom had to offer on behalf of the woman a so-called marriage obligation in the form of a sum of money. This was to be delivered in case of the death of the man or after a divorce. According to Deuteronomy 24:1, only the husband was allowed to dissolve a marriage, an act which could be accomplished by issuing a letter of divorce to the wife, if he discovered anything disgraceful about her. The document had to indicate the name of the husband and the wife, the date, and the explicit affirmation of the husband that his wife is herewith free and is allowed to contract a new marriage with anyone. Two other men had to witness and sign the document. As to the question of what constituted sufficient grounds for divorce, the opinions of the scholars in Scripture were divided. While the school of Shammai considered divorce justified by the unfaithfulness of a wife to her husband, the followers of Hillel held the view that even if something about the wife simply displeased the husband, this was shameful and thus was a basis for divorce (cf. p. 118). In actual practice, of course, it was not possible for men arbitrarily to dissolve a marriage, because they were obligated to pay the divorced wife the marriage obligation and to raise another sum of money to enter into a new marriage. For this reason polygamy, which according to Old Testament law was permitted, was also rare in well-to-do circles.

Women were regarded as inferior to men. They could not appear in public as a witness before a court or take an active part in the cultus. In the temple area they were permitted to go only as far as the court of women and were allowed to share in the synagogue worship only by listening, not by actively participating. Women were required to observe the prohibitions of the Law, but they were not required to keep all of the commandments nor to study the Law. Hence it is understandable that R. Judah in the second century A.D. said that the Jew should daily utter three thanksgivings:

> Blessed be he who did not make me a Gentile. Blessed be he who did not make me a woman. Blessed be he who did not make me an uneducated person [that is, in matters of the Law]. [For it says in Isaiah 40:17]: "All Gentiles are nothing before him." [Blessed be he] who did not make me a woman, for a woman is not obligated to keep the commandments. [Blessed be he] who did not make me an uneducated person, for the uneducated person does not fear to commit sin. (Tosephta Berakhoth VII. 18).

Like the women and children, *slaves* had to observe the prohibitions of the Law but not all the commandments. A Jewish master had to release Jewish slaves in the sabbath-year, i.e., at the latest after seven years. Because the Jewish slave was protected by the Law, Gentile slaves who had to serve under Jewish masters usually sought to gain the protection of the Law by turning to Judaism and becoming proselytes. Since there were only a few rich people in Palestine, the number of slaves was never large. As a rule, when Jews became slaves to Gentile masters, their countrymen and comrades in faith strove to buy their freedom as soon as possible. Thus many Jews who were taken away into foreign countries as prisoners of war were freed after a time. Usually they remained in the Diaspora; but some returned to the homeland, and in Jerusalem there was a synagogue of the Libertines, i.e., those who had been set free (Acts 6:9).

2. The Temple Cultus in Jerusalem

In the time of Jesus the *temple* in the holy city had lost none of the great significance which it had always held in the history of Israel. The Maccabean fight for independence against Hellenistic foreign influence had been undertaken in the interest of preserving its sanctity; and the groups of the devout who in the following period sought to compel strict observance of the Law were concerned that the temple cultus should be carried out precisely according to the prescriptions of the Law. But while the Pharisees were able to ensure that the Sadducean priesthood substantially conformed to Pharasaic views, the community that gathered around the Teacher of Righteousness was not able to establish its interpretation of the Law and had to leave Jerusalem (pp. 99–100).

Under the rule of King Herod the temple was completely restored, and the temple area was enlarged to twice its earlier size after a correspondingly larger area had been sufficiently secured by the erection of retaining walls. For this undertaking no costs were spared and an impressive sum of money was committed. Work began in the year 20/19 B.C., and ten years later it was possible to dedicate the new temple. The construction continued on the great work for decades, however, and it was completed only shortly before the beginning of the revolt against the Romans in A.D. 64. "Anyone who has not seen Herod's building has not yet seen anything beautiful," a proverb contends. And when Jesus stood with his disciples before the temple in Jerusalem—so the gospel writers tell— they called his attention to the greatness of the building with wonder and amazement: "Master, see what marvelous stones and buildings!" (Mark 13:2 par.)

The temple did indeed offer an impressive sight to its viewers. Anyone going up to Jerusalem could see from a long way off the elevated temple, which in its brilliance looked like a snow-covered hill. Having come through the gates of the city and approached the temple area, one first came into the outer court, which was open even to Gentiles. The outer court was surrounded by a wall on the inner side of which covered colonnades traversed the length and width of the entire temple square. The columned porch which was located on the east side was called Solomon's Porch because it was said to have been built by King Solomon (cf. John 10:23; Acts 3:11). In the outer court there was considerable activity, as was necessitated by the daily sacrifice and the visits of the many pilgrims coming to the feast. Since the Jews who came to the temple from a distance could not bring a sacrificial animal with them on the journey, provision had to be made for them to buy an unblemished animal, which they then could offer as a sacrifice, at the holy places. For a long time the Tyrian coinage had been used within the temple area, but because the pilgrims did not have this money available, they had to change the coins which they brought with them into the coins that were legal tender in the temple area. For this reason, moneychangers were authorized by the priests currently holding office in the temple to sit in the forecourt of the temple. Merchants offered doves for sale, so that even the poor could bring to the altar at least a small sacrifice (cf. Mark 11:15-19 par.; John 2:13-17).

The outer court was separated from the inner court by enclosures on which were posted warning placards. These were inscribed in Greek and Latin: "No foreigner may enter the enclosure and the walls around the temple. Anyone who is found here unlawfully is responsible for his own punishment by death which will follow." This warning was carefully heeded even by the Roman occupation forces, and any trespass on the sacred precincts was avoided. At the entrance to the inner forecourt lay many beggars who hoped for charitable gifts from the visitors to the temple (cf. Acts 3:2). Jewish women were permitted to enter its eastern precincts, but the western part was reserved for Jewish men, because only they could participate in the cultus. On the columned portico which surrounded the court of women were situated offering boxes in which people placed gifts for the temple cultus (cf. Mark 12:41-44 par.). In front of the temple stood the altar of burnt offering; inside stood the golden altar of incense, the constantly burning seven-branched lampstand, and the table of shewbread, on which twelve new loaves were placed every sabbath. The holy of holies, which was separated from the rest of the temple by thick curtains, might be entered only by the high priest when on the great Day of Atonement he had to perform the expiation of sins for all Israel. The ark of the covenant, which had once stood on this spot, had been lost during the destruction of Jerusalem by the Babylonians in 587 B.C. When it became possible two generations later to rebuild the temple, this place was left empty. Hence from that time on, the blood of the goat which was offered by the high priest for the sins of Israel on the great Day of Atonement, instead of being sprinkled on the ark, was sprinkled on the stone upon which the ark had once stood.

The members of the priestly company, led by the *high priest,* conducted their service in the temple. In spite of all the abuse to which the office of the high priest had been subjected during the political events in the second and first centuries B.C., it continued to be highly regarded. The high priest, the head of the Sanhedrin, was ranked highest in the Jewish community. He alone could perform the cultic acts on the great Day of Atonement in order to make expiation for the sins of the people. Only on this one day of the year was he obliged to exercise his office, though it was customary for him to conduct the cultic rituals on sabbaths, in the festivals of the new moon, and in the three great pilgrim festivals. Each day he had offered at his own expense an oblation, which appointed priests performed for him. Philo of Alexandria bears witness to the high esteem enjoyed by the high priests in the eyes of all Jews; he writes:

> It is true that, when considered with all the others, the high priest is little, but he becomes much when he is alone, [that is, he becomes] the entire court of judgment, the entire council, the entire nation, the great throng, the whole human race, yea, more, to tell the truth, a kind of intermediate being between God and man. (*De somniis* II. 188)

Under the high priest were the *chief priests,* who like him came from the prominent Sadducean families of Jerusalem. The ruler of the temple functioned as the representative of the high priest; he was the overseer of the temple cultus and exercised police power in the entire temple area. The leaders of the various priestly divisions, the temple overseers (to whom the Levites were subordinate), and the treasurers always lived in Jerusalem and also held influential positions in the temple and in the city.

The great majority of the *priests,* however, lived with their families outside of Jerusalem in smaller towns and villages in the country. They were divided into twenty-four "courses," each of which had to serve one week. When the week was over, the group was replaced by another and returned home; in the same way the Levites, who along with the priests were responsible for one week at the temple for the singing and various other services, rotated their obligations (cf. Luke 10: 31-32).

A priest had to be of unquestionable priestly ancestry and was permitted to marry only a woman of pure Israelite blood. He had to be free from physical defects, according to the prescriptions of the Law, and he could not allow himself to become unfit for cultic activities through any ritual contamination, such as contact with a dead person or animal or through bodily discharges. Among the priests it was determined by lot which responsibilities should be carried out by each individual (cf. Luke 1:8-9). Before daybreak a herald called out with a loud voice: "You priests, enter upon your service." It is told that the Jewish king, Herod Agrippa, who ruled over all Palestine from A.D. 41 to 44, was once on a journey and at a distance of three Persian miles—about ten American miles—could hear the call of the herald, and sent him gifts as a sign of appreciation. As soon as the priests heard their call, they hurried to make the preparations for punctual performance of the cultic activities. Each day they lighted an offering of incense compounded of various aromatic spices, and each day an unblemished one-year-old lamb was sacrificed on the great altar of burnt offering. In addition to these, private sacrifices were offered by individual Jews as a sign of their thanksgiving to God (cf. Luke 2:24).

On the major feast days great throngs of pilgrims came to Jerusalem, their numbers often considerably larger than the approximately twenty-five thousand inhabitants of the city. Finding accommodations for all of them was possible only because the citizens of Jerusalem were obliged to provide hospitality to foreign pilgrims without charge, for Jerusalem was regarded as the possession of all Israel. A person who uttered his prayer here received a special promise; for, it is said later in the Midrash on the Psalms (Midr. Ps. 91, § 7), "He is like one who prays before the throne of glory; for there [in Jerusalem] is the gateway of heaven and the open door to the hearing of prayer."

In the spring the *Feast of the Passover* was observed in Jerusalem. It was celebrated in recollection of the liberation of Israel from captivity in Egypt, and every family or group of pilgrims had to engage in careful preparation (cf. Mark 14:12 par.). The room in which the Passover was to be observed had to be searched and cleansed of anything leavened; for long ago, at the time of the exodus from Egypt, people had eaten only unleavened bread (cf. Exod. 12:1-28; I Cor. 5:6-8). The room had to be large enough to allow all the participants to indulge in the joy of the feast and to recline while eating. An unblemished, year-old male lamb was taken to the temple, slain in the inner forecourt, and then cooked and carefully prepared according to the prescriptions of the Law. These preparations for the Passover meal were performed in the course of the afternoon of the fourteenth of Nisan and had to be completed before evening. When the new day began at sundown—as was regularly the case with the Jewish calendar—the Passover liturgy and the Passover meal were observed in the circle of the family or the celebrating group.

The Mishnaic tractate *Pesahim* tells about the course of the feast. The regulations concerning it were first written down in the second century A.D., but the manner of observance could not have been significantly different in the time of Jesus from the way it is described in the Mishnah. It begins with a prefatory utterance which the father speaks over the first cup of wine; then people partake of a relish which is made of green and bitter herbs. Then the meal is served, but it is not yet eaten. A second cup of wine is poured, but it is not yet drunk; for now follows the actual Passover liturgy, in which the father answers the questions of his son. The son says: "How is this night different from all other nights? For on all other nights we eat both leavened and unleavened bread, but on this night only unleavened bread. On all other nights we eat meat that is roasted, boiled, or cooked; but on this night only roasted. . . ." In response, with a reference to the experience of Israel at the time of the exodus from Egypt, it is explained why the foods used in the Passover differ from those that are otherwise customary. The unleavened bread is eaten because Israel had to leave Egypt so hastily that there was no time to wait until the leaven had caused the dough to rise. Bitter herbs were eaten as a reminder that the Egyptians made the lives of the ancestors in Egypt bitter. And only roasted meat might be eaten at the feast. In this way the Passover was observed, for in every generation man is obligated to regard himself as though he had come out of Egypt; for it is said, "Because of what the Lord did for me when I came out of Egypt" (Exod. 13:8). Therefore we are obligated to give thanks, to extol, to praise, to glorify, to lift up, to laud, to bless, to exalt, and to celebrate the one who did these great things for our fathers and for us, who led us out of slavery to freedom, out of sorrow to joy, out of affliction to the day of feasting, out of darkness to a great light, and out of the yoke of bondage to deliverance. And we shall lift up our voices before him in a hallelujah. (Mishnah Pesahim X. 5)

Then follows, as a song of praise, the first part of the so-called *Hallel* (e.g., Ps. 113 or 113–14). After this the second cup is drunk. Only now is the main meal eaten, introduced by the prayer of the father of the house over the unleavened bread; in this part of the meal the Passover lamb is eaten, along with unleavened bread and bitter herbs. A prayer over the third cup ends the feast. At the conclusion of the entire ceremony, the second part of the *Hallel* is recited, that is, Psalms 114 (or 115) through 118 (cf. Mark 14:26 par.); a word of praise is then pronounced over the fourth cup, which is now served. The sequence of events with which the writers of the Synoptic Gospels have framed their account of Jesus' last meal with his disciples presupposes the occurrence of a Jewish Passover observance (Mark 14:12-17, 26 par.). Nevertheless, it does not necessarily follow from the theological interpretation that is given thereby to the first celebration of the Lord's Supper, that the words of the Supper (which in the earliest period of the Christian church were handed down without the subsequently added narrative framework; cf. I Cor. 11:23-25) have to be understood in terms of the context of a Passover observance.

When the temple was destroyed in A.D. 70, it was no longer possible to slay and prepare the Passover lambs. Since then the feast has been observed by Jews throughout the world without a lamb. The hope is kept alive, however, that sometime the day may come when people will once again bring Passover lambs to the restored temple and observe the feast in the holy city. Just as God once liberated his people from captivity, so also in the future deliverance he will redeem them. This hope is given expression in the cry with which the Passover observance is concluded: "Next year in Jerusalem!"

Fifty days after the Passover comes the *Feast of Pentecost* (cf. Acts 2:1; 20:16; I Cor. 16:8), which was observed as an offering of firstfruits. These were brought to the temple as the first harvests of the field "to give thanks for the past time in which we were not compelled to suffer the plagues of lack and hunger, but rather lived in a fruitful year, and for the future, because for it we are supplied with provisions and food, and hopeful of filling our houses with God's gifts" (Philo, *De specialibus legibus* II. 187). People also sought to connect this feast with the history of Israel by celebrating the giving of the Law on Mt. Sinai at Pentecost. The significance of the feast was able to survive the destruction of the temple and is preserved to the present day.

The *Feast of Tabernacles* took place in the autumn (cf. John 7:2). In solemn procession the people marched around the altar, voiced thanksgiving to God for the harvest, and presented a water libation. For seven days they lived in small tents in remembrance of Israel's journey through the wilderness. When after A.D. 70 these activities likewise could no longer be conducted at the temple, people could still erect their tents anywhere, and in this way could continue to observe the Feast of Tabernacles.

Also in autumn, in addition to these three pilgrim feasts which were celebrated at the temple in Jerusalem, there was the great *Day of Atonement,* which was of great importance for the entire nation. The high priest performed the ritual of expiation prescribed in Leviticus 16; he first sacrificed a goat for the expiation of his own sins and then conferred the sins of the people upon a second goat and sent it out into the desert (cf. Heb. 7:1–10:18). After A.D. 70 this rite too could no longer be performed, and since then the Day of Atonement has been observed as a day of penitence on which the people fast (cf. Acts 27:9) and confess their sins.

For the entire Jewish community, the temple, where the sacrifices were offered daily and to which thousands of pilgrims streamed for the great pilgrim festivals, was the holy place. The Jewish Christian community also continued to hold to the temple as the place for worshiping God (cf. Matt.

5:23-24; 17:24-27; Luke 24:53; Acts 2:46; 3:1-10 *et passim*).
Times of dire distress did not interfere with the punctual
daily performance of the religious service. During the siege
of Jerusalem by the Romans, the daily sacrifices were faithfully offered to the very last (cf. p. 50). When the splendid
building went up in flames, the visible center of the faith was
lost. Judaism's survival of this fearful catastrophe was possible
only because its religious life was not bound solely to the
temple cult, but drew its tenacity and strength from other
sources as well.

The story is told that soon after the destruction of Jerusalem
by the Romans, the famous scholar R. Jochanan ben Zakkai
visited the ruins accompanied by his pupil Joshua. When
they saw that the sanctuary in which the expiation was made
for the sins of Israel lay in rubbish and ashes, R. Jochanan
said that they did not need to be troubled about this; for
they had an expiation which was of equal worth to everyone,
the performance of the works of love, for it is written, "I
desire love and not sacrifices" (Hos. 6:6; Aboth Rabbi Nathan
4). What is to be counted among the works of love and how
these must take place is declared by the Law, whose commandments are taught in the synagogue.

3. The Synagogue

The *beginnings of the synagogue* lie hidden in obscurity.
One would expect that the Jews, who after the conquest of
Jerusalem in 587 B.C. had been carried away to Babylon and
were compelled to live there in exile, would have established
places for themselves where they could hear God's word and
commandments. Yet we are lacking any more definite accounts
of any such development. The first certain testimonies come
from the third century B.C.; at that time there were already
synagogues in the Egyptian Diaspora. Then for the second
century B.C. a synagogue in Antioch is mentioned. Thus the
origin of the synagogue is to be sought in the Diaspora, where
the Jews lived scattered among peoples of other faiths. Far
removed from their homeland, they had to secure a place
in the foreign land where they could gather for worship. The
institution of the synagogue then was quickly embraced not

only in the Diaspora but also in Palestine, so that in the days of Jesus there was a synagogue in every locality inhabited by Jews. In larger cities like Jerusalem, but also in Rome, Alexandria, and Antioch, there were several synagogues in which worship services were held, the Law was studied, and the children were taught. The relationship between the Law and the synagogue became so self-evident to the Jews in New Testament times that people thought there had always been synagogues. Hence it could even be said in the book of Acts that "from early generations" Moses has had those who preached him in every place, where he is read in the synagogues on every sabbath (Acts 15:21 RSV).

The *synagogue building* in which the community gathered was usually a long, rectangular house which faced toward Jerusalem. At the entrance stood pitchers of water so that everyone who wished to enter the synagogue could perform the ritual cleansing. The room for prayers was plainly and simply arranged. A niche held the scripture-scrolls, which were brought out for use in the services. In earlier times a portable wooden shrine was used, but later a shrine for the Torah was built into the wall on the side toward Jerusalem. A special place was provided for prominent people in the worship services. The scholars sat on the seat of Moses (Matt. 23:2) with their backs to the Torah shrine and faced the people in such a way that everyone could see them. In many synagogues the floor was adorned with mosaics which represented ornaments, the signs of the zodiac, or even biblical scenes. In excavations at Dura-Europos, a city on the west bank of the Euphrates, a synagogue was discovered which had been built and decorated in the third century A.D. The walls of this synagogue are covered with a whole cycle of pictures on biblical narratives. These paintings were affected by Oriental, Roman, and Western influences, and are evidence that the Judaism of the Diaspora did not close itself off from the culture of its environment that did not share its faith. Even in Palestinian synagogues—for example, in Beth-Alpha —there are pictures of animals and men. Thus Judaism by no means everywhere and always interpreted the biblical prohibition of images (Exod. 20:4) to mean that every portrayal of living beings was forbidden. Where pictures were used in the synagogue, their purpose was to glorify the past actions of the God who had marvelously led Israel, his people, and therefore would also guide them in the future.

The synagogue served the local Jewish *congregation,* which was responsible for its maintenance. The management of the external concerns of the synagogue community usually lay in the hands of a board of directors consisting of three members. The only officials of the synagogue were the president and the servant. The president, or *archisynagogos,* who was chosen from among the most prominent men of the community, was responsible for conducting the service of worship in an orderly fashion (cf. Luke 13:14). He decided who should lead in prayers and do the reading, and ensured that suitable persons were present to deliver sermons (cf. Acts 13:15). The servant of the synagogue brought the roll of the Scripture (cf. Luke 4:20), and it was he who asked the members chosen by the president to conduct prayer, song, or preaching. The instruction of the children was also often entrusted to him. When punishments such as lashing (cf. II Cor. 11:24) were to be inflicted upon individual members who had transgressed the Law, the servant of the synagogue had to carry them out. Such sentences were pronounced by a panel of three judges when a person had repeatedly committed a deliberate offense against the Law, for example, by grossly disregarding the rules concerning cleanliness. The number of lashes could not exceed thirty-nine; this limit was observed in order to be sure that in no case was the rule of Deuteronomy 25:3, where forty lashes were mentioned, exceeded. The alms which were asked of the members of the community (cf. Matt. 6:1) were collected by persons specifically designated for that purpose. Priests and scribes did not hold any special office in the community, though the lecture of a rabbi was thankfully heard, and people gladly invited a priest who was present to pronounce the blessing. In order for a service of worship to be held in the synagogue, at least ten men had to be present.

The *service of worship* in the synagogue included the confession of the one God, prayer, the reading of the Scripture, and instruction concerning the will of God. The confession of the God of Israel and the priestly blessing had had their fixed places in the temple liturgy also. After the destruction of the holy place the memory of the temple was kept alive in the synagogue. A seven-branched lampstand, such as had originally stood in the temple, was set up in the synagogue. Prayer was offered with the same regularity as the sacrifices that had previously been offered in the temple (cf. Acts 3:1), and people besought God that the temple might be restored. Hence the synagogue was also called "a sanctuary in small measure" (cf. Ezek. 11:16), the place of prayer which keeps open the way for the rebuilding of the temple. On the sabbath, but also on weekdays, especially on Mondays and Thursdays, and at the time of the great feasts, people joined together in worship.

The content of the worship service, whose basic features have remained unchanged from the time of Jesus to the present, is divided into two parts: a first part, with a stronger liturgical stamp, and a second part, consisting of instruction. First one utters the "Hear, O Israel," which the Jew recites morning and evening every day as a confession of the one God of Israel. This confession consists of three passages of scripture, whose exact delineation was finally established by scholars after A.D. 70; it is identified by the beginning of the first passages as the *Shema* (meaning "Hear"):

> Hear, O Israel; the Lord our God is one Lord. And you shall love the Lord your God with all your heart, with all your soul, and with all your strength. And these words which I command you this day shall be written on your heart, and you shall teach them to your children and shall talk of them when you sit in your house and when you walk in the way, when you lie down and when you rise up. You shall bind them on your hands for a reminder and wear them on your forehead as a sign. And you shall inscribe them on the door posts of your house and on your gates. (Deut. 6:4-9)

These prescriptions were understood and applied literally; for the recitation of the Shema and for prayer, people wore the so-called phylacteries on the forehead and the wrists, and on the doorposts of the houses they affixed a capsule (Hebrew: *mezuzah*) which contained a small scroll with the text of the Shema. These verses from Deuteronomy 6:4–9 were followed by a passage from Deuteronomy 11:13–21, which contains the promise of divine blessing upon the land and repeats the command to write these words on the doorposts and the gates. The words from Numbers 15:37–41 constitute the conclusion and inculcate the requirement that the Israelites make tassels on the corners of their garments, so that they will remember God's commandments. For "I am the Lord, your God, who brought you out of the land of Egypt, that I might be your God—I, the Lord, your God" (Num. 15:41).

The plea "Hear, O Israel," which is introduced and concluded with utterances of praise, is followed by the so-called Eighteen Benedictions. This prayer consists of eighteen petitions. One part of its wording must already have been established in the days of Jesus (cf. II Macc. 1:24–29). It has been handed down in two versions, a Babylonian one, which was acquired by Judaism from the Jewish communities in Mesopotamia and was well accepted, and an older Palestinian one, the text of which was discovered in an ancient synagogue in Cairo at the end of the last century (cf. p. 94). Although the two versions agree in basic content, they differ in details, particularly in the fact that various expansions and enlargements are found in the Babylonian recension.

The main part of the prayer is enclosed by two groups of three utterances of praise. The first three and the last three benedictions call on people to praise God (the following quotations throughout follow the earlier Palestinian version):

> Praised be thou, Lord our God and God of our Fathers, God of Abraham, God of Isaac, and God of Jacob, great, mighty, and awesome God, most high God, creator of heaven and earth, our shield and the shield of our fathers, our trust in all generations. Praised be thou, shield of Abraham. (First Benediction)

> Thou art the hero, who dost bring down the lofty, the mighty one, and the one who dost judge the violent, the eternally living one, who causest the dead to arise, who causest the wind to blow and the dew to fall, who dost care for the living and dost give life to the dead. May help come to us in a moment. Praised be thou, Lord, who dost bring to life the dead. (Second Benediction)

> Holy art thou, and awesome is thy name, and there is no God but thee. Praised be thou, Lord, holy God. (Third Benediction)

Each of these is voiced by one leading the prayers, and after each one the congregation responds, "Amen" (i.e., "That is certain"), and thus identifies itself with what has been said in the prayer (cf. I Cor. 14:16). The twelve petitions which make up the main part of the prayer are related on the one hand to everyday needs, and on the other hand to the messianic age, which God's mercy, it is hoped, will bring about:

> Forgive us, our Father, for we have sinned against thee. Uproot and take away our shortcomings from before thine eyes; for great is thy mercy. Praised be thou, Lord, who forgivest much. (Sixth Benediction)

> Bless this year to our good, O Lord our God, in all the things that it brings forth, and speedily bring in the year of the time of our redemption. And give rain and dew upon the earth and satisfy the world out of the treasures of thy possessions. And bless thou the work of our hands. Praised be thou, Lord, who dost bless the years. (Ninth Benediction)

When, at the end of the first century A.D., the final separation of church and synagogue took place, the Twelfth Benediction acquired the following wording:

> May there be no hope for the apostates, and mayest thou speedily uproot the insolent government [Rome] in our days. And may the Nazarenes [Jewish Christians] and the *Minim* ["Jewish heretics"] die in a moment, may they be blotted out of the book of life and not be enrolled with the righteous. Praised be thou, Lord, who dost humble insolence.

Since this curse upon the Christians was pronounced in the worship service of the synagogue, they were finally excluded from the Jewish communities and forbidden to enter the synagogues (cf. Luke 6:22; John 9:22; 12:42; 16:2). The Thirteenth Benediction, which begs for God's mercy for the proselytes, is followed by the petition that the eschatological salvation be brought about:

> Have pity, O Lord our God, in thy great mercy, upon Israel, thy people, and upon Jerusalem, thy city, and upon Zion, the

dwelling place of thy glory, and upon thy temple and upon thy dwelling and upon the kingdom of the house of David, of thy righteous Messiah. Praised be thou, Lord, God of David, who dost build up Jerusalem. (Fourteenth Benediction)

Three Benedictions whose content is once again expressed in more general terms stand at the end of the prayer. The priestly blessing according to Numbers 6:24–26 is inserted between the last two utterances of praise. If a priest were present at the synagogue service of worship, it was his place to pronounce the blessing. But if no priest was present, the blessing was pronounced by a member of the congregation in the form of a petition addressed to God. The congregation responded again with "Amen." Then the prayer concluded with the last Benediction:

Bestow thy peace upon thy people Israel and upon thy city and upon thy possession, and bless us all always. Praised be thou, Lord, who dost create peace.

The instructional portion of the service is composed of the readings and the exposition of the Scripture. For the readings, which were from the most important part of the Old Testament, the Torah (i.e., "the five books of Moses"), a definite order was gradually formed, in which the sections of the Law (Hebrew *parashiyyoth*) were planned for the whole year. Any Jewish man might come forward during the worship service and read from the Scripture. It was forbidden to give the Scripture from memory; for the wording of the Law might not be altered under any circumstances. Since the people could no longer readily understand the ancient Hebrew language, it became necessary to translate the biblical text into the Aramaic vernacular. Next to the reader stood an interpreter who repeated the sentences of the Torah in Aramaic, verse by verse. These Aramaic translations, which were in part literal but in part also paraphrases, assumed a more definitive form in the oral tradition. Only in the fifth century A.D. did these so-called *Targums* (i.e., "translations" [of biblical books]) begin to be written down, but a long process of oral tradition preceded their being fixed in written form. It must be assumed that in the time of Jesus there was already a more or less common version of the Aramaic translation of the biblical text. Thus for example in Mark 4:12 a quotation is cited from Isaiah 6:9–10 whose wording at the end corresponds, not to the Hebrew Bible, but to that of the Targum. In the Old Testament version it speaks of an utter hardening of the people: "lest they should see with their eyes and hear with their ears, lest they should understand with their hearts and turn and be healed." But Mark 4:12 follows the wording of the Targumic version of the prophetic saying: "that they should see and yet not see, hear and yet not understand, *unless* they turn and it be forgiven them." Thus here the possibility of conversion which can lead to forgiveness is not completely excluded, but is still kept open. From this similarity between Mark 4:12 and the prophetic Targum it may be concluded that the Aramaic translation, which only later came to be written down, is based upon an ancient tradition which in this passage certainly goes back to the days of Jesus.

The reading from the Law was followed by another lesson read from the prophetic books. The order of the prophetic texts had not yet been established in New Testament times, so the reader could choose the passage which he wanted to read. Since the service of worship concluded with this second reading of the Scripture, the reading from the prophets was called *Haphtarah* ("dismissal"). To be sure, a homily could be appended to a reading of the Scripture; for any male member of the community was permitted to preach. Jesus made use of this right, as is portrayed in Luke 4:16–30 in a vivid description of the worship service in the synagogue in Nazareth. Jesus stands up to read. The scroll of the prophet Isaiah is handed to him, he opens it, reads the words from Isaiah 61:1–2, rolls up the scroll, gives it to the servant of the synagogue, and sits down. Seated, Jesus delivers the homily; the eyes of all those present are attentively fixed on him. The homily, to general amazement, contains only the one provocative sentence: "Today this passage of scripture is fulfilled in your ears" (Luke 4:21).

The homily must often have consisted of a periphrastic explanation of the biblical text, into which other biblical passages were readily woven. Examples of explication proceeding verse-by-verse are afforded by the biblical commentaries among the Qumran writings. Many samples of synagogue sermons have been handed down in the rabbinical literature. Thus it is told, for example, of R. Nehorai, who lived about the middle of the second century A.D., that he once delivered the following homily: "An Israelite woman was passing through the Red Sea, and her child was with her, and it was crying. Then she stretched out her hand and plucked an apple or a pomegranate in the middle of the sea and gave it to the child." This vivid ornamentation of the story of Israel's passage through the Red Sea is confirmed with a reference to a saying in the Psalms: "For in Psalm 106:9 it is said, 'He led them through the flood as through a pasture.' Just as in a pasture there is no lack, so also nothing is lacking in the flood. This is that which Moses said: 'The forty years that the Lord, your God, was with you, you lacked nothing' (Deut. 2:7). For they only needed to mention something, and it was produced before their eyes" (Midrash Rabbah on Exodus XXI.) Embellished exegesis includes anecdotes, parables, and graphic portrayals. Explanations of the Law are enhanced by being connected with other biblical passages, or by references to events from the lives of famous biblical scholars. The broad tradition of expositions of the Scripture (which were collected for individual books) was the literary antecedent of the so-called *Midrashim* (i.e, "studies," or "expositions"). The first *Midrashim* were written down by rabbis in the second century B.C. In the following centuries an abundance of literature of this type appeared. In Hellenistic synagogues, sometimes artistically constructed lectures were delivered in which various sayings from popular Hellenistic philosophy were incorporated (cf. pp. 127–28).

As the place where the Law was taught, the synagogue was also the locus of the school, and therefore was frequently called the *house of instruction*. Sometimes one and the same room served for worship and for instruction, but often a separate school building was situated beside the synagogue. The children were guided in the reading of the Law by a teacher, and were introduced to its understanding. In addition to the elementary school, study of the life of the scholars was also pursued; this too had its place in the synagogue or in the school building. There the scribe imparted to his pupils the fine art of the exposition of the Law. The synagogue was the center of the community life, so that people also gathered there to consult with each other concerning community affairs and to discuss all the questions that affected the life of the community.

4. Scripture, Law, and Tradition

The group of writings from which the divine will was to be discerned for the Jewish community had to be unequivocally established. In the fourth century B.C., at the latest, the editing of the *five books of Moses* had been brought to a conclusion; for the Samaritan community, which separated itself from the Jewish cultic community in Jerusalem, continued to hold the Pentateuch as Holy Scripture, in common with this Jewish community. Hence the Pentateuch's definitive form must have been established before the separation of the Samaritans from the Jews (cf. p. 18). The Torah enjoys unassailable authority in Judaism; its holiness and position are comparable to none. According to the view later developed by the rabbis, it was preexistent; before the creation of the world it was present with God. The rest of the books of the Old Testament ranked below the Torah. While the Torah was already existent in heaven, before it was delivered to Moses without any human collaboration, the other writings were written down by men under divine inspiration. Therefore the Law unequivocally deserves the highest rank, and all other scriptures only receive their authority from it. Canonical recognition is ascribed to them solely on the basis of their agreement with the Torah.

In the *collection of the prophetic books* the rabbis distinguished between the Former Prophets and the Latter Prophets. The Former Prophets included the historical books of Joshua, Judges, I and II Samuel, and I and II Kings; the Latter Prophets are the writings of the major prophets Isaiah, Jeremiah, and Ezekiel, as well as those of the twelve minor prophets from Amos to Malachi. The group of prophetic books was already closed in the second century B.C. For when the book of Daniel appeared (cf. p. 67), it could no longer be accepted among the Prophets; instead, it was placed with the books of Ezra and Nehemiah and the Chronicler's historical work at the end of the Old Testament Canon. Mention is made of the Law, the Prophets, and the rest of the books received from the fathers, in the prologue of the book of Jesus Sirach (Ecclesiasticus), which the grandson of the author translated into Greek at the end of the second century B.C. This presupposes the finalization of the Law and the collection of the prophetic books, but not yet of the third part of the Old Testament. In the New Testament reference is frequently made to the scripture or to the Law as the scripture's most important part. The Law and the prophets also are often mentioned (cf. Matt. 5:17; 7:12; 11:13 par.; Luke 16:29, 31; Rom. 3:21 *et passim*). Only in Luke 24:44 do we find the threefold designation of "the Law of Moses, the Prophets, and the Psalms." Although the final and definitive delimitation of the Canon occurred only shortly before the end of the first century A.D., both the writings of the Qumran community and the New Testament bear witness to the fact that in the time of Jesus the group of canonical books was actually already closed; for they quote from all parts of the Old Testament.

The books "which make the hands unclean" (Mishnah Jadaim III. 5) are to be regarded as sacred writings. They possess almost a material sanctity, so that a person who has touched them must perform a ritual washing of the hands. Profane writings, on the other hand, do not have the effect of rendering the hands unclean. The sacredness of the scriptures means that special attention must be given to their scrolls. When a scripture-scroll is worn out and is to be taken out of use in the worship service, it may not simply be thrown away; instead, it is first hidden in a special place and later carefully buried along with other rolls of scripture, in order thus to prevent its desecration.

The question as to which books possess this character of holiness was still under thoroughgoing discussion among the rabbis near the end of the first century A.D., since in some cases it was still a matter of dispute how the boundaries of the Canon should be drawn. Thus there were doubts whether chapters 40–48 in the book of Ezekiel, in which a picture of the future of the community of Israel is sketched, are really in harmony with the comparable parts of the Torah. According to tradition, this problem was solved by the scholar Hananiah ben Hiskiah. He sat down, had three hundred vessels of oil brought for his study lamps—so it is said—and thought through the discrepancies until he finally succeeded in demonstrating complete harmony between the book of Ezekiel and the Torah (Babylonian Talmud, Sabbath 13*b*). Further, there was dispute over the book of Koheleth, whose skepticism about life aroused distrust. Since at the beginning and end of the writing (of which King Solomon was believed the author) was a summons to fear God and keep the commandments, agreement with the Law could be discerned and the book could be acknowledged as canonical. Difficulties were also presented by the Song of Solomon. But since the view prevailed that the love songs of the book were to be understood in a figurative sense and to be connected with God's relationship to Israel, the reservations which had been raised with respect to this writing could be eliminated and its canonical recognition assured. With these decisions Palestinian Judaism brought the long process of the formation of the Canon to a close. The Hellenistic synagogue, on the other hand, did not as sharply discriminate between canonical books and writings that arose later and used, for the Septuagint, a more comprehensive collection of books, which they employed even in worship services (cf. p. 130). Only when Judaism renounced the Septuagint, which in the meantime had been taken over by the Christians, did the more narrowly conceived Canon of the Palestinian synagogue prevail.

According to the teaching of the rabbis, the Torah which God gave to Israel has been handed down from generation to generation: "Moses received the Torah on Sinai and handed it on to Joshua, and Joshua to the elders, and the elders to the prophets; and the prophets handed it on to the men of the Great Synagogue" (Mishnah Aboth I. 1). The Law which Moses once received embraces the written and the orally transmitted Torah as it has been handed down in an unbroken succession of scribes in that it was "received" and "handed on"—as the technical language states it—in each successive generation (cf. I Cor. 11:23; 15:3, *et passim*). To be sure, the validity of the oral Torah required precise and detailed substantiation through provision of an exegetical foundation in the Pentateuch for the articles of the tradition or by deriving them from the written Law. The tradition which was thus demonstrated was not inferior in importance to the word of the Scriptures, since the one harmonious divine will in fact is expressed in the written and in the orally transmitted Law. Although the Sadducees disputed this interpretation and appealed to the written Torah alone (cf. pp. 75–76), the authority of the tradition, which was defended primarily by the Pharisees, who held it in high regard as the "tradition of the elders" (Mark 7:3), prevailed and then after A.D. 70 came to be generally acknowledged.

The unfolding of the tradition was accomplished to a large extent by means of exposition of the Scriptures. The *Halakah,* i.e., "the guidance as to how one should walk," was in constant need of further expansion in view of demands for examination and decisions made by newly emerging questions on the Scripture. Since the rules of the Torah frequently contained only general definitions or gave only a few specific directions, the current import and meaning of the Scripture had to be deduced in learned discussions from time to time. For example, when it says, "You shall keep the sabbath day holy" (Exod. 20:8), it had to be determined more precisely what is forbidden on the sabbath, and what is allowed. What regulations are to be observed in contracting marriage and in divorce? What governs the conditions of cleanness and uncleanness? May one offer a Passover sacrifice even when the Feast of the Passover falls on a sabbath, when one is forbidden to do any kind of work? Hillel solved this problem, which is not considered in the Pentateuch, by arguing as follows: If it is permissible on the sabbath to present the sabbath offering, how much more then may the Passover sacrifice be offered on the sabbath (Babylonian Talmud, Pesahim 66a). Hillel discovered this answer, which established his fame, by drawing a conclusion linking the lesser to the greater and thus applying one of the exegetical principles according to which the exposition of the Scripture is to be performed.

Thus the *exposition of the Scripture,* which was of such great importance for bringing out the current validity of the Law, was by no means performed arbitrarily, but with specific rules which were first summarized and described particularly by Hillel. The aforementioned inference from the lesser to the greater was among these rules. Another principle is the conclusion from analogy, which can appear something like the following: "Dough-offering and dues are a gift for the priest, and the heave-offering is a gift for the priest. So just as one does not offer the heave-offering (to the priest on a festival day), so also one does not offer the dues" (Mishnah Betzah I. 6). One can also reason from the general to the particular; further, when a certain word recurs in a second biblical passage, this passage can be utilized to expound the former one. Significance came to be attached also to the view that every biblical passage which stands in close proximity to another must be interpreted in terms of this other passage. In Numbers 25:1 it is said that "while Israel dwelt in Shittim the people began to play the harlot with the daughters of Moab" (RSV). This raises the question of who then led the Israelites astray into harlotry. The answer is found by adducing the context: Since Numbers 22–24 speaks of Balaam as the one who is said to have been prompted to curse the Israelites, Balaam is also regarded as the one responsible for having led the Israelites astray into harlotry (Midrash Sifre Numeri; § 131). The exegetical rules that had been summarized in seven principles under Hillel were further developed in the following period; and in the second century A.D. they were expanded by R. Ishmael into thirteen prescriptions. In this connection careful attention was given to the rule that in the exposition of scripture not the slightest significance was overlooked. Even the iota, as the smallest letter, or a little hook with which a letter was adorned might not be disregarded (cf. Matt. 5:18). And if a Hebrew word is written with an additional consonant as bearer of a vowel, this too is not to be overlooked. For it is precisely through observation of the fine points of scripture that the scribe sharpens his vision, his ability to discern the hidden sense of the Torah and to render its meaning for the present time. Indeed, the rabbis also knew and occasionally employed the allegorical interpretation of scripture which was practiced in abundant measure in Hellenistic Judaism. However, they used it far less often than the Hellenistic synagogue (cf. pp. 134–35).

Examples of how the rabbis practiced the art of interpreting scripture are found in the New Testament. Thus Jesus proves from the Torah in dialogue with the Sadducees, who deny the resurrection of the dead, that God raises the dead; for God is the God of Abraham, Isaac, and Jacob, and therefore cannot be the God of the dead, but only of the living (Mark 12:26–27; cf. pp. 75–76). Paul repeatedly employs the inference from the lesser to the greater, as for example he argues in Romans 5:15: "For if through the transgression of the one [that is, Adam] the many [that is, all men] died, so were God's grace and his gift through the grace of the one man Jesus Christ bestowed abundantly upon the many [that is, all men]." The rule that two different biblical passages in which the same word appears are reciprocally explanatory underlies the argument of Romans 4:3–8: Abraham's faith was reckoned to him for righteousness (Gen. 15:6), and this means simply "To the man to whom the Lord does not reckon sin" (Ps. 32:2), so that justification by faith necessarily is to be understood as forgiveness of sins. And the apostle can occasionally emphasize as do the rabbis the principle that attention must be given even to the smallest details of the biblical manner of expression. Thus in Galatians 3:16 he points out that it is not an accident when scripture speaks of Abraham and his seed and uses the singular "seed" rather than the plural; for thereby it is indicated that the one descendant, namely Christ, is signified.

The exposition of scripture was significant not only for revealing the current validity of the Law, but also for further developing the *Haggadah*. The Haggadah is distinguished from the Halakah, the directions about the proper conduct according to the Law, by the fact that it contains all the non-Halakic interpretation of scripture. Thus it contains edifying narration and elaboration as well as actual description of the content of faith and hope not connected with commandments of the Law. The diverse formulations of eschatological hope, therefore, are to be counted as part of the Haggadah and the various versions of biblical stories in the later tradition as well. When, for example, it is said that Moses was trained in all the wisdom of the Egyptians (Acts 7:22), in this matter the Haggadah goes beyond the biblical text, which does not mention this. Again, the names of the Egyptian magicians who opposed Moses are known, although the Old Testament does not give them (II Tim. 3:8; cf. CD V. 18-19). Numbers 20:7–13 tells of the miracle of the water yielded from a rock which Moses wrought in the wilderness, and then in Numbers 21:16–18 it is said that after long wandering the people came to a fountain, of which it is remarked: "This is the fountain of which the Lord said to Moses, 'Call the people together, and I will give them water.' " Out of these brief references, then, the Haggadah spins a lengthy story: the fountain which Israel reached in the desert had followed them in their wanderings, had gone with them into the valleys, and had reascended with them to the high places (cf. I Cor. 10:4). The occasion of the delivery of the Law to Moses on Sinai is extolled in the narrative tradition with the declaration that the Law had come to Moses through the mediation of angels, and in this fashion the worth of the Torah is affirmed (Acts 7:53; Gal. 3:19). Legendary stories are naturally inspired by the lives and deaths of great men, so that, for example, we are told how after the death of Moses, Michael and Satan contended for his body (Jude 9). In I Kings 17:1 it is said that the drought will continue until God speaks to the prophet Elijah, and in I Kings 18:1 this is followed by the statement, "But after a long time, in the third year, the word of the Lord came to Elijah." In the later reiteration of the Elijah stories, this indication of time is made more explicit with the statement that the famine in Elijah's time lasted three and a half years—one half of the number seven (Luke 4:25; James 5:17).

The Haggadah offers vivid examples of what a life lived according to the Law is like, and in this way it supplements the Halakah, which claims unconditional preeminence, because in it the commandment of the Law is expounded. Since in the course of life new questions are constantly being raised that call for consideration and response, the study of the Law and the working out of a casuistry that could make reference to a prescription of the Law in answer to every conceivable query could never cease. The material of the tradition, from which the exposition of the Law originated and then expanded, became so abundant that it soon became almost impossible to survey its wealth completely. Originally the entire tradition was transmitted orally; and a major aspect of the study of the scribes consisted in imprinting upon the memory the material of the tradition. While the strict law-observing community of Qumran set about making records of the Halakah which developed out of their study of scripture, people in the Pharisaic circles at first held to the rule of not putting the orally transmitted Torah in writing. However, in the first half of the second century A.D. people began to collect, to sift, and to write down the overflowing abundance of the constantly increasing Halakic tradition. This process of arranging required so much time that only in the latter half of the second century A.D. did the *Mishnah* emerge as the collection of the valid Halakah, and then its final editing was undertaken under R. Judah-ha-Nasi near the end of the second century A.D. The word Mishnah signifies "the teaching to be learned through repetition." The material was written down in sixty-three tractates, and these were combined into "six divisions" (Hebrew *sedarim*), each of which contains tractates that are related in subject matter.

The first division bears the name "Seeds." Its tractates are related primarily to agriculture, the tithing of the produce, and so on. Of special significance is the first tractate *Berakhoth,* which contains discussions of when prayers are to be offered and praises uttered as a sign of thanksgiving to God. The second division, which contains prescriptions for the "Set Feasts," is composed of such important tractates as "The Sabbath," *Pesahim* (i.e., "Feast of Passover"), and *Sukkah* ("Feast of Tabernacles"). In the third division, "Women," the various regulations concerning betrothal, marriage vows, divorce, and the handling of a case of adultery are treated in detail. In these prescriptions no distinction is made between civil and religious law, but because God's law covers all areas of human life, instructions for the conduct of the feasts and of worship, as well as prescriptions by which everyday life is to be regulated, are derived from it. Therefore it is not surprising that in the fourth division, "Damages," which concerns things as well as persons, there is detailed discussion of civil law, the application of justice, and the infliction of punishments. The fifth division deals with "Hallowed Things," that is, the various sacrifices and their presentation in the temple. Although the holy place had been destroyed, the rabbis conducted intensive discussions about the cultus and its conduct, in order always to be ready and able to reestablish the temple worship in full accord with the commandments of the Torah. Cultic prescriptions also determine the contents of the sixth division, which bears the superscription of "Cleannesses." When a vessel is clean, when it is unclean, what is to be considered in the appearance of leprosy, how immersions for the attainment of ritual purity are to be performed, and what is to be observed in washing the hands are established in all details. The abundance of material which is collected in the tractates of the Mishnah is not arranged according to strict topical logic, rather it is evident throughout that the statements derive from the oral tradition. Frequently there is a loose connection of ideas, but occasionally there is no connection at all between individual passages.

A few sentences from the tractate "Sabbath" may be cited as examples of the Mishnah's casuistic style of argument in which the concern for giving precise instructions for every conceivable case is evident. The biblical commandment to rest on the seventh day calls for more precise exposition of how exactly to observe the rest and what is to be regarded as work, which must be forbidden under all circumstances. Thus it is said: "A tailor may not go out with his needle near twilight [that is, before the beginning of the sabbath], lest he forget and go out [that would be work on the sabbath]. A scrivener may not go out with his pen; and a man may not search his clothing for vermin [for no animal may be killed on the sabbath]. And one may not read by lamplight [lighting a lamp would be work]" (I. 3). There is not an unequivocal opinion on all questions, but often the schools of the scholars reach different conclusions: "The School of Shammai says that [on the eve of the sabbath] one may not soak ink, dyestuffs, or vetches [which serve as fodder] unless [there is time] enough for them to be completely soaked that day. But the School of Hillel declares that it is permitted" (I. 5). The manifold individual rules which the rabbis established to forbid work on the sabbath have been summarized in some lists of instructions. The following catalog sets forth the most important of these enumerations:

The main classes of prohibited work are forty less one: sowing, plowing, harvesting, binding sheaves; threshing, winnowing, cleansing; grinding, sifting, kneading, baking; shearing wool, washing, beating, dyeing, and spinning it; weaving, making two loops [on the loom], twisting two threads, separating two threads; tying a knot, loosening a knot, sewing two stitches, tearing in order to sew two stitches; hunting a gazelle, killing it, skinning it; salting it, curing its skin, scraping the skin, cutting it up; writing two letters, erasing in order to write two letters; building, tearing down; putting out a fire, lighting a fire; striking with a hammer; carrying anything from one area into another. These are the main classes of work, forty less one. (VII. 2)

These rules then require still more explicit instruction on particulars. For example, with regard to the work which is done in the extinguishing of a lamp the instructions read:

If a person puts out a lamp [which would mean, as work, an offense against the sabbath commandment] because he fears the Gentiles, robbers, or an evil spirit [for evil spirits as well as robbers are attracted by the light], and when he does it so that a sick person may sleep, he is guiltless [in spite of the offense]. If [he does it, however,] to save the lamp, or to save oil, he is guilty. But Rabbi Jose declares him guiltless in all [cases] except that of the wick, because thereby he makes charcoal. (II. 5)

This last statement alludes to one's quickly extinguishing the wick so that with the charring that forms on the end of the wick he will find it easier to light it again later.

Alongside the Mishnah, in which the directions regarded as normative were collected, there arose a similar collection which incorporated propositions of the scholars that had not been included in the Mishnah. This work acquired the designation *Tosephta,* i.e., "supplement," or "addition." Nevertheless the Tosephta represents an entirely independent work which contains pieces that either are not found in the Mishnah at all or offer propositions that more or less significantly differ from those of the Mishnah. Thus in the *Tosephta* is assembled pertinent material from the scholarly discussions of the first and second centuries A.D. which supplements the Mishnah— that is, it explains, contradicts, or offers variants to it—so that in this collection are found many ancient traditions which did not gain general acceptance.

However, the question of how the instructions of the Law are to be understood was by no means finally resolved with the codification of the accepted Halakah as it had been undertaken in the Mishnah. Instead, the discussion continued, because people had to concern themselves with the innumerable individual difficulties of applying the Law, which the rabbis from the third to the fifth century A.D. discussed in connection with the didactic propositions summarized in the Mishnah. Thus, for example, the list of the thirty-nine main types of work forbidden on the sabbath was expanded, down to the most minute details, by specifying six subclasses of work for each of the main types. In this fashion a closely woven network of regulations, almost beyond comprehension, was formed. The scholarly reflections, however, were also expanded with a variety of haggadic material, containing edifying exposition of scripture, anecdotes about events in the lives of famous scholars, and all sorts of other interesting narratives. This extensive body of material was arranged as *Gemara* (i.e., "information that has been learned") with the respective individual propositions of the Mishnah tractates as commentary on them. Finally, in order to maintain these many-layered traditions, there arose in the fifth century A.D. the *Talmud* (i.e., "the teaching"), which we have in two different versions. The first version is the so-called Palestinian Talmud (also called the Jerusalem Talmud), which acquired its definitive form in the schools of Palestine. It is significantly shorter than the collection that was written down about the end of the fifth or the beginning of the sixth century A.D. and was produced in the schools of Mesopotamia. This version, the so-called Babylonian Talmud, which was distinguished by the wealth and variety of traditions it contained, then came to be recognized throughout worldwide Judaism as the authorized version of rabbinical teaching. As the Talmud—which it came simply to be called—it was studied over and over, explained, and later published in artistic, printed editions.

The great number of individual rules into which the Torah was developed in the rabbinical teaching—248 commandments and 365 prohibitions, thus a total of 613—may seem to be beyond one's capacity to survey. Hence it is understandable that when the famous Shammai was once asked by a Gentile how many laws the Jews actually have, Shammai answered: "Two; the oral and the written Torah." But then when the same question was posed to Hillel by a Gentile, with the statement that the latter would become a proselyte on the condition that Hillel would teach him the entire Torah while he stood on one foot, Hillel said: "Do not do to another person what is unwelcome to you; this is the entire Torah, and the rest is interpretation" (Babylonian Talmud, Sabbath 31a). The one obligatory will of God, which is made specific in the multiplicity of the individual commandments, is contained in the written and orally expanded Law, which finds its exposition in innumerable particular regulations. The Law, which was created by God even before the foundation of the world, is of eternal validity. God himself studies the Torah daily. And when the Messiah comes, he will not bring a new Law, but in company with his people will study the Law and will secure for it universal application and acknowledgment. Hence it is only through the Law that man can gain and enjoy communion with God. For "if two sit down and concern themselves with the words of the Law, the *Shekinah* (i.e., "God") dwells in their midst" (Mishnah Aboth III. 2).

5. God and Man

Judaism possesses neither a detailed system of dogmatics nor a confession of faith which contains a concise doctrine of God. For Judaism, to speak of *God* means to speak of his Law, through which God's will and commandment are made manifest. Therefore, who Israel's God is and what he demands of her is not explained to her in a systematically developed doctrine of God, but rather in the exposition of the Law. Whatever the Jew experiences daily is understood by him as a gift of God. If he experiences something good, he has occasion to rejoice, and when he partakes of food and drink, he utters a brief prayer of thanksgiving. The wording of these utterances is established for the individual occasion. If he is enjoying the fruits of the tree, he is to say: "Praised be thou, Lord,

King of the world, who dost create the fruit of the tree!" If a person drinks more than a thimbleful of wine, he is to say: "Praised be thou, Lord, King of the world, who dost create the fruit of the vine!" And if he eats of the fruit of the earth or bread in an amount more than the size of an olive, the blessing is: "Praised be thou, Lord, King of the world, who dost create the fruit of the soil [or: who dost cause bread to come from the earth]!" (Mishnah Berakhoth VI. 1). With these words the Jew confesses his God as the Lord of the world who has created the earth and men, preserves them, and provides them with his gifts.

Since God has made known his will in the Word, there is no other source of revelation besides this Word. It is true that people could recount all sorts of marvelous occurrences, things which have happened in history and are happening even in the present, but in their evaluation of them they maintained a surprising caution. The history of Israel was elaborated on a grand scale: for example, the tradition of the passage through the Red Sea—Israel passing through steep, towering walls of water—or of the handing-down of the Law at Sinai with innumerable hosts of angels in attendance. Devout and righteous men were able, by virtue of special powers, to perform *miraculous deeds*. Thus, for example, the following incident is told of the famous scholar Rabban Gamaliel II, who taught about the beginning of the second century A.D., when he was once traveling on board a ship. A storm arose, and the rabbi became terrified because he saw in the storm a punishment for his having collaborated in imposing excommunication upon his opponent R. Eliezer b. Hyrcanus. In prayer to God he declared that he had not done this at all for his own honor, but solely and exclusively for the sake of God's honor, so that conflicts might not be multiplied in Israel. When this prayer was finished the sea became calm (Babylonian Talmud, Baba Mezia 59*b*; con., Mark 4:35-41). Frequent reports are given of sick people who are miraculously healed. Thus Josephus describes the expulsion of a demon, performed by a man named Eleazar in the presence of the Emperor Vespasian, his sons, the commanders, and other soldiers, and witnessed by Josephus himself as well:

He [Eleazar] held under the nose of the possessed man a ring in which was enclosed a root which Solomon had mentioned; he had the sick man to smell it, and thus drew the evil spirit out of him through his nose. The possessed man immediately collapsed, and Eleazar then adjured the spirit, by pronouncing the name of Solomon and the proverbs composed by Solomon, never to return to the man. But in order to prove to those present that he actually possessed such power, Eleazar set up close-by [a vessel or a basin filled with water and commanded the evil spirit, upon leaving the man, to upset this container and thus convince the beholders that it had indeed left the man. This in fact happened, and thus Solomon's wisdom and knowledge became known" (*Jewish Antiquities* VIII. 46-49; con. Mark 1:23-28 par.; 5:1-20 par., etc.).

Although miraculous deeds were firmly entrenched in the legends which gathered about past events and the lives of great men of God, the rabbis were conservative in their opinions of the miracles. No one doubted the possibility or the actuality of them, but they never were recognized as definitive proof for use in reconciling disputed doctrinal questions, which are rather to be decided according to the Law and its exposition. A miracle acquires significance only when this significance can be demonstrated from exegesis of scripture. It is true that people expected the coming messianic age to be filled with God's miraculous activity, but they did not conceive of the messiah as a miracle worker. He must demonstrate his position not by miracles but by the fulfillment of scripture.

Thus according to Judaism's conviction, one can learn who God is and what he demands of man only from his Word, from which Israel knows that he is king of the world and rules over all men. But the heathen do not know his Law and therefore are ensnared in idolatry and immorality. Against the gods and idols which they venerate, sharp polemic and sometimes biting ridicule are hurled. There is no reality behind their images, unless perhaps it is the apparition of demons (cf. I Cor. 8:4; 10:20; Rev. 9:20-21). Only the God of Israel is the sole true God, whose holiness was spoken of with great reverence. One does pronounce the *name of God,* lest one incur guilt for any kind of misuse or desecration.

Because with the knowledge of a name power can be exercised or magic practiced in a dangerous fashion, no one may infringe upon the loftiness of the name of God, even in the remotest way. In the Qumran texts God's name (Yhwh—Yahweh) usually is written in old Hebrew script or is indicated by four dots, and in the earliest manuscripts of the Septuagint, Yahweh is also written in old Hebrew letters. When the biblical text was read aloud, the phrase "the Lord" was always used instead of God's name. Only once each year might the high priest pronounce the name of God—during the liturgy of the great Day of Atonement. Then the priests who were standing near to him fell down in reverence, but the singing of the temple choirs was so loud that no one could hear the voice of the high priest.

Since the name of God was carefully avoided, various periphrastic labels were employed. Very often he was called "the Holy One, praised be he," or "the Most High," "the Eternal One," "the Almighty," "the Exalted One," "the Lord of Heaven," and so on. Some chose other designations for referring indirectly to God. Thus they sometimes spoke of heaven when God was meant. Hence the kingdom of heaven, as it is usually called in the Gospel of Matthew, means nothing other than the kingdom of God. And when it is said that there will be joy among the angels in heaven over a sinner who repents (Luke 15:7, 10), this really is speaking of God's joy. When Jesus poses the question to the scribes whether the baptism of John is from heaven or from men, this means "either from God—or only from men" (Mark 11:30 par.). Mention frequently is made of "the Power" to refer to God, as for example when it is said that the Son of man will sit at the right hand of power (Mark 14:62 par.). In the Targums, which repeat the Old Testament text in an Aramaic paraphrase (cf. p. 164), "the Word" (i.e., of God) frequently replaces the name of God. There is also frequent mention of "the dwellingplace" (i.e., of God) or of "the Name." Finally, a common paraphrase of the name of God consists in the use of passive expressions to denote God's activity. This kind of expression is found in many passages in the New Testament, as for example in the Beatitudes when it is promised to those who mourn that they shall be comforted (meaning God will comfort them), to the hungry that they shall be filled (God will fill them), and to the merciful that they shall obtain mercy (God will be merciful to them) (Matt. 5:3-10; Luke 6:20-23).

As the Holy One who rules over all the world, God is far removed from men. Since he sits enthroned in heaven like a great king whom one dares to approach only in humble submissiveness, one does not say that God rejoices, but, instead, that there will be joy in the presence of the Father in heaven (Matt. 18:14), or in the presence of the angels of God (Luke 15:10). God does not come into contact with the world directly, but enlists the service of intermediate beings and emissaries. He lets his voice sound forth from heaven when there is some special message to proclaim (cf. Mark 1:11 par.; 9:7 par.; *et passim*). Ordinarily, however, he employs the *angels,* who encircle his throne and, as his servants, await his bidding. The seven archangels are especially prominent among the hosts of angels. Gabriel is the bearer of divine tidings (Luke 1:19, 26), and Michael is the warrior who battles for the people of God (Dan. 10:13, 21; Rev. 12:7; Jude 9). The great throngs of angels are divided into groups and classes, so that they are always ready for service. According to popular conception there is a guardian angel, not only for the entire nation of Israel, but also for every individual person. This guardian angel guides the person and intercedes for him before God (cf. Matt. 18:10). Its appearance is so like that of the person whom it protects that one could be taken for the other (cf. Acts 12:13-15).

Satan and his host stand on the other side, in opposition to God and his angels (cf. p. 57). To be sure, Satan is not regarded as a counterpart equal to God, but as a fallen angel who now leads the powers of darkness; his power nevertheless is threatening. He reigns over a well-organized kingdom (cf. Mark 3:24 par.) and through demons and sinister forces exercises his power as the ruler of this world (John 12:31 *et passim*) or the god of this world (II Cor. 4:4). He leads the hosts of evil spirits who assail men and cause plagues and illnesses (cf., e.g., Mark 5:1-20 par.). But even though their undertaking is terrifying, still it can in no way endanger

God's rule. He is and remains the Lord who has created the world, guides it to its very end, and calls to account all men.

The idea of God's future *judgment* shapes the belief and the action of the devout Jew, who knows from the law of his God what he has to do here upon earth and what will be asked of him someday during the judgment. Man is given the task of obeying God and doing his will; he remains accountable, body and soul, as a servant to his Lord. This responsibility of man is described by the rabbis in a graphic parable: A king owned a lovely orchard in which he had placed two watchmen, one lame and the other blind. One day the lame man said to the blind man, "I see some fine fruit in the garden; come, let me ride on you, so that we can get it and eat it." Then the lame man mounted the shoulders of the blind man, and they got the fruit and ate it. Some days later the owner of the orchard came and asked the two of them where the fine fruit was. The lame man answered that he had no feet to enable him to walk. And the blind man said that he had no eyes to enable him to see. Then what did the owner of the orchard do? He put the lame man on the blind man and punished them together. The application of this parable is this: "So also does the Holy One, praised be he, proceed; he takes the soul and places it in the body, and then he punishes them together" (Babylonian Talmud, Sanhedrin 91 *a/b*).

Since judgment is pronounced on the basis of works, the devout are concerned to attain in their lives and deeds the requisite righteousness which then can be affirmed and acknowledged in the judgment. It is not only through fulfillment of the commandments, but also through the performance of voluntary works of charity and the giving of alms that one gains merit that can be pleaded before God's judgment bar. Therefore the Jew is happy for every opportunity that is offered him to do good: to feed the hungry, to give drink to the thirsty, to show hospitality to the stranger, to clothe the naked, to visit the sick and imprisoned (cf. Matt. 25:31-46), to comfort the sorrowful, and to bury the dead. According to the conviction of the Pharisees, whose views determined popular opinion, it is entirely possible for man to live and act righteously, to fulfill the Law, and, therewith, to stand before

God. Therefore in looking back upon his Jewish past Paul can say that with regard to righteousness in the Law he had been blameless (Phil. 3:6), and a Pharisee refers in prayer, not without pride, to the works which he has performed (Luke 18:9-14).

Although through Adam's deed the fate of death has come upon all men, they still have freedom of and responsibility for the will. For "Adam is the occasion solely and exclusively for himself; but we all have become Adam, each one for himself" (Syr. Bar. 54:19). Thus Adam's transgression is constantly repeated in the offense of each individual man, who is thrust into a battle which he must wage for the sake of the good and against the evil. According to the teaching of the Qumran community, we must fight against falsehood and for the truth, against the darkness and for the light; in this struggle the individual finds himself predisposed by fate toward either the spirit of truth or wickedness (cf. pp. 104–5). The doctrine of the good and evil impulses was developed in Pharisaic circles. While the evil impulse is native to man from birth, the good impulse only begins to function when one is thirteen years old and as *bar-mitzvah* (i.e., "son of the commandment") possesses sufficient knowledge of the Law to be able to act on one's own responsibility. By virtue of the good impulse man is then able to contend with evil and to conquer sinful desire. The evil impulse "says to man today, 'Do this,' and tomorrow, 'Do that,' until at last it says, 'Worship other gods'" (Babylonian Talmud, Sabbath 105b). But this impulse must be resisted; for only one who masters his impulses is strong (Mishnah Aboth IV. 1).

While in the Qumran community a radicalized interpretation of the Law was held, according to which all the commandments and regulations are to be maintained without exception or limitation (cf. pp. 103–4), the rabbis were of the opinion that merits are reckoned and may offset offenses. If at the end the merits predominate, the judgment is pronounced in terms of righteousness. R. Akiba sums up this doctrine in the following picture:

All is given against a pledge, and the net is cast over all living; the shop stands open and the shopkeeper gives credit and the

account book lies open and the hand writes and every one that
wishes to borrow let him come and borrow; but the collectors go
their round continually every day and exact payment of men with
their consent or without their consent, for they have that on
which they can rely; and the judgement is a judgement of truth;
and all is made ready for the banquet. (Aboth III. 17; quoted
from *The Mishnah,* tr. Herbert Danby [London: Oxford University Press, 1933] p. 452)

Thus God keeps a reckoning of the deeds of a man, and later
sends the angels as his agents to collect the debts. If at the
end there is a positive balance, the way is opened for the
righteous to the banquet in the future kingdom of God.

Since even the pious person can never wholly escape the
danger of committing an occasional offense against God's
commandment or of acting thoughtlessly, it is important to
provide *atonement* for offenses, in order in this way to secure
compensation for faults and failures. Only those deeds which
are committed by oversight can be expiated; deliberate wickedness can have no atonement (Num. 15:22-31). In the
Mishnah is assembled a catalog of the various possibilities of
atonement which are given to man: "The Sin-offering and
the unconditional Guilt-offering effect atonement; death and
the Day of Atonement effect atonement if there is repentance.
Repentance effects atonement for lesser transgressions against
both positive and negative commands in the Law; while for
graver transgressions it suspends punishment until the Day
of Atonement comes and effects atonement" (Yoma VIII. 8;
Danby, *Mishnah,* p. 172). Thus reference is made first of all
to the cultus, to the offerings and the Day of Atonement. It
is true that after the fall of the temple the cultus could no
longer be practiced, but the way to atonement for Israel is
not closed as a consequence. Crucial significance, therefore,
is attributed to repentance, whereby man turns away from
wrongdoing and turns back to God. R. Eliezer gave the advice
that a person should repent one day before his death. But
when his pupils asked how a person could know on what day
he would die, the teacher responded: "So much the more
must he repent today, for he may die tomorrow. Thus it
follows that he spends all his days in repentance" (Babylonian
Talmud, Sabbath 153a). The last and best opportunity for

atonement is given to man by death. Even a criminal who because of his deeds has been condemned to death and is to be executed can find atonement if at the place of execution, before he is stoned, he responds to the demand that he confess his sins and says, "May my death be an atonement for all my sins" (Mishnah Sanhedrin VI. 2). Just as a man can, during his lifetime, pay the well-deserved penalty for his sins through the sufferings which he accepts as God's dispensation, so to a still higher degree is guilt atoned for by death, so that at the last "all Israel has a share in the future world" (Mishnah Sanhedrin X. 1).

But what are we to make of it when a righteous man, who has not incurred guilt for any transgression, likewise must suffer? This question, which Job's friends had already discussed thoroughly but had not been able to solve, is answered to the effect that the suffering of the righteous is borne vicariously for Israel. This teaching finds its clearest expression in the reference to the martyrs who surrendered their lives during the Maccabean uprising: "They became, as it were, a substitute for the sin (i.e., the sin-stained soul) of the people. By means of the blood and the death of those devout men, which served as atonement, divine providence has delivered the previously severely oppressed Israel" (IV Macc. 17:22). While dying, the pious man, who remains faithful to the Law to the very death, prays: "Be gracious to thy people, and let the punishment which we are suffering for them suffice. Let my blood serve as a cleansing for them, and take my soul as a substitute for their soul" (IV Macc. 6:28-29). The atonement which the righteous achieve with their guiltless life and death benefits the entire nation. Because—as R. Ammi later (about A.D. 300) concisely declares—there is no death without sin and no suffering without guilt (Babylonian Talmud, Sabbath 55a), the innocent death of the righteous can benefit all Israel.

The concept of *God as gracious* is by no means unknown to Judaism. The Qumran community is able to say that the devout man lives solely by the mercy of God, whose grace is demonstrated in his having placed man under the Law by which he is to live (cf. pp. 107–8). The Pharisaic-rabbinic teaching sees the expression of God's love in his act of giving the Law at Mount Sinai; for thereby he created for his people the possibility of doing good works, gaining merit, and achieving righteousness. At the judgment the merits of a man will be placed on one side of the balances, and his faults on the other. If it happens that merits and faults are in balance, then God will add a little bit on the side of the merits, to tip the scales in the man's favor. How the gracious God acts is described later (about A.D. 300) by R. Zeeira in a parable which is strikingly reminiscent of Jesus' parable about the workers in the vineyard (Matt. 20:1-16) and which most clearly diverges from it precisely at the crucial point. When a gifted scribe, R. Bun ben Chijja, died at the age of twenty-eight years, R. Zeeira sought, in his eulogy, to solve the riddle of this early death.

> With what can R. Bun ben Chijja be compared? It is as in the case of a king who hired many laborers. Among them was a laborer who because of his work was highly deserving. What did the king do? He took him with him as his companion on his rounds. In the evening every worker came to receive his pay. He gave this man full pay along with the others. Then the laborers muttered and said, "We worked the whole day long, and this man worked only two hours, and he gave him as much pay as he gave us." Then the king said to them: "This man did more work in two hours than you did throughout the whole day." Thus in twenty-eight years R. Bun achieved in the Torah what a good pupil cannot learn in a hundred years. (Palestinian Talmud, Berakhoth II. 5c).

God keeps his accounts, not in the manner of freely bestowing goodness, but rather by precise balancing of achievement and reward. A person who lives according to the Law therefore may trust in the Law; for the way to life is opened by the righteousness which is gained through the Law.

6. The Coming Salvation

In the Eighteen Benedictions which every Jew utters daily, a prayer is addressed to God that he will have mercy upon Israel and upon the kingdom of the house of David, of the righteous Messiah (cf. p. 163): "Blow the great trumpet for our liberty and raise a banner to gather together our exiles. . . . Bring back our judges as before and our counselors as at the beginning, and be king over us, thou alone" (Tenth and Eleventh Benedictions). It is true that the one God whom Israel confesses is already the King and Lord of the world, but his lordship still is hidden from the world and is not recognized by the peoples. Therefore the hope of the pious is oriented to the future in which God's glorious rule will become manifest to all the world, and they beseech God: "May thy glory become manifest and thy sublime majesty become well known. . . . And now speedily make known thy glory and do not tarry with what hath been promised by thee" (Syr. Bar. 21:23, 25).

Quite diverse conceptions of the actualization of the future salvation were held in Judaism. Sometimes the introduction of the time of salvation was thought of as God's miraculous deed, and sometimes it was thought of as the work of an *anointed one* who was to appear and to work at God's commission. For the Jew the only binding demand was the obligation to follow the instructions of the Law. With respect to the eschatological hope, no particular outlook was prescribed; thus no unitary teaching about last things was established, and variously conceived expectations stood side-by-side without any interrelation.

In many circles of the Jewish nation during the time of Jesus and the first Christians there was a lively hope that God's anointed one would soon appear. Again and again certain men attracted followers who saw them as the coming Messiah. Two such pseudo-messianic movements are mentioned in Acts 5:36-37: a certain Theudas arose, and some four hundred men followed him, but "he was killed, and all his followers were scattered and destroyed." After him came Judas the Galilean, "and he drew many people away after him, but he also perished, and all who had followed him were scattered." According to Acts 21:38, when Paul was arrested, he was asked by the Roman centurion who had taken him into custody whether he was the Egyptian who recently had incited four thousand of the Zealots to revolt and led them into the wilderness.

The most popular view regarding the messianic transformation had been developed among the Pharisees, who had suffered grave disappointments under the kingdom of the Hasmoneans and the alien rule of the Romans (cf. pp. 30–34). Under the impact of these events the ancient promises had gained new force: someday God would cause the anointed ruler to arise, after the example of David, to liberate Israel and lead her to glorious brilliance. He would raise up for David a righteous branch (Jer. 23:5; 33:15; Zech. 3:8; 6:2), and a shoot would come forth from the stump of Jesse (Isa. 11:1). But above all, people recalled the divine promise which had been given to the family of David through the prophet Nathan: God would not withdraw his favor from David's descendants, but would give stability to his house and kingdom and would establish his throne forever (II Sam. 7:12-16). Attached to this promise from God was the hope by which the people were able to turn away from the present with its misfortune and look toward the future when God's gracious deeds would become reality.

This expectation found its clearest expression in the Psalms of Solomon, which arose in Pharisaic circles about the middle of the first century B.C. Before a detailed picture of the coming age of the Messiah is drawn, the confession of the God of Israel is expressed: "Lord, thou thyself art our king forever and eternally" (Ps. Sol. 17:1). In view of the severe suffering which has come upon the nation with the conquest of Jerusalem by Pompey, God is reminded of his ancient promise: "Thou, Lord, hast chosen David to be king over Israel, and thou hast sworn to him concerning his seed for all time, that his kingdom shall never cease from before thy face" (17:4). Even though because of the sins of the people godless men could rise up against Israel, still God's promise remained in force. Hence the prayer is addressed to him: "See to it, O Lord, and let their king arise for them, the Son of David, at the time which thou hast chosen, that he may rule over thy servant Israel" (17:21). When the coming ruler is called by the name of the great King David, this is an indication that the prediction of Nathan will find its fulfillment. Just as God once equipped and strengthened David, so will he also gird the eschatological liberator with strength, that he may cleanse Jerusalem of the heathen, smite the sinners with a staff of iron, and destroy the heathen with the word of his mouth. For "he will not allow injustice any longer to dwell in their midst, and no one who knows evil may dwell among them" (17:27). He will rule over them as the "great king, taught by God, and in his days no injustice will occur among them, because of all of them are holy, and their king is the anointed one of the Lord" (17:32). When it is expressly emphasized here that the future ruler of Israel will be taught by God, this is an indication that the picture of the Messiah was drawn by people faithful to the Law, who expected, above all, that God's emissary would be obedient to God's commandment, would know his will, and would make the Law the only standard for his actions. At the end of the detailed description of the messianic salvation the appeal to God is made once again: "May God soon let his favor come upon Israel; may he save us from defilement by unholy enemies. The Lord himself is our king forever and eternally" (17:45-46).

The hope that the Son of David would liberate his people and would reprove the heathen for their godlessness, would punish unrighteousness, and would expose wickedness (IV Ezra 12:32) was so universally shared that the title "Son of David" could be used by the rabbis consistently as a designation for the Messiah without requiring any further definition. The expectation was maintained and carried beyond the destruction of Jerusalem by the Romans, and it continued to be a fixed part of the prayers which are addressed to God that he might send the branch of David and cause his anointed one to appear.

Other opinions also were held besides this one dominant view of the coming of the Messiah; some of these supplemented this picture, and others contradicted it. Various mention was made of a forerunner of the Messiah who would announce his coming and prepare the way for it. Usually the returning prophet Elijah is named as the forerunner (cf. Mal. 3:23-24; 4:5-6); in Qumran people spoke only of the coming of a prophet of the end-time (1QS IX. 11). The figure of the bearer of salvation who follows the messenger could also be conceived of as an *eschatological priest* who would gather together the people liberated from uncleanness and sin. Unlike David or the prophet, his activity becomes relevant only after

Paradise has been restored. Then will the sword that threatened Adam be taken away, the saints will be allowed to eat of the tree of life, the power of evil will be eliminated, and Belial will be bound; thus the community of the consummation can live unassailed in the joy of Paradise and the Lord will be well pleased with his beloved for all eternity (Test. Levi 18).

While in the eschatological expectation held by the Qumran community the conception of a messianic high priest is linked with that of the royal anointed one (cf. p. 108), many Jews thought that the emissary of God who would appear in the last days would simply be the prophet or the returning Moses. The prophet who is to come into the world (John 6:14; cf. also John 1:21) will appear in fulfillment of the promise of Deuteronomy 18:15: "The Lord your God will cause to arise among your brethren a prophet like me [i.e., Moses], whom you will heed."

The apocalyptic portrayals of the transition from this perishing eon to that coming world of God's own people either do not mention a Messiah at all, or they speak of the *Son of man*, who in God's presence stands ready to descend on the clouds of heaven at the end of time, to pronounce judgment, and to lead the righteous into blessedness (cf. pp. 60–61). Here the deliverer is not thought of as an earthly phenomenon of high sanctity, but as a supramundane figure who will issue from the celestial world.

The question of when the kingdom of God will come was raised throughout the Jewish community, and signs from which one could discern whether the messianic age was already being announced were sought (cf. Luke 17:20). The rabbis answered this question by saying that through strict obedience to the Law Israel could hasten the coming of the future salvation. If all Israel would truly repent, the dedemption by the Messiah would then come to pass. Since the day of liberation was delayed, many surmised that the Messiah would remain completely hidden and perhaps no one would recognize him (cf. John 7:27); others said that he had already been born and had appeared but had not been recognized. In such ways they expressed the disappointment over the fact that history and the present time disclosed nothing of the signs of the messianic age. Yet the hope remained alive in Judaism that at the end, God would have mercy upon his people and would take note of their misery.

As different as these views about the Messiah and the time of salvation were, common to all of them was the conviction that the one anointed by God would appear as a ruler and judge, would exalt the lowliness of Israel, drive out the heathen, and establish the kingdom of glory. But nowhere do they speak of a *suffering Messiah* who because of the sins of the people would take upon himself humiliation and death. Where the relationship of man to God is determined entirely by the Law, where people seek after righteousness under the Law and know no other way to salvation outside the Law, there can be no place for a suffering Messiah who takes upon himself the guilt of others. Only when the frightful events during the Jewish War (A.D. 66–70) and the revolt under Bar Cochba (A.D. 132–135) had struck a severe blow at Judaism and the expectation that the Messiah would soon appear was shattered did a few scattered persons begin to think that God's anointed one must suffer and die. In addition to the Messiah, Son of David, there is occasionally mentioned a messiah, son of Joseph, who must fight hard battles as a warrior and die in battle. A later legend tells that R. Joshua ben Levi, who lived in the third century A.D., once met the prophet Elijah and asked him when the Messiah would come. The prophet answered that he should ask him himself, and he would find him at the gate of Rome, where he would be sitting among the poor lepers. They unbind the sores of their leprosy all at once, and bind them up again all at once; but he unbinds them and rebinds them one at a time, for he thinks, "If I am wanted, there must be no delay" (Babylonian Talmud, Sanhedrin 98a). Afflicted with sickness, sitting hidden among the wretched ones, the Messiah holds himself in constant readiness for the hour when he will be called by God. Even these words, which speak of a Messiah burdened with misery, say nothing of his suffering for the sins of others. But he has surely entered into the community of suffering with all Israel, who is patiently waiting for redemption.

The Christian community, which proclaims the crucified and resurrected Jesus as the Messiah, transferred to its Lord all the titles of dignity and honor which stood side-by-side without having been similarly linked to the eschatological expectations of Judaism. The Lord is not only called the Christ (or Messiah) and Son of David, but also the high priest, the prophet, and the Son of man. It is not through the messianic hope of Judaism, (which presents a rich diversity of conceptions) but through the Christian confession that the various designations of the Messiah are first assembled into a unity. This was accomplished by the event of the cross (to which these designations were now without exception related), which profoundly reshaped messianic designations and gave them new content; for they at last came to describe the uniquely lofty character of the humiliated Messiah who has died for our sins in accordance with the Scriptures (I Cor. 15:3). In the multiplicity of its messianic images, Judaism did not know of an anointed one of God who becomes the friend of tax collectors and sinners and in dying takes upon himself the guilt of the world. But the Christians believe in the crucified and resurrected Messiah as the living Lord. Nevertheless, belief in the Messiah is never spoken of in Judaism; belief, as confidence in the truth of God's word, is rather one good work among many in the life of the devout. Therefore no more specific reflections upon the person of the Messiah are undertaken; the eschatological expectation is oriented, not to the messianic person, but to the messianic age which he is to bring, and to the work which will be performed at God's bidding. When he shall appear, the glory and splendor which God wills to bestow upon his people through his instrument will dawn. Hence the Messiah will be the executor of salvation, not its ground, meaning, or content.

The earlier expectation of an earthly messiah-king and the apocalyptic hope which is oriented to the change from one age to another were not originally linked. Yet when the question was later posed as to how these different conceptions are interrelated, the attempt was made to reconcile them in the following manner: first the Davidic Messiah will appear, and he will liberate and rule over Israel, but his rule will be limited and will constitute only the beginning of the eschatological events. After one last assault by the hostile forces this eon will pass away, the dead will be raised, and the Son of man will judge all mankind; thus God's new world can arise, and some will enter into life, and others into eternal death. In this way there arose the idea of a *messianic interregnum* which is to precede the end of this world and the coming rule of God. According to IV Ezra 7:28-29 the Messiah will rule for four hundred years, but then he and all who have breath will die. When the whole world has remained for seven days in the silence of the primeval time the dead will arise and the final judgment will take place. Thus the time of the Messiah on earth represents only a preliminary stage of the splendor that will dawn after the end of the old eon. The length of the interregnum is variously calculated in Jewish apocalyptic. Where the number one thousand is given, it is derived from the idea of a cosmic week, according to which world history is to take its course for six thousand years and the great cosmic sabbath is to prevail for the last thousand years (cf. p. 58). This expectation of a messianic interregnum found its way in a christianized form into the Revelation of John (cf. Rev. 20:1-10). This could happen all the more readily since according to the primitive Christian proclamation Jesus was called Messiah-King as well as Son of man, and all expectation of the future was linked exclusively to his name.

In the hard struggles of the Maccabean period the urgent question had been raised about whether the righteous ones who fell in battle could not participate in the future salvation. The answer was first conceived in the conviction that both devout individuals and martyrs from Israel's history would be raised from the dead to share in full salvation (cf. II Macc. 7). Sinners, on the other hand, would remain in death: "The sinner's ruin is eternal, and he will not be thought of when he [i.e., God] visits the devout. This is the lot of the sinners eternally; but those who fear the Lord will arise to eternal life, and their life [is passed] in the light, and [it] will never be exhausted" (Ps. Sol. 3:11-12). Soon, however, the idea of the *resurrection* in connection with the future judgment as portrayed in apocalyptic was expanded to the extent that not only do the righteous arise to blessedness, but all men are to be raised from the dead, to give account before

God's judgment seat. In Ethiopic Enoch 22 it is said that all of the dead of the underworld, the righteous and the ungodly, will arise to judgment. The only exceptions are sinners who have been murdered, who by their death have already achieved sufficient expiation for their guilt and therefore have no more need of appearing before the judgment bar. The Similitudes of the Ethiopic apocalypse of Enoch (chapters 37–71), the visions of the apocalypse of Ezra, and the Syriac apocalypse of Baruch (30:1-5; 50:2–51:3) then presuppose the general resurrection of all the dead. When the body is placed in the grave after death, the soul of man is taken to a heavenly place, where it tarries in an intermediate state. But at the last day the bodies will be taken out of the graves and the souls will be reunited with them (cf. pp. 59–60).

As the Sadducees rejected the belief in the resurrection of the dead (cf. p. 75), so also the teaching of the Qumran community represents the earlier form of the eschatological expectation, indeed referring to God's victory and the salvation which is to be bestowed upon the sons of light, but nowhere speaking explicitly of a resurrection of the dead. The hope is that the sons of truth "will have a superabundance of peace so long as days continue, and fruitfulness of seed with all eternal blessings and eternal joy in everlasting life and a crown of glory with garments of splendor in eternal light" (1QS IV. 7–8). Even though the question of how there can be participation in salvation beyond death is not discussed, the one who prays says: "I praise thee, Lord, for thou hast redeemed my soul from the pit, and from the underworld of the abyss thou hast lifted me up to eternal heights" (1QH III. 19–20). Then when after the destruction of Jerusalem in A.D. 70 the Pharisaic scribes alone determined the teaching of the synagogue, the hope of the resurrection of the dead (cf. p. 75), so also the teaching of the Qumran by praising the God of Israel who raises the dead.

After the judgment, for all who may enter into blessedness, eternal life will begin—eternal life sometimes being conceptualized as an exalted continuation of earthly life from which burdens and troubles now are removed. There is eating and drinking in festive banquets (Eth. Enoch 62:14 *et passim*), and sickness and distress are banished (IV Ezra

8:53). Eternal life, as distinguished from life of this world, unfolds without any temporal limitation, because the rule of death is broken (Syr. Bar. 21:22-23 *et passim*). More over, there will be no more sin after the evil impulse which resides in man is extinguished along with death. According to other expressions, eternal life is in no way comparable to earthly life, because the conditions under which men lead their earthly existence will be eliminated. In the future world—so the rabbis occasionally say—there will be neither eating nor drinking, neither begetting nor propagation, neither buying nor selling, neither envy nor enmity and strife; but the righteous will sit with their crowns on their heads and will enjoy the splendor of the *Shekinah* [i.e., "of God"] (Babylonian Talmud, Berakhoth 17a).

In Hellenistic Judaism, it is the Greek influence that causes the belief in the *immortality of the soul* to be appropriated to the extent (cf. p. 124) that the hope of eternal life also took on a different significance. Its beginning is now no longer necessarily simultaneous with the resurrection of the dead, but has its inception at the moment the immortal soul is released from the body and is taken up into imperishability. Immediately after death the hour of judgment and retribution strikes, and it is decided whether the way to eternal life is open or closed.

Common to the manifold conceptions concerning salvation and the various expressions of the hope of eternal life is the conviction that eternal life is bestowed upon men in the next world as the gift of God, who alone is eternal. Faith and pious conduct, obedience to the Law, or a virtuous life are the conditions prerequisite to attaining the future saving gift of eternal life.

PART II
The Hellenistic-
Roman Environment
of the New Testament

CHAPTER 1
Politics and Society in the Roman Empire
in the First Century A.D.

The seemingly boundless empire which Alexander the Great had assembled through his expeditions of conquest soon disintegrated after the early death of the young Macedonian king. Nevertheless, in the territories ruled by the Diadochi, who divided Alexander's legacy among themselves, the pervasive influence of the Greek language and customs continued undiminished. Syria and Egypt were ruled by Hellenistic kings, and the populace learned the language of the Greeks and adapted themselves to their customs and manners. Then after the Romans emerged victorious from the severe conflicts with Carthage, they (from the middle of the second century B.C. on) increasingly directed their attention toward Greece and the East. In the encounter with Hellenism they appropriated the art and science of the Greeks and, through their political successes, continued to extend the sphere of their power. In the first century B.C. Syria and Palestine became subject to Roman rule, so that now the entire eastern part of the Mediterranean world was brought under the dominion of Rome. Thereby, the Romans everywhere effectively assumed the succession of the Greeks. In so doing they felt it their obligation to provide for the preservation of the heritage that had fallen to them, whereupon Hellenistic Roman culture and civilization became firmly established and further disseminated through the stable medium of the powerful Roman Empire.

1. The Roman Empire Under the Rule of the Caesars

After Caesar had finally succeeded in conquering his adversaries, thereby augmenting his power, and just as he was reaching for sole rulership, he was murdered (44 B.C.). Yet Caesar's murderers were able to maintain their power for only a short time. Octavian and Antony, who had formed an alliance to fight those who had murdered Caesar, quickly put an end to their rule. The victors divided the empire: Antony took over the rule in the East, lived in Alexandria with the queen Cleopatra, and from there also determined the destiny of Syria and Palestine; Octavian ruled over Italy and the western part of the empire, from his seat in Rome. Yet this arrangement was not to last, as dissension soon arose between the two rulers. In the war that resulted Octavian emerged victorious, Antony's fate having been sealed by his defeat in the sea-battle at Actium (31 B.C.). From that time on, Octavian was the sole ruler of the wide Roman Empire.

Italy and the provinces had suffered severely during the many battles and conflicts. Many families had been torn asunder, and the men sent to foreign countries as soldiers. The populace had suffered great privation; agriculture and trade languished. The upheavals had affected even the most remote corners of the empire. It was necessary at any given time to accommodate oneself to the person who was currently in power. And if a sudden change occurred, one had to take care to gain quickly the favor of the new ruler. Thus the Jewish King Herod became adept at quickly comprehending every change in the political situation and in alternating sides when he judged it necessary (cf. pp. 37–38). The experience of these painful years filled the populace of the entire empire with a profound yearning for peace. In Italy as well as in the provinces people hopefully anticipated the arrival of a ruler who would finally stamp out the flames of war.

Octavian, who as victor over Antony fell heir to unlimited power, became the creator of this greatly desired peace. Since it was only as leader of the army that he could ensure the continuation of peace, he received, as *imperator,* the command of the troops. He appeared in public as the advocate of Roman tradition. Although he alone had executive power, he respected the Senate and reinvested it with its ancient rights. Non-Romans who had come into the Senate in Caesar's time were excluded so as to enhance the esteem accorded the supreme authority. Octavian's position was strengthened by the elevation of his adoptive father Caesar, at the Senate's decree, to a place among the deities. Thereafter Octavian called himself the son of the divine Caesar, *imperator Caesar divi filius.* Although the old Roman constitution had been put into effect once again, the power of government in fact lay wholly in Octavian's hands. When in the year 27 B.C., he publicly and officially renounced all the special powers that had been transferred to him and gave them back to the Senate so that the old order might be restored, the Senate asked him to retain his position, that he might protect the peace and continue to care for the welfare of the state. Thereupon Octavian reassumed the powers which he had just resigned to the Senate. Thus there arose a new form of government. It is true that the Senate remained Rome's supreme authority, but Octavian was the first citizen of the state who as the *princeps* guided its destiny. He added to his name the one of Augustus and thus emphasized the unique dignity of his position; for until that time this designation (meaning "the exalted one") had been employed only as a surname of deities. It is true that Octavian guarded against breaking with the Roman tradition that sharply distinguished between gods and men, but by allowing himself to be called Augustus, he unmistakably gave the impression that his position of power was of incomparable loftiness.

The highest priestly office of the *pontifex maximus* was transferred to Augustus in 12 B.C. on the basis of a popular referendum, and in 2 B.C. the list of honorary titles was once more expanded when Augustus was designated by the Senate as *pater patriae*. In a report given shortly before his death, in which he considered his policies in retrospect, Augustus proudly emphasized that his honors had been given to him by the Senate because of his courage and mildness, justice and piety. His influence was supreme, but his official power was no greater than those with whom he shared every office.

From 27 to 23 B.C. Augustus each year had the office of consul entrusted to him. Although another consul shared the office with him, the leadership was his alone. Later his position was so greatly strengthened that he exercised the office of consul only now and then. The army remained loyal to him since the soldiers, who in large part were recruited from Italy, could expect wages, advancement, and good allowances only from the Caesar, and the officers, who came from the Roman nobility, could count on achieving promotion and success through Augustus. Of course he had to be responsible for the considerable expenses which the maintenance of the standing professional army required. He was able to do this because after the victory over Antony and Cleopatra he had taken over Egypt as his personal possession and was thus by far the wealthiest man in the empire—notwithstanding that he committed his great wealth to the well-being of the state. He not only bore the responsibility for the maintenance of the army, but also imported grain from Egypt to be distributed among the Roman proletariat. These were kept in good humor by bread and games (*panem et circenses*) and were always ready, when called upon, to hail Caesar, to celebrate the festivals which he established, and to pay homage to him.

Augustus deployed the legions to the boundaries of the empire, to protect the endangered territories. Only the Praetorian Guard, which was responsible for order and for the protection of Caesar, remained in Rome. The provinces were administered by governors; in this arrangement, the Hellenistic cities in the eastern part of the empire were allowed a considerable degree of self-government for their own affairs, in accordance with traditional laws of the cities. The supervision of the old provinces rested with the Senate, which also had to name the governors and as a rule sent a consul, after the completion of his year in office, to a province as proconsul. Thus it is related in Acts 18:12 that the proconsul Gallio came to Corinth to assume the office of governor of Achaia (A.D. 51). The newly won provinces such as Egypt, on the other hand, were not under the jurisdiction of the Senate, but as imperial provinces were directly subject to Caesar, who alone determined who should hold office as his governor. The great commonwealth of the empire also included allied principalities which were dependent upon Rome. Thus King Herod could rule in Palestine only with Rome's permission; and when he died, his testament had to be confirmed by Augustus before it could take effect (cf. pp. 40–41). If a prince in a country dependent on Rome did not conduct himself properly, he could be removed from his office and his territory placed under the supervision of a Roman procurator (cf. p. 42).

The skillful and moderate policies with which Augustus ruled the empire met with almost universal approval. After the long-lasting terrors of the wars, peace had finally returned in all localities, and the Romans did not undertake any further conquests but concerned themselves instead with securing the stability of the empire and strengthening its borders. Throughout the empire Augustus was celebrated as a peaceful ruler. Thus in an inscription made in 9 B.C. at Priene in Asia Minor it is said that people wished to mark the beginning of the year with Caesar's birthday; for divine providence had brought the highest fulfillment to human life, "in that it gave us Augustus, whom it filled with power for the well-being of men, when it sent him to us and our descendants as savior, who would put an end to war and would set everything in order." The glad tidings that issued from his victorious rule had begun with the news of the birth of the ruler: "The birthday of the god was for the world the beginning of good news [Greek: *euangelia*] that came forth because of him." Where such homage was offered to him in the eastern provinces of the empire, Augustus received it, but he did not demand a similar veneration in the West or in Rome. Since he wanted to be recognized as the peaceful ruler who with wisdom and goodness advanced the well-being of men, he also gave ear to various complaints that were brought to him from throughout the broad empire and intervened to help oppressed peoples, punish guilty persons or remove insensitive governors and rulers from offices (cf. p. 42).

Throughout the empire new cities were founded; temples, theaters, waterworks, and other public facilities were constructed; and, most importantly, roads were built. Military police provided security on the Roman roads at dangerous places, so that one could travel quickly and safely without anxiety about attacks from robbers; and the sea lanes were protected by Caesar's fleet, so that shipping went unmolested by pirates. Consequently trade and commerce flourished and expanded far beyond the boundaries of the empire, to the Atlantic, the Baltic, and Africa. The rights of Roman citizenship were extended beyond Italy to deserving inhabitants in the provinces. Any citizen of the empire could travel about freely, and a small customs charge was assessed only at the boundaries of the provinces. A feeling of security was given to the populace of the entire empire, and people were at last free from threats to life and limb.

Hand in hand with the outward fortification of the empire went Augustus' measures for instituting internal reform. He had represented the victory over Antony as a triumph of the old Roman virtues over foreign influence from the East. Now he sought to counter the decline in morals evident everywhere in Rome, to bring back courage and justice, and to maintain discipline and morality. In the search for pleasure, many Romans remained unmarried, numerous marriages remained childless, divorces were common, and the great host of slaves, both men and women, presented a constant temptation to immorality. In order to stem this development, laws were issued for the protection of the Roman family: all men between twenty and sixty years of age and all women between twenty and fifty years were to be obliged to marry. In order to promote families, it was decreed that unmarried people could not inherit property, married people who were childless could inherit only one-half of estates, and fathers with numbers of children were to be preferred in the competition for offices. Yet these measures failed to achieve their aim, since people sought in various ways to circumvent the legal prescriptions. Marriages were contracted in name only, and the decline in morals could not be stemmed so that a more thoroughgoing reformation could be achieved. The depiction in Romans 1:18-32 of the moral conditions of the Hellenistic-Roman world is indeed extreme, but to a large extent it must have corresponded with the actual circumstances.

The reorganization of the empire that was accomplished during the long and peaceful reign of Augustus was so well established at the end of his life that it continued after his death. When Augustus died in A.D. 14 at the age of seventy-six, his adopted son Tiberius, an experienced commander and prudent politician who was already fifty-six years old, took over the government. The arrangement of the principate had gained such approval that Tiberius was able to assume the succession without any opposition from the Senate. Actually Augustus had not originally marked him as his successor, but since other possibilities had been shattered, he had finally destined him for this position. Tiberius had experienced many disappointments, and he worked in a secretive and reserved way. As ruler he undertook to fulfill his obligations strictly and conscientiously by methodically and purposefully continuing the policies of his predecessor. But he lacked the creative mind that had enabled Augustus to succeed in his work. Because of his strictness and a certain insecurity Tiberius was not skillful in dealing with people, and he made many enemies. During his reign the orderly administration of the empire continued. Under Tiberius' rule Pontius Pilate was installed as procurator in Judea and Samaria (A.D. 36), John the Baptist appeared in Palestine (cf. Luke 3:1), and Jesus of Nazareth pursued his work in the country until he was handed over by the Jews to the governer in Jerusalem, condemned to death, and executed by the shameful punishment of crucifixion.

Tiberius was followed by *Caligula* who, when he took over the rule, was only twenty-five years old (A.D. 37). In contrast to his predecessor, he behaved as a Hellenistic ruler and surrounded himself with a circle of corrupt young Hellenistic princes, one of whom was Herod Agrippa, who through Caligula's favor achieved influence and rule in Palestine (cf. p. 45). Caligula's dissolute life and his absurdly exaggerated striving for godlike exaltation of the ruler's position hindered him from fulfilling the tasks of his office. He did not even hesitate to demand that the Jews set up his statue in the temple in Jerusalem (cf. p. 46). His designs were thwarted, however, by his sudden death. During the few years of his rule he had made so many enemies that a palace revolution put an end to his regime (A.D. 41).

The Praetorian Guard summoned *Claudius*, uncle of Caligula, to be caesar (A.D. 41–54). He was a reasonable man who strove to govern conscientiously. He carried on extensive correspondence with the officeholders in the provinces of the empire in order to be informed about local conditions and to exert an influence upon them. In a detailed document which he sent to the city of Alexandria he approved the erection of statues of himself and his family at various locations in the city and then continued: "I do not approve of the appointment of high priests nor the building of temples; for I do not want to cause offense to my contemporaries, and it is my opinion that the shrines and the like are exclusively the prerogative of the gods, which are their due at all times." Since conflicts had arisen in Alexandria between the Jewish and non-Jewish populace, Claudius admonished the Alexandrians:

> that on the one hand you be tolerant and friendly toward the Jews, who have dwelt in the same city for a long time, and not desecrate any of the rites which they perform in the worship of their gods, but allow them to follow their customs as in the time of the divine Augustus, which I, after I have listened to both sides, have likewise approved; and on the other hand I explicitly command the Jews not to strive for more privileges than they possessed earlier. . . . If you desist from these things and are willing to live with each other in mutual forbearance and friendliness, I on my part will show the same benevolent concern for the city that was shown to you by my predecessors. (London Papyrus 1912)

It is true that in this decree Claudius is unmistakably guided by the effort to deal justly with both parties, but in Rome he took steps against the Jews, because conflicts arose among them. Suetonius relates: "He expelled the Jews from Rome because, under the instigation of a certain Chrestus, they were constantly causing unrest" (Claudius 25). From this unclear account it is to be inferred that because of the message concerning Christ, controversies had arisen among the Jews. The report erroneously cites the frequently used slave name Chrestus to identify the person guilty of instigating the disturbances. Actually, however, it must have been the proclamation that the crucified Jesus of Nazareth was the Christ, the Messiah of Israel, that caused the outbreak of these disturbances, which Claudius unhesitatingly understood as justification for expelling the Jews from the capital city. Perhaps not all the members of the Jewish community who lived in the world capital were forced to leave Rome, but it is certain that they were forbidden to hold services and meetings in the synagogues. The Jewish Christians were also affected by this decree (cf. Acts 18:2). Then under Nero the edict of Claudius was lifted, so that the Jews were allowed to return to Rome.

In A.D. 54 Claudius was poisoned by his wife Agrippina, who wanted to eliminate him in order to bring to the throne her son *Nero*, who was born of her first marriage and had been adopted by Claudius. The change in government was successfully accomplished without upheaval. Since the new ruler was only seventeen years old, affairs of office were at first conducted by Praetorian prefects and the philosopher Seneca, one of the wealthiest and most influential men in Rome. The years of their regency went well. But when Nero himself took over the rule, he abandoned all restraints. He liked to appear publicly as an artist, represented himself as a friend and patron of Greek culture, and strove to clothe his lofty position as ruler with divine splendor. He ruthlessly removed men who might hinder him. The first persecution of Christians in Rome arose at his instigation. After a dreadful fire in which many houses were consumed (A.D. 64), the rumor spread (and stubbornly persisted) that the fire had been set at Nero's command. To divert suspicion from himself, Nero sought to produce people who could be blamed— in this confining himself to the Christians—and condemning to death all whose property people coveted. Tacitus writes:

In the execution, sport was made of them by putting them in animal skins and letting them be torn to pieces by wild dogs.

Others were nailed to crosses or condemned to death by fire, after nightfall burning like torches. For this show Nero had provided his own park, and at the same time he arranged circus games, where he mingled with the people dressed as a wagoner or rode about in a chariot. (*Annals* XV. 44)

Nero even murdered members of his own family. Matters finally became so bad that a conspiracy was formed against him, and he took his own life (A.D. 68). His sudden end was hailed by many with jubilation; but others were perturbed and suspected that it was not true that he was dead, that he was still alive and hiding somewhere. Thus arose the expectation that he would return from out of the East at the head of a Parthian army, or that he would be raised from the dead to a new life. These ideas that were widespread among the people exhibit the features with which the book of Revelation portrays the figure of the beast from the abyss that will appear as the fearful ruler of the last times (Rev. 13:1-18; 17:12-17).

With the death of Nero the rule of the Julian-Claudian house came to an end. In Spain Galba was summoned by his soldiers to be caesar, in Rome the Praetorian Guards wanted to place Otho in power, and in Germany the legions declared Vitellius to be Nero's successor. None of the three men, however, achieved recognition throughout the empire, so the threat of renewed civil war arose. Then *Vespasian*, who was with his legions in Palestine and was chosen by them as leader, succeeded in taking over the rulership and, supported by the army, in bringing about peace and order (A.D. 69). Vespasian continued the policy of renewing the principate that had been initiated by Augustus and secured the succession in office of his sons. When he died in A.D. 79, his son *Titus*, the conqueror of Jerusalem, became emperor, and in A.D. 81 he was followed by his brother *Domitian* (A.D. 81–96). Domitian emphasized that his power as ruler was unlimited, sought to exhibit the sanctity of his person publicly, and liked to hear the people greet him and his wife in the amphitheater on the day of the great festal banquet with the cry, "Hail to our lord and his consort! (Suetonius *Domitian* XIII). He demanded blind submission to his commands from everyone. Any hint of resistance was suppressed, but he could not restrain the growth of dislike and hostility toward him. For the Romans did not want a tyrant for a ruler, but looked for a man who would conduct the government as a servant of the state. When Domitian in A.D. 96 fell victim to a conspiracy, the era of the Flavian ruling house came to an end. Although a diversity of conflict and tension had consistently arisen in the course of the first century A.D. and caused significant disruption in Rome, still the empire established by Augustus proved stable. In the provinces the Roman administration worked reliably, and did not greatly suffer in the aftermath of events taking place in the capital city.

After Domitian's death a change came about, for the Senate chose as emperor a man who came from an old Roman family who also fit the model of a ruler imbued with Stoic ideas. With Nerva (A.D. 96–98) begins the succession of caesars who were committed to the teachings of the philosophers and sought to actualize these teachings for the benefit of the commonwealth. The Stoic ideal of the ruler, which prescribed that the best man should rule and should conduct his office as a servant of the commonwealth, prevailed. Nerva adopted the general Trajan, who then took over the government as his successor in A.D. 98 and ruled until A.D. 117. By the procedure of adoption it was assured that from the group of candidates under consideration the most capable one could be chosen and destined to become the next ruler. Trajan was concerned with humane government. When Christians in Asia Minor were being persecuted because of their faith and the emperor was asked how an official should proceed against them, it was his counsel to act with caution and reserve, and not to use the powers of office to search out the Christians. If accusations were made against them, the matter was to be pursued, but anonymous denunciations were to be disregarded. Anyone who publicly abjured the faith and offered sacrifice to the gods was to be pardoned, but those who did not were to be punished severely (Pliny the Younger *Epistle* X. 96). Toward the end of Trajan's reign a revolt of the Jews broke out in the eastern part of the empire; this uprising claimed the lives of Jews particularly in Egypt, and it finally was crushed.

Trajan was followed by *Hadrian* (A.D. 117–138), who saw

himself as a cosmopolitan ruler. He frequently traveled about the empire and particularly liked to stay in Greece. He had buildings erected everywhere, and was concerned with the prosperity of the provinces. The determined resistance of the Jews was once again aroused by his prohibition of castration, which was extended also to circumcision, and by the directive to erect a shrine for Jupiter Capitolinus on the site of the ruined temple in Jerusalem. This resistance led to the revolt under Bar Cochba (A.D. 132–135; cf. pp. 52–54). Then from A.D. 138 to 161 *Antoninus Pius* reigned, a ruler highly regarded by the entire populace of the empire. Nor was the esteem accorded *Marcus Aurelius*, the philosopher on the throne of caesar (A.D. 161–180), any less. Filled with the desire for truth and constantly absorbed in questions of philosophy, he strove to preserve peace and to enhance the prosperity of the empire. Yet he was not spared the task of having to take sword in hand to defend the boundaries of the empire against attacks from the East and the North.

The succession of rulers who were committed to the Stoic concept of humanity and strove to the limit of their powers to remain faithful to this ideal came to an end with Marcus Aurelius. To be sure, they did not succeed in preserving peace everywhere; internal and external conflicts made military intervention a necessity. But under the humane rule of the caesars a salubrious existence was granted the empire. The boundaries remained secure, so that internal building was able to continue and the development and expansion of Hellenistic-Roman culture to proceed undisturbed.

2. Social Conditions in the Roman Empire in the First Century A.D.

The Roman Empire was a cosmopolitan commonwealth, within whose wide-ranging fortified borders the Hellenistic-Roman culture, now a homogeneous product of its Greek and Roman heritages, could unfold without hindrance. Everywhere in the East and to a large extent also in the western part of the empire, people spoke and understood Greek, which since the time of Alexander the Great had become the universal language of commerce in the Mediterranean basin.

In the course of further development, a certain simplification of Attic Greek (that which was spoken in Athens in the time of the tragedians and Plato), the so-called *Koine* (i.e., "the common language"), had emerged, thereby contributing to universal understanding. It was not written and spoken everywhere with grammatical correctness, and individual words from Oriental languages and from Latin were mixed with it. But everyone strove to master Greek sufficiently to make it apparent that they belonged to the Greeks and not to the barbarians. People looked upon barbarians in contempt because their language resembled a succession of incomprehensible sounds ("bar-bar"), and everyone wanted to claim for himself a share, even though a modest one, in the culture of the Greeks.

Hellenistic culture had its base in the cities of the empire, where lines of trade and commerce intermingled and a person could develop a wealthy and easeful existence. Every city strove to achieve distinction by means of its buildings—to provide open plazas after the example of Greek architecture, to erect temples, to lay aqueducts, to construct public baths, and to create theaters and sport centers. Wealthy citizens often committed a large part of their assets to the improvement of their city and in exchange for this donation were permitted to erect their statues on one of the columns on the main street. Their wealth made it possible for them to spend their days as spectators in the theater or at the games. Competitive games, which were conducted by Greek cities from early times, took place in the Roman period as well. Many of the competitors made a vocation of sport and enjoyed recognition and an enthusiastic following for their victories. In Rome the masses frequently streamed into the great amphitheater of the Colosseum to watch and to take pleasure in the fights of the gladiators or of wild animals.

The language of the Greeks was used not only in Egypt, Palestine, and Syria, but in Rome as well. The Greek culture had infiltrated the country much earlier through Greek settlements that had existed in the southern part of Italy for some centuries. Yet it was only after the Romans had conquered Greece and numerous slaves who spoke the Koine had been brought from the East to Rome that the Greek language gained a firm foothold in the capital city itself. The Romans were aware that politically powerless Greece was culturally superior to them, and they willingly opened themselves to the rich intellectual treasure that flowed to them from Hellas. People learned the language of the Greeks, read their literature, and strove to imitate their poetic art, in order to apply these to materials drawn from the history and lives of the Romans.

The innumerable *private letters* that are extant from the Hellenistic period attest the wide dissemination of the Koine in East and West alike. Letters were written on papyrus, the writing material provided by Egypt for the whole empire. A letter was usually kept short, so that it could be put on a single sheet of papyrus, which then was rolled up and fastened with a seal. On the reverse side of the sheet the name and address of the intended recipient were written. The beginning of the letter named the sender and the addressee and added a greeting which expressed a wish for the well-being of the recipient. At the close of the letter there was another formula-like expression referring to the health of the reader. The body of the letter comprised only a few sentences, containing brief messages, as may be seen in a letter written from Egypt in A.D. 25:

Theon sends greetings to the highly esteemed Tyrannos. The bearer of this letter, Heraclides, is my brother, in whose behalf I most urgently beg you to take him under your patronage. I have also written to your brother Hermias asking him to present him to you. You will do me a great favor if you grant him your good will. Above all, I pray that health and the best success may be granted to you, along with protection against sorcerers. Best wishes. To Tyrannos the *dioikete* [i.e., an official].

Short private letters were usually written in the sender's own hand. Wealthy people would dictate to a secretary who would make some notes on a wax tablet from dictation, then work out the letter and present it for signature. Important pieces of writing were dictated verbatim because exactness of form was crucial (cf. Rom. 16:22), and then the conclusion would be written in the sender's own hand (cf. Gal. 6:11).

The government's postal service provided only for official needs, but one could send private letters by means of travelers, who would quickly carry them to their destination (cf. Rom. 16:1-2). The individual traveler would usually make his journey on foot, along the well-built roadways, but wealthy people and merchants would travel by wagon. Shipping was necessarily interrupted during the winter because of the dangerous storms, and from the middle of November to the middle of March it was completely at a standstill; but even earlier in the autumn ships could get into trouble at sea because of the sudden outbreak of storms (cf. II Cor. 11:25; Acts 27:14-44).

The *Roman administration*, to which all parts of the empire were subordinate, granted to the local authorities a certain amount of independence. Nevertheless the Roman governor held a supervisory position and could intervene any time he deemed it proper to do so (cf. p. 42). It was not uncommon for the Roman officials to use their position shamelessly to enrich themselves during their period of service in the provinces. Often they succeeded unhindered in returning home with rich booty; sometimes, however, complaints were made against them, so that they had to answer to Roman courts. The supreme judicial authority lay in the hands of the emperor, who issued decrees for every province through his governors and other officials, and could take into his own hands cases that were difficult to resolve locally. If a Roman citizen was involved in a trial, he could, at any time, appeal to the caesar and demand that the issue be decided in Rome (cf. Acts 25:6-12). This demand had to be granted and the case then referred to a Roman court that stood under the immediate oversight of the caesar.

In order to achieve a more exact basis for the *taxation* of the native population, in various parts of the empire a census was undertaken for which all of the inhabitants were compelled to register, indicating their hometown and details of property owned. At the time that the Jewish prince Archelaus was removed from office, in A.D. 6, and Judea was placed under a Roman governor (cf. pp. 42, 83), Quirinius, the Roman commander in Syria, ordered that a general census be undertaken in Syria and Palestine (Josephus *Jewish An-*

tiquities XVII. 355; XVIII. 1–10, 26). This directive created disturbances among the Jewish population that were further intensified due to the instigation of nationalist groups. But the Romans prevailed, and the orders of the governor were carried out. It is possible that the range of the census was to include the territories that remained subject to the rule of Herod's sons. Lists for the purpose of taxing the populace were made in Egypt also. Yet these measures were not taken at the same time, and nothing is known of a decree of Augustus that a general census should be made throughout the empire at a particular time (Luke 2:1).

Production and trade were carried on for the most part by slaves. The *slave* did not count as a person, but as chattel, with which the master could deal as he chose. He could decide on purchase or sale, could specify punishment, and, in general, could treat a slave as he wished. To be sure, certain restrictions were imposed by Roman law which forbade the grossest kind of mistreatment. Nevertheless the legal rights of slaves remained quite minimal. Only judges were allowed to decide whether a slave might be condemned to fight with the wild beasts; and a bureau was established where slaves could register complaints about mistreatments that they had suffered. Although a slave might not contract a marriage, still, tacit acceptance was usually given to a marriagelike arrangement between men and women, and such couples were not separated by force. Often it was even possible for slaves to amass certain sums of money which they could control themselves. But the unlimited legal power of the master was not diminished thereby.

The number of slaves was considerable, since many prisoners of war had been brought to Rome as booty and then sold there. The price of a slave was small; hence well-to-do people could own great numbers of slaves and could have them working by the hundreds on their *latifundia*, in businesses, and in distribution centers. Anyone who wanted to be successful had to be able to claim at least a dozen slaves. While their numbers at first were swelled significantly by the military conquests, they grew still further through natural increase; for children of slaves remained in the station of slaves. Their value was calculated according to their physical

212

health and their general abilities. Slaves who had been faithful to their master frequently were rewarded by him with emancipation. In other cases they were given the chance to accumulate a sum of money with which they could then purchase their liberty. The purchase of freedom often took place in this way: the money would be deposited in the temple of a deity, and then when the priest of the temple handed over to the erstwhile master the sum of money that had been entrusted to him, liberty was granted in the name of the deity. A document attesting the emancipation would be issued concerning this purchase of freedom. In the text of these documents, which are found in great numbers (for example, in the shrine of the Pythian Apollo at Delphi), it was always stated that the owner of a slave—both were identified by name—had sold the slave to Apollo for so many *minas*, so that he might now be free for the rest of his life to do as he would. The person freed could, according to his choice, return to his homeland or remain in the country where he was. Since it was a common occurrence in Rome for slaves to be given their freedom, the composition of the city was considerably altered thereby. If a master was a Roman citizen, his emancipated slave also received Roman citizenship. Many of the latter quickly rose to great wealth and influence in the city and attained positions of eminence.

Through the Stoic doctrine, which attributed to all men a divinely governed nature, the view that even slaves are persons and deserve to be treated humanely gained acceptance. Yet not even Stoic philosophy ventured to suggest the possibility of abolishing the institution of slavery, because people obviously could not imagine how commerce and public life could survive without it. Besides, a general emancipation of slaves presumably would have meant that overnight many people would have been plunged into misery and abandoned to utter ruin. Hence the question as to the fundamental rightness of slavery was nowhere raised, and the slave remained dependent upon the good will of his master. If his master was benevolent, things went well for him; if he provoked the master's wrath, he had reason to be afraid. It was not uncommon for slaves to slip away and attempt to gain freedom on their own initiative (cf. Philem. 10–16). An escaped slave could find asylum in a sanctuary or could attempt to lose himself in a large city and there make his way by begging and thievery. If he was captured, he had to be returned to his master. Then he could expect harsh punishment.

Through the varied impact of the Hellenistic world upon Rome, life in house and *family* underwent many changes. Originally the Roman family was structured along strictly patriarchal lines; the father was its head and made the decisions. Marriage, which usually took place at an early age, was arranged by the father and was solemnized in the presence of witnesses in a ceremony by which the bride became subject to the will of the husband. The old order, however, was fundamentally changed with the establishment of marriage by consent, for then marriage could be entered into without any further formalities and could be just as easily dissolved. In this arrangement essentially the same rights were conceded to the woman as to the man, so that she, as well as he, could sue for divorce. With the relaxation of morals throughout Rome, the practice of adultery, prostitution, and the Greek pederasty also became common and even a cause for boasting. A life of indulgence and luxury, which paralleled the growth of wealth, contributed to the collapse of the old Roman morals; people strove to be like the Greeks in every respect.

The *education of the children*, likewise, was made to conform to the Greek pattern. From this time on, Rome was no longer satisfied with the strict military training of earlier times; instead, the growing youth had to be made familiar with the intellectual world of the Greeks. Since there were no general schools, the families themselves had to provide for the education of their sons. A slave was made responsible for the daily supervision of the lad, accompanying him to his instruction, protecting him, keeping an eye on him for proper behavior, and, if necessary, correcting him. This slave was called the pedagogue—not in the sense of a teacher, but rather in that of a disciplinarian (cf. Gal. 3:24)—whose only duty was to see that his charge behaved properly. The task of educating the boy was committed to the teachers. Among the Greek authors to whom he was exposed, Homer occupied first place; in addition to an introduction to literature, music and training in sports were cultivated. Special importance was attached to training in rhetoric, which had already been developed by the Greeks into a lofty art. The less creative the philosophical thought, the more prominent was the cultivation of oratorical skill. Since in the Hellenistic period there were hardly any subjects that had relevance to major policy-making, people turned their attention to questions of everyday life or the practice of law, or took pleasure in skillful, formal discourse which did not necessarily have any significant content. The Romans benefited intellectually from the rhetoric of the Greeks and were not only able to make particular use of it in matters of law, but also to influence the course of political events. The speeches and writings of Cicero are abundant evidence of this; for they demonstrate his ability to utilize the philosophical legacy of the Greeks, to turn the sharp weapon of the right word against his political opponents, and to exert, by means of his speeches, an influence upon public issues.

Even in the field of *science* the Romans were pupils of the Greeks. The latter had acquired fundamental knowledge in mathematics, had taken up the rudiments of astronomy as they had been developed in Babylon, and had explained the courses of the celestial bodies and the order of the universe. The art of medicine had achieved a high level of proficiency, so that the skill and artistry of Greek physicians were everywhere admired and treasured. The Greeks had traveled in foreign lands, described customs and ways of life, studied the various species of the animal world, and pursued botany and zoology. They had carefully handed down the writings of the classical authors, analyzed texts with philological exactness, and explained the structure of language. Art and science, which had attained a high level of development in the Hellenistic world, were highly regarded by the Romans, whose minds were turned primarily to practical matters; but the Romans were not able to contribute to the advancement of pure research. It is true that they appropriated Hellenistic art and adopted the Greeks' building methods but they did not know how to maintain the conditions under which, alone, the unhindered development of the mind is possible. Thus the presently existing, imported intellectual heritage continued intact; but for a long time no further advance was made beyond appropriating the insights that the Greeks had gained in philosophy, philology and the natural sciences.

3. The Cult of the Emperor

In the East, the rulers had been regarded as sons of the deities and had been venerated as such since antiquity. It was from the hand of the deity that the king had received the law by which he governed his people; hence, by virtue of his own origin and the divine authority bestowed upon him, he had unlimited power. His office was received directly from the gods and therefore was both lofty and unassailable. Through the king the deity discloses himself to men, becoming visible through him and in him, and thereby coming into association with them.

The Greeks did not share these ideas, which were widely held in the East. For in their libertarian way of thinking, they knew of no divine exaltation of the ruler whom all his subjects must serve as slaves; and the gods whom they venerated are not separated from men by a sharply drawn boundary. Important men can be elevated from the human sphere into the divine and be placed as heroes in the company of the gods. And if prominent men can be accepted into the company of the gods, then conversely, the gods sometimes appear on earth in human form. The account in the book of Acts of the reception of Paul and Barnabas in Lystra shows how potent and widespread were these ideas in the Hellenistic period. When Paul had healed a man who had been a cripple since infancy, and the crowd saw how the healed man leaped up and walked about, they cried: "The gods have taken human form and have come down among us" (Acts 14:11). The miracle had convinced them of the epiphany of the gods. Because Paul was the spokesman, they called him Hermes, the messenger of the gods, and identified Barnabas, who remained silent, as Zeus (Acts 14:12).

Through the victorious expeditions of Alexander the Great, who led his armies far and wide through the eastern countries, the Greeks encountered the oriental version of the divine kingship. When the Macedonian king sought out, in Egypt, the famous oracle of the god Amon at the oasis of Siva to inquire about the future, he was addressed by the high priest as "the son of Amon," which the Greek understood as being equivalent to "the son of Zeus." Alexander not only accepted this homage, but from that time on regarded himself as son of the most high God. When he suddenly died soon thereafter, this unexpected end made his work appear, in the eyes of his contemporaries, even greater. After the deceased king had been buried in the city of Alexandria which he had built, a cult with its own priesthood was founded, honoring him as the founder of the city and the son of Amon who had been raised to the level of the gods. Not only in Egypt, but also in other places people began to pay cultic veneration to him, so that in Asia Minor and even in Athens temples were erected to the invincible god. It is true that all along the Greeks had been familiar with the idea that gods could appear on earth as men and divine men could perform miraculous works; but until that time they had never bowed to a ruler as an epiphany of deity.

The *diadochi*, who divided Alexander's legacy among themselves, also sought to claim for themselves the divine dignity which had been accorded to the great king. The trilingual inscription on the Rosetta stone, from the year 196 B.C., bears witness to the homage paid to the Ptolemies, who just after Alexander's death provided for the establishment of his cult in Egypt. Ptolemy V is extolled with-lofty phrases as the one "who has brought order to Egypt, . . . who has made the lives of men happy, the living image of Zeus, son of Helios, the eternally living Ptolemy, favorite of Ptah, god upon earth, who, being god stems from god and goddess, . . . who has brought peace to Egypt, who gave her all her laws, founded temples and altars, and set upright those who needed help, and thus exemplified the nature of a benevolent god." In the Seleucid Empire, within whose boundaries various nationalities lived, the religious exaltation of the king served to fortify the state, which was held together at least in part by the officially promoted ruler-cult. And Demetrius Poliorcetes, king of Macedonia, was saluted with these words: "Hail to you, son of the almighty god Poseidon, son also of Aphrodite! The other gods are far away or have no ears or do not exist or do not inquire after us. But we see you bodily present, neither wooden nor stone, but truly being. Therefore we pray to you." These testimonies to the ruler-cult as it was established and promoted for reasons of state in the Hellenistic realm express the universal yearning for peace which would create a happy and secure life. The ruler who was able to satisfy this longing was hailed as a divine manifestation.

The more the populace of the Roman Empire suffered from the effects of prolonged civil war in the first century B.C., the more strongly did the surging desire for an end to war manifest itself. This hope was given powerful impetus when Octavian and Antony succeeded in destroying Caesar's murderers and dividing the rule over the empire between themselves (41/40 B.C.). It was at this time that the Roman poet Vergil composed his famous *Fourth Eclogue,* in which he gave expression in mythical language to the yearning of mankind. He referred to the expectation, widely held in the East, that a child sent from heaven would appear, who would bring in a new era in which peace and joy would reign:

> He will live as God and observe the heroes of ancient times
> walking among the Gods; they will behold him in amazement.
> Peace he will bring to the world, governing it with the
>   Father's power.

In his kingdom of peace, marvelous things will take place:

> The goats themselves come home with udders full,
> No longer will the herds of grazing cattle fear the lion,
> Even from the cradle sprouts a wreath of flattering flowers.
> The serpents also will disappear; harmful, poisonous plants
> will vanish; the fields of Assyria will yield balsam in
>   abundance.

These paradisiacal conditions will accompany the appearance of the child, whose birth, therefore, is hailed with rejoicing:

> Now, offspring of Jupiter, dear child divine,
> Already comes the time; assume the dignity sublime!
> See the heavy burden of the world convulse and heave,

Lands and seas' breadth alike, and the depths of heaven,
See how they all rejoice at the golden age that now appears.

When the yearning for the restoration of true peace was
fulfilled by the rule of Octavian, in many of the eastern parts
of the empire people greeted his rule as a marvel of divine
manifestation; yet in the Orient the blessed ruler had long
since been revered as a savior. This designation had already
been given to Caesar in some places when he stood at the
height of his power. Thus in a popular decree composed in
Ephesus in 48 B.C., he was called "the god on earth, descended
from Ares and Aphrodite, and universal savior of human
life." In Rome they did not use such lofty words, but as early
as 42 B.C. the Senate had decided to include the deceased
Caesar among the gods as *Divus Julius*. Although the unique
glory attached to the memory of Caesar was to some degree
inherited by Octavian, his adopted son, Octavian, as a clever
politician, acted with prudence and moderation and did not
demand that homage be paid to him as to a Hellenistic god-
king. However, by the very fact that he allowed the surname
Augustus to be transferred to him in a ceremonial act of state
he unmistakably expressed the view that his position was one
of incomparable loftiness (cf. p. 199). In the Oriental provinces people lauded his work with unreserved use of the
traditional mythological language, identifying him as the
savior and deliverer who had been sent to men and marking
his birthday as the beginning of the good news that had gone
forth to all the world (cf. p. 201). Augustus allowed temples
to be erected to him in Asia Minor, though he exacted a
condition that they be dedicated to both him and the goddess
Rome, in order in this way to bind the eastern part of the
empire more closely to Rome.

When Augustus died in 14 B.C., there was no question that
he would now likewise be placed among the deities. Witnesses
were immediately brought forth who stated that they had
seen the deceased ruler ascending toward heaven. Augustus'
successor preserved his memory by means of cultic veneration,
but refrained from claiming such veneration for himself
during his lifetime. When permission was asked of Tiberius
that Spain be allowed to build a temple to the emperor and

his mother, he refused the request on the grounds that he was a mortal man, although divine honors were due to Augustus, the true savior of humanity. Claudius also made the same decision.

Caligula and Nero, however, abandoned all reserve. Caligula was pictured on coins with the halo of the sun-god Helios, and Nero was represented as Apollo. Yet the way in which these two emperors conducted themselves after the pattern of the Hellenistic divine kingship met stiff resistance in Roman circles. Roman tradition was characteristically in harmony with the skeptical irony with which the dying Emperor Vespasian mockingly said, "Alas, I am surely becoming a god." However, his son Domitian, who ruled at the end of the first century A.D., was of a different mind (cf. p. 206). He issued his instructions as divine commands by introducing official documents with the words, "Our lord and god commands that the following be done" (Suetonius *Domitian* XIII), and he required that everyone who spoke with him or wrote to him greet him with this reverential form of address. Anyone who resisted this felt the force of his wrath. Thus he had his kinsman, the consul Flavius Clemens, put to death, and exiled Clemens' wife Domitilla for atheism. Their guilt apparently consisted in their having refused to recognize the emperor as god. Throughout the empire Domitian had imperial portraits set up, and in Ephesus he had a great temple built, with a larger-than-life-size statue of the emperor. This development is presupposed in the book of Revelation. While most of the inhabitants of Asia Minor were very willing to pay cultic reverence to the ruler because it was their custom to view him as a manifestation of the deity, for the Christians it was impossible to designate a man as lord and god. For them there was only one Lord of all lords and only one King of all kings (Rev. 17:14; 19:16), who alone is to be venerated and worshiped.

The cult of the emperor, which spread further and further in the Roman Empire, served primarily political aims; for the Romans did not prevent the many peoples who lived in the empire from worshiping their traditional gods, but, rather, granted them full freedom to practice the old traditional religions. The worship of the ruler was primarily a sign of political submission, expressed in cultic form. Since the Jews were an ancient people with a venerable religion, they were not required to participate in the cult of the emperor. As a substitute, until the outbreak of the Jewish war, a daily sacrifice for the emperor was offered in the temple. Even after the Jewish war the rights that had been guaranteed to the Jews were maintained. At first the authorities in various places also counted the Christians as Jews or regarded them as a Jewish sect. But as soon as Jews and Christians became separate from each other, the Christians forfeited the privilege of sharing in the rights which the synagogue enjoyed. Although the Christians acknowledged the authorities of the state as representatives of the order established by God, they could not possibly participate in a cultic veneration of the ruler; thus conflicts, persecutions, and grievous sufferings fell upon the church again and again, until, in the days of the Emperor Constantine, the caesar bowed his knee to Christ.

CHAPTER 2
Religious Movements and Intellectual Currents in the Hellenistic-Roman World in the Time of the New Testament

1. The Gods of the Greeks and Romans

The gods whom the Greeks venerated embodied forces and powers that are at work in nature. Zeus hurls lightning-bolts and makes the thunder roll, Poseidon rules the sea and arouses the tempests, Apollo sends illnesses and gives cures, Aphrodite awakens love and symbolizes beauty. In green groves, in fountains and streams, and in the darkness of the forest rule the gods and goddesses; fertility and blessings come from them, but so do drought and punishment. Alongside the deities that produce order and law stands the god Dionysus, who moves about reeling and staggering and can be recognized thereby by his worshipers. He possesses in spendthrift abundance the gifts of nature bestowed upon men, so that the wine does not fail but spouts from a never-failing fountain. While the deities of the Orient are masters of fate, the gods of the Greeks are not, and are distinguished from men only by the fact that they are immortal and possess far greater powers than men.

Cities and various associations of men have their special deities. The goddess Athena protects the city of Athens, and Artemis is venerated in Ephesus (Acts 19:28). Yet they are not connected with just a single city; the gods, the Homeric epic tells, were venerated by Greeks everywhere. Splendid temples were erected to them, in which representations of the gods were displayed. It is by means of the image that the deity is present and enters into connection with men

222

through mysterious hints or significant instructions that issue from it. In the Orient the deities were frequently represented as great and fearful beastlike figures; the gods of the Greeks, on the other hand, are genuine, ordinary men. In the Orient the image of the god stood in the holy of holies, to which only consecrated priests have access; the Greeks, however, knew nothing of such strict separation. Ordinarily there was no separate priestly order among them, rather, the priestly functions were performed by individual members of the community who had been appointed for this service, and the sanctuary was open to any Greek who wished to come before the image of the god and worship there.

It is the will of the gods that city and society should live according to well-defined order. City and society see to it that the lawful pattern of life is preserved, and the gods stand guard to prevent violation. It is wicked and impious to rebel in impudent pride against the gods and in insolence to disregard the limitations that are set for mortal man. *Hubris* therefore is the real offense for which one can incur guilt in relation to the gods and for which punishment quickly follows. The veneration that is due to the gods is satisfied by participation in the cultic observances that are established by tradition and custom. A weekly day of rest and celebration, like the sabbath among the Jews, does not appear among the Greeks or the Romans. Yet a considerable number of feasts and festivals were scattered throughout the entire year, so that there were frequent occasions for resting from labors and for paying homage to the gods. The high festivals that were observed by the Greeks in honor of their gods were connected with games that were conducted at regular intervals and were shared in by all of Greece. The most famous were the Olympic games, which took place every four years and were both a sacrifice to the gods and a competition for victory in sports. The winner was assured universal acclaim. Every two years the Isthmian games were held at Corinth; these likewise drew many participants and spectators (cf. I Cor. 9:24-27).

The shrine of the deity was usually erected on an elevated site overlooking the city or else high in the mountains. At the temple the sacrifices intended for the gods and consecrated to them as gifts were offered. The intestines of the slaughtered animals were burned on the altar, and the edible parts were given to the priests or were sold as meat. One could not secure any meat that had not in some way come into connection with the cultus, since at least a small part of every beast that was slaughtered was burned for the deity. Cultic meals frequently were held in the temple areas; people invited kinsmen and friends to these occasions. As many papyri attest, these often were requested, by written invitation, to come to the house of the god at a certain hour to share in a merry feast. Thus a considerable part of the social life took place in and around the temple (cf. I Cor. 10:20-21, 25-28).

The sacrifices that were burned for the gods served to satisfy the obligation owed to them, but they were also intended to influence the gods to send good fortune to men or to avert the possibility of disaster and destruction falling upon the city. In ancient times, human sacrifices were also occasionally offered to ensure the gracious disposition of the gods. Later, animal sacrifices usually took the place of these, yet in some Greek cities the old custom of performing expiation by the sacrificial offering of a man was preserved. If this expiatory sacrifice was to be successful, the victim had to be ready to die voluntarily. Consequently they sought out for this purpose poor men and promised them a full year of the best of life and good food at the city's expense. This enticement prompted some who led a wretched existence to agree to this bargain and to sell themselves as scapegoats, who, after a year spent in luxury, had to surrender their lives in expiation for the community (cf. I Cor. 4:13).

The Romans equated the gods whom they had worshiped since antiquity with the Greek deities, so that Jupiter became Zeus; Juno, Hera; Venus, Aphrodite; Mercury, Hermes; Neptune, Poseidon; and so on. The earlier Roman tradition told of no myths concerning the gods. But when the Romans established the correspondence between their gods and those of the Greeks, they also appropriated the abundant myths that had been developed in Hellas; and in this way the Roman gods, who protected the sanctity and inviolability of the traditional order, acquired a history.

Since the cult was and remained an affair of the state (for

whose well-being it was conducted in the accordance with the calendar) the state was concerned to further its practice. It is true that in the course of the first century B.C., with the strong influence of the Hellenistic and Oriental world on Rome, the care with which the cultic obligations were fulfilled had significantly diminished; but under the reign of Augustus renewed energy was devoted to the cultivation of the traditional religion. Numerous temples were restored, and the office of priest was once again elevated to a position of honor and charged with guarding, through reverential regard for the gods and the obligations owed to them, the Roman legacy against the alien influence exerted by enlightened Hellenistic thought and disintegration of morals. Of course, the success of this policy could not be longlasting, because the stance and manner of life of the Romans had already undergone transformations too profound to permit people to return to the old ways. The influence of foreign cults that came to Rome out of the Orient proved to be so strong that it could no longer be suppressed.

Even in the Hellenistic-Roman period the cultic ministry in the temple was performed with care, although many joked about the conduct of the gods or expressed doubts about the ministry. Even though the belief in the gods was weakening, great buildings in their honor were still being constructed in Italy and Greece, in the Near East, and in North Africa. The significance attributed to divine oracles and instructions continued undiminished. The flight of birds was carefully observed for omens; in the carving of sacrificial animals, the intestines were studied for hints of the future. Before making difficult decisions, or before beginning a journey or important undertaking, one would seek to learn the will of the gods. If the first attempt did not provide a clear and encouraging verdict, one could once again slaughter sacrificial animals and repeat the study of the intestines. At certain shrines one could address questions to the deity and learn from the oracle that was then issued what the divine will might be. Since antiquity, all the Greeks had sought out the oracle of Apollo at Delphi. They would apply to the priests with the petition for a decision, the priests would then present the questions to the Pythia, a priestess, who sat on the golden tripod and with the powers of a seeress probed and fathomed the instructions of the god. Many people sought information about personal concerns—help in time of illness or counsel in managing difficulties within the household and family—but political questions were also posed to the Pythia. Before laws were promulgated the carefully weighed judgment from Delphi was often sought, in order to ensure acting in accordance with the will of the god.

The temple in Delphi bore the inscription, "Know thyself." This sentence urged man to be aware of the limits that are set for him and to admonish him not to be presumptuous and in impious pride disregard the power of the gods. Man should and must be conscious of the fact that he is mortal and that he is granted only a brief span of existence. It is true that in the Hellenistic period the old religion had suffered a serious loss of power, but the question concerning simply the divine, which determines the basis of all that is, remained a vital one. Even though it is not known whether there actually was an inscription "to the unknown god" on an altar in Athens (Acts 17:23), still there were many people who were seeking an answer to the question about the unknown god. To a large extent people regarded the sun-god Helios as the deity that guides all things, while philosophers spoke of a god whose governance is discernible in nature. Alongside the cult of the old gods and a rising monotheism existed a varied array of popular notions about the intervention of divine powers and mysterious forces that guide the destiny of men. This popular belief was far more influential than the official cult of the gods in molding people's lives in the Hellenistic-Roman period.

2. Popular Belief and the Idea of Fate

In the ancient world, the belief that one could experience divine assistance through miraculous events was widely held. The cult of the god of healing, Asclepius, who was worshiped and invoked for help by innumerable persons, had already been practiced in ancient times at various places in the Mediterranean world. After the great plague that afflicted Athens in 420/419 B.C. it was also introduced there. The sign of

Asclepius was the serpent; for originally he had been venerated in Thessaly as a chthonic serpent-god. His central shrine was in Epidaurus, where large buildings were constructed in the Hellenistic period. Near the temple there were large halls for beds, where the sick lay down to rest and receive healing while they slept. Cripples could walk again, mute persons regained their speech, and blind ones recovered their sight. Miraculous experiences and the healing skill of physicians brought recovery to many people, who then demonstrated their gratitude to the shrine by giving gold or silver representations of the healed organ or member, or presenting gifts to the temple. Asclepius was extolled as the god of the healing arts and as the savior who helps men and guides them with tender care.

Marvelous occurrences are set in motion by men who are endowed with special power and radiate divine energy. Where they pass through the countryside, the fields turn lush and green, sick people become healthy, and other extraordinary things happen. When Vespasian came to Alexandria soon after the beginning of his rule, a blind man begged the emperor to moisten his eyes with his saliva, and a lame man asked him to touch his leg with his, the emperor's, heel. It is related that the emperor complied with these requests and healing power flowed into the afflicted ones, so that they were cured of their ailments (Suetonius *Vespasian* VII). The philosopher Apollonius of Tyana, who traveled around Asia Minor as a teacher in the first century A.D., was extolled as a wonder-worker who was able to alleviate suffering and to heal the sick. It is told that once in Athens a young man, whose manner of life was so dissolute and disreputable that people had composed ditties about him, was listening to the philosopher's lecture. When this young man broke out in loud, immodest laughter, Apollonius looked at him and said, "It is not you that blasphemes here, but the evil spirit by which you are possessed." Then the story continues:

He actually was possessed, without being aware of it. He laughed when no one else laughed, wept without cause, and sang and talked to himself. The people thought that his licentious youth was to blame for this; but the truth is that he was being guided by an evil demon, and he appeared, in his impiety, as drunken. Now when Apollonius looked at him still more steadily and wrathfully, the demon cried out, like a person who is being branded or otherwise tortured, and swore that he would leave the youth and never again attack a man. But when Apollonius angrily addressed him, as an angry master might address a shamelessly wicked servant, and commanded him to come forth visibly, he cried, "I will throw down yonder statue," and pointed to a statue in the king's portico. Then the statue started moving and fell over. What fear and wonder! Who could describe it all! But the young man rubbed his eyes like someone just awakening, looked toward the sun, and was embarrassed because all eyes turned toward him. From that time on he no longer appeared wild and unrestrained as previously, but his healthy nature appeared, as though he had been treated by medicines. (Philostratus *Life of Apollonius* IV. 20)

As this story demonstrates, the generally accepted view was that the peculiar behavior of this young man was to be traced to the influence of demons which, as spirits of superhuman power, intervene in the lives of men. Demons could be favorably inclined toward men and could lend them assistance; but countless numbers of them were also evil spirits desiring to injure men and enslave them. The exorcist possesses power over them, so that by virtue of his extraordinary insight and healing ability he is able to drive out the evil spirits. His success is exhibited before all eyes when the exiting demon overturns a statue and the young man who is liberated from the demon stands there in full health, filling the witnesses of the event with wonder and amazement (cf. Mark 1:23-28 par.; 5:1-20 par., *et al.*)

Since the career and destiny of man are dependent upon supraterrestrial powers, it is of great importance to gain a more precise knowledge of these powers. Therefore people observe the stars to deduce from their courses the laws of the macrocosmos and, from this, to draw conclusions for insight into its destiny. For the lot of the individual man is written in the stars. The knowledge that the Babylonians had acquired about the course of the heavenly bodies was pursued further by the Greeks and deepened by their mathematical skills. In the Hellenistic period people combined the results achieved by science with so many sorts of popular notions and magical practices that a varied mixture of astrology developed. While the art of astrology could only be practiced by educated people who knew how to carry out the calculations, there were still many soothsayers who claimed to be able, for a small fee, to interpret the future from the stars for simple folk. The horoscope was produced to secure information about the fate of people. Certain days, which gave promise of ill fortune, were avoided; occasions which seemed to stand under a good star were seized upon. Superstitious fear made people look to the heavens with anxious concern. They felt themselves so bound to the cosmic forces and powers that they were obliged to receive their guidance, to discern and carefully follow their laws, to guard against injury and peril, and to make skillful use of the days and hours favored by the celestial powers. Writings and books served to disseminate bits of astrological information which a well-informed man could utilize when he had an important question to decide or a difficult task to undertake. In one bit of astrological counsel, for example, we read:

> When Saturn is in triangulation with Mars, this signifies misfortune. Jupiter in triangulation or in conjunction with Mars causes promiscuity and adultery; when Mercury also stands with them, lust and debauchery result. When Mercury stands in conjunction or in triangulation with Jupiter, this produces favorable activities or business ventures. . . . When Mars appears in triangulation with Mercury and with Saturn, this brings good fortune, and will make for great achievements. (Papyrus Tebtunis 276)

Under the influence of the knowledge gained in astronomy and geography a change in the view of the world was wrought. While in earlier times people had visualized the earth as a flat disc above which the heavens arched like a giant shell and beneath which the underworld was spread, now they regarded the earth as a sphere encircled by the seven planetary spheres and the heaven of the fixed stars. The souls of men ascend into the celestial world when they are separated from the body at the moment of death. The body remains on earth, but the soul ascends to the heights where it undergoes purification and perfection. The idea that one can gain information from the stars about the fate to which the soul is destined gained influence even in Rome. It is true that there was an ancient edict expelling interpreters of the stars from Rome, but the caesars so strongly believed in this practice that they forbade unauthorized persons to consult the stars concerning the imperial destiny and immediate future. Yet they had inquiries made for themselves and had their horoscopes charted in order to procure possibly beneficial instruction.

People sought to gain influence over the course of destiny by means of sorcery and magic. Grave significance was attributed to dreams; one had to be on guard against evil spirits and injurious forces in order not to fall victim to their machinations. Various precautionary measures, like the wearing of amulets to ward off the demons and to prevent their access to the body, served to protect one against harm. Mysterious magical phrases, greater in supposed power according to the strangeness of their sound and the number of times they were repeated, on the one hand, kept away evil spirits and their effects, and on the other, brought good fortune. Many syllables were combined to form long, almost unpronounceable verbal monstrosities, and extraordinary impact was attributed to words from foreign languages. In Egypt, the country in which magic had been especially highly developed since antiquity, traditions from various languages and religions came together, yet people all the more readily adopted and mingled these traditions since in this way a mysterious significance could be ascribed to the expressions and formulas which one uttered in order to achieve a particular goal. Individual words and names from the Old Testament-Jewish tradition were specially selected for inclusion in this variegated patchwork; consequently even non-Jewish magicians invoked the God of Abraham, Isaac, and Jacob, to assure themselves of assistance. Thus without hesitation they disregarded the Old Testament commandment prohibiting abuse of God's name and its use for purposes of magic (Exod. 20:7; Deut. 5:11, *et passim*), and thus we read in a long text which summarizes rules for magicians:

> For those possessed by daemons, an approved charm by Pibechis.
> Take oil made from unripe olives, together with the plant
> mastigia and lotus pith, and boil it with marjoram

(very colourless), saying: "Joel, Ossarthiomi,
Emori, Theochipsoith, Sithemeoch, Sothe,
Joe, Mimipsothiooph, Phersothi, Aeeioyo,
Joe, Eochariphtha: come out of such an one (and the other usual
    formulae)."
But write this phylactery upon a little sheet of
tin: "Jaeo, Abraothioch, Phtha, Mesen-
tiniao, Pheoch, Jaeo, Charsoc", and hang it
round the sufferer: it is of every demon a thing to be trembled at,
    which
he fears. Standing opposite, adjure him. The adjuration is
this: "I adjure thee by the god of the Hebrews
Jesu, Jaba, Jae, Abraoth, Aia, Thoth, Ele,
Elo, Aeo, Eu, Jiibaech, Abarmas, Jaba-
rau, Abelbel, Lona, Abra, Maroia, arm,
thou that appearest in fire, thou that art in the midst of earth and
    snow
and vapour, Tannetis: let thy angel descend,
the implacable one, and let him draw into captivity the
daemon as he flieth around this creature
which God formed in his holy paradise.
For I pray to the holy god, through the might of Ammon-
ipsentancho.

(Paris Magical Papyrus lines 3007–3029; quoted from *The New
Testament Background: Selected Documents,* ed., with introduction, by C. K. Barrett. [New York: The Macmillan Company,
1957] pp. 31–32)

Names of Egyptian deities, Old Testament names, and con-
coctions of words that do not offer any particular meaning
have been woven together into a peculiar fabric which,
in the range and multiplicity of its symbols, for any circumstance will supply the appropriate magical term whereby power
can be exercised over the spirits and influence exerted upon
the destiny of men.

   The cosmopolitan philosophy that prevailed in the boundaries of the Roman Empire left it to individual choice to
determine which deities one would call upon and which religious persuasion one would embrace; thus was provided an
open and free realm which the individual had to fill in for
himself. A more or less clearly developed notion of fate, often
coupled with superstitious views, was frequently the result.

The figure of Tyche, signifying the fortune that is either given to men or denied them, enjoyed general popularity. Everyone hoped for a favorable destiny and sought to secure signs that good things would come to him and his kinsmen.

The brevity of human life was universally and painfully felt. Some concluded from this that one must strive to enjoy every day of sunshine, because the end could come as suddenly and early as tomorrow. Others were filled with skepticism, and many lived more or less tranquilly, not bothering with these more serious thoughts.

The views of what would come after death were diverse. Among the common folk the old view still persisted that the deceased enter into the dark underworld and there lead an existence as shades. The conviction that only in the heavenly world would the immortal soul attain the fullness of its real destiny was widespread. Thus the day of one's death was regarded as the birthday of one's eternity, because the spirit leaves the body and returns to the divine world. According to popular view, the soul of the deceased remained for three days in the vicinity of the tomb before departing to the heights (cf. John 11:39). Many people, however, doubted the expectation of a life after death and plainly declared that there was no hereafter, and death, therefore, marked an irrevocable end. The diversity of views is reflected by the inscriptions on the tombs, whose words engraved in stone were intended to preserve the memory of the deceased and to admonish passersby to reflect. In remembrance of the departed person, family and friends gathered at regular intervals, for example on his birthday or on the anniversary of his death. During their lifetimes, wealthy people often established a foundation intended to provide for the future celebration of memorial meals. The dead, it was believed, required the regard that is attested by the caretaking of their burial places and by reverent remembrance.

3. The Mystery Religions

Superstition and notions of fate, the yearning for miracles, and fascination with astrology and magic, all of which found numerous adherents in the Hellenistic period, make it evident that people were in the throes of deep anxiety and uncertainty about life. Threatened by powers and demons, by illnesses and unforeseen strokes of fate, one lived in suspense and fear and felt subject to overpowering forces against which one could not assert oneself. People strove, through all sorts of practices and precautionary measures, to arm and protect themselves against fate. The question of how to escape a dismal turn of events or to liberate oneself from fear required an answer. This answer was given to them by the mystery religions, which promised deliverance to man, by offering him a saving power that afforded resistance to suffering and even to death. We speak of "mysteries," because the religious communities that assembled for particular cultic activities maintained a strict silence about the content and meaning of those activities, a silence that could not be breached in interactions with any uninitiated person. As a result of the carefully maintained secret discipline, only scanty accounts have been handed down; yet what scattered references and allusions exist suffice to describe the nature and import of the mystery religions.

In the Hellenistic period Oriental cults appeared throughout the Mediterranean area: the cult of Osiris and Isis, from Egypt; the veneration of Adonis, which was native to Syria; the Phrygian cult of Attis and of Cybele; and the cult of Mithras, from Persia. When these various religions encountered each other, there was a widespread tendency to equate the deities revered in each. No matter what the most high god was called, the reference was the same. The one lord of the world could be addressed by all the various names. Thus, the religions that were carried by their adherents into other countries were not set in opposition to each other, but were amicably intertwined. They entirely accepted the practice of belonging to several religious communities at one and the same time in order to achieve contact with divine power and to be filled with it in manifold ways. The mystery communities were formed by the free choice of their members. Freemen and slaves, Greeks and foreigners, men and women were all accepted without regard to their different social positions; for all of them were conscious of being bound as one in the veneration of the cult's deity. Although the cultic myths of the individual mystery religions were of diverse origin, and the forms of worship variously constructed, it is still possible to discern certain basic features common to all the mystery communities notwithstanding their peculiarities.

During the cultic celebration the fate of the deity whom the believer confessed was enacted. The center of worship was not the word, expressed in proclamation, but the drama. Only those persons who had undergone an initiation were admitted to the observances of the mystery community; all others were excluded. Although in principle the initiation could be granted to any man regardless of his status or his nation, in some mysteries people who did not meet specific conditions were excluded. Thus, for example, in Eleusis, neither barbarians (who had not mastered the Greek language) nor murderers were permitted initiation. Any person who is introduced to the mysteries is thereby set apart from the mass of the uninitiated. Sacred formulas or symbolic signs are imparted to him, with the help of which the initiates can identify each other. It is true that the form of the initiation is different for each of the individual mystery religions, but they all have in common the idea that through the initiation, a person is reborn to immortality.

While the ancient Greek religion portrayed the gods as free from suffering and death, the deities of the mystery religions do experience the fate of suffering and dying. Just as nature's vegetation grows and flourishes in the spring but dies in the autumn, so also the deity passes through the metamorphosis of becoming and passing away. It must endure suffering, yet perseveres, then to be raised to new life. By the initiates' participation in the drama, in the fate of the deity, they are involved in its fate and are filled with divine power. In the worship service the cry is addressed to them:

> Salvation comes to God. You, his initiates, are comforted;
> Salvation from your woes is granted also to you.

This liturgical expression is reported by Firmicus Maternus, who, after his conversion to Christianity, engaged in sharp polemic against the errors of the heathen religions. He reports that after the image of the god has been placed backwards on a bier and is mourned with cries of lamentation, light is brought into the dark room. The priests anoint the throats of all, who are weeping and wailing, and whisper to them, in slow murmurs, the summons to rejoice over the salvation which has come to the deity and now is imparted to the believers also (22:1-3). The deliverance which they are granted is inalienable, so that all to whom it is given can never be lost, whatever may happen. Therefore the initiate can henceforth be certain of living under the protection of the deity and of being possessed of immortality.

Since the cultic myth that is unfolded in the activity of worship portrays the process of becoming and passing away, of the death and life that is manifested by nature, it is not related to a particular historical event, but illustrates an always valid truth. Its content "never happened, but always is" (Sallust *On the gods and the world* IV) and is handed down in varied form, on the basis of the respective prehistory experienced by the sacred narrative in the individual mystery religions. Mysteries were not foreign to the Greeks, who in the age of Hellenism were acquainted with the religions that came from the Orient. The god *Dionysus* had long been familiar to them as a deity who was experienced in exuberant intoxication encompassing the heights and depths of life and transported its believers into a state of ecstasy. His cult had already reached Italy as early as the second century B.C., but it met with stout resistance there. Its adherents were accused thus:

> Among them, it is the acme of religion to regard nothing as sinful. The men prophesied like insane persons, with ecstatic bodily movements; the women, in the costume of the Bacchantes and with hair dishevelled, ran to the Tiber carrying blazing torches; and they would plunge the torches in the water and bring them out again still burning (because they contained live sulphur mixed with calcium) People were said to have been carried away by the gods (Livy *Ab urbe condita* XXXIX. 13).

The celebration of mysteries had been practiced in *Eleusis* since antiquity. The cultic myth tells that Ceres, the daughter of the goddess of vegetation, Demeter, had been seized by Hades, the ruler of the underworld. Yet Zeus had had mercy, and it had been agreed that for eight months Ceres should remain on the earth with her mother, but then return to the underworld for four months. Thus the myth portrays the growth and flourishing of fruits as well as their harvest and secret storage in buried containers. In the search for her lost daughter—so the story continues—the deeply troubled mother came to Eleusis. In gratitude for the hospitable reception given to her there, she taught the king of Eleusis the art of growing wheat and initiated him into the sacred mysteries. The mysteries, which transport the mythical event to the present by means of cultic enactment, promise those who participate in them that in the world beyond they will experience deliverance and a better fate. Of course the opinions of the Greeks were highly divergent as to the value of the mysteries, as is clearly shown by the critical judgment of Diogenes. When the Athenians demanded that he submit to the sacred rites, and said to him that in Hades the initiates would have precedence over all others, he retorted that this was ridiculous. For it would be utterly ludicrous for such eminent men as the victorious Spartan King Agesilaus and the famous Theban general Epaminondas, who had not been initiated, to have to walk around in the mire, while fellows of no account should dwell in the aisles of the blessed, solely because they had received the initiation (Diogenes Laertius VI. 39).

The cult of *Isis* and *Osiris* (or *Serapis*), which gained a broad following, is of Egyptian origin. The myth is attested in various formulations, and is most clearly described by Plutarch in his writing on Isis and Osiris. According to this, Osiris once ruled as god-king on the Nile; but his brother Typhon devised a strategem to supplant him. He secretly measured Osiris' body and had a beautiful, richly ornamented chest made to Osiris' size; then, on a festive occasion, Typhon promised to give this chest to the person who would fit it exactly. By means of this promise he persuaded Osiris to lie down in the chest. No sooner had he lain down than the conspirators rushed in, locked the chest, poured molten lead over it, carried it to the river, and threw it in the water. Isis, the sister and consort of the victim, sorrowfully searched for the dead Osiris, finally found him at Byblos, opened the casket, put her face against the face of the corpse, kissed it, and wept. When Typhon learned of this, he had Osiris' corpse divided into fourteen pieces and scattered about during the night. Yet Isis found the pieces and put them together again, so that Osiris could enter into the underworld and there assume rule as a god. His son Horus went forth to do battle against his enemies and defeated Typhon; but Isis—the myth concludes—bore Osiris (who still cohabited with her after his death) a son, Harpocrates, in a premature birth. Therefore she is represented and worshiped as a mother with her child.

In the cultic observance the *mystai* go out weeping to search for the dead Osiris. Exultation is voiced with the cry, "We have found him!" Now the sorrowing is at an end; for death is transformed into life. Osiris rules in the underworld as the judge of the dead, before whose throne all departed ones must appear. Just as the body of Osiris was carried to the river, so also must every deceased person be borne across the Nile into the kingdom of the dead. In the Hellenistic era, at the prompting of the Ptolemies (cf. p. 22), the name of Osiris was changed to Serapis, so as to create an equivalence between this name and the supreme deity who was venerated by Egyptians as well as by Greeks. The god Serapis was equated with Zeus, the father of gods and of men, and was extolled as savior and deliverer, who gives aid to all men. Isis stands beside him as the divine mother, who came to be so highly regarded that she gradually surpassed the importance of the god, was gloried as the noble essence of all gods, and was worshiped as the one goddess, who encompasses all.

A hymn to Isis, the divine mother, praises her as the helper of men in all the ways of their lives:

Thou holy one, perpetual help of the human race, who are ever merciful to quicken the mortals, thou dost show to the poor in their misery the sweet tenderness of a mother. Not a day nor a nighttime rest, nor even a moment passes by without thy deeds of kindness, whereby thou dost watch over men on sea and on land, driving away the storms of life and extending thy helping hand, with which thou dost untwist the inextricably tangled threads of destiny, dost calm the storms of fate, and dost restrain the injurious course of the stars. The celestial beings honor thee, and those in the underworld revere thee; thou dost cause the firmament to turn, thou dost give light to the sun, thou guidest the world and dost tread Tartarus under foot. To thee the stars respond, the seasons recur, the gods rejoice; the elements serve thee. At a sign from thee the winds blow, the clouds bestow the moisture, the seeds sprout, and the sprouts grow. The birds that fill the skies, the wild creatures that range the hills, the serpents that hide in the earth, and the fish of the sea, all tremble at thy majesty. Yet I am too weak in spirit to sing thy praise, and too slight in ability to bring thee an offering. I do not have at my command the abundance of language needed to say what I feel of thy glory, not even if I had a thousand mouths and as many tongues, not even in an eternal flow of unwearying discourse. Hence I will do what I can, one who is devout but in other respects poor. I will keep thy divine countenance and thy holy majesty forever in the secret inner chambers of my breast and before my eyes. (Apuleius *Metamorphoses* XI. 25)

The divine mother, to whom homage was paid in procession and in religious celebrations, symbolized the faithful care which man knew protected him from the attacks of fate. Since the divine mother was so widely esteemed and her fame so great, with the encounter between religions that took place in late antiquity, Christianity appropriated various features from the religion of Isis and blended them with the emerging devotion to Mary. Those who belong to the divine mother are addressed by the priest with these comforting words: "May fate now go its way and seek another opportunity to exercise its rage and cruelty. For a hostile fate possesses no power over those lives the majesty of our goddess has taken into her service" (Apuleius *Metamorphoses* XI. 15).

Anyone who wishes to be initiated into the mysteries of Isis must first receive brief instruction, undergo a bath of purification, and then for ten days abstain from eating any meat or drinking any wine until, on the evening of the tenth day, the initiation is performed. The novice is clothed in a linen garment and at sunset is led into the holy place. Because of the command of silence that was imposed upon all mystai, the cultic ritual itself is nowhere described. However, in the *Metamorphoses* of Apuleius the experience to which the initiate is subjected is expressed in allusions which obviously said enough to those familiar with it: "I came to the boundaries of death and crossed the threshold of Proserpine; I traversed all the elements and then returned; at midnight I saw the sun in a blinding white light. I approached the gods above and the gods below face to face and worshiped them in close proximity" (Apuleius *Metamorphoses* XI. 23). Thus in the initiation the descent into the underworld and the ascent into the heights is enacted, so that death and life are traversed and through the cosmic pilgrimage divine powers are imparted to the *myste*. On the morning after the completion of the solemn ritual he appears before the people clothed in a twelve-fold stole, and shows himself to them in the splendor of the sun-god. By means of the initiation he is born a divine being, filled with power and surrounded with radiant light. Henceforward in the service of Isis he must follow her directions and behave ethically, in order that one day he can stand before Osiris, the judge of the dead. Since the Isis mysteries were able to combine ethical earnestness with the initiation into the secrets of the divine mother, they exerted a powerful attraction.

The *cult of Adonis*, which portrays the mystery of death and life, is native to Palestine and Syria. Women clothed in the garments of Aphrodite sowed seeds of quick-sprouting plants in vessels covered with only a thin layer of soil. These trays were exposed to the sun on the roofs of houses, so that the seed grew quickly and then soon withered. Thus the flourishing and dying of the god were represented in a parabolic fashion.

The cult of *Cybele* and *Attis*, which allows one to undergo the divine experience in delirium and ecstasy, comes from Phrygia. These features of the cult of Attis, which first spread in Asia Minor and then throughout the Mediterranean area, exhibit various similarities with the worship of Dionysus, which in the Hellenizing of the cult of Attis was not without influence on the further development of the latter. Cybele, originally native to the mountain region, is portrayed as the great divine mother on the throne, with two lions beside her. The cultic myth, which tells of the encounter of the goddess with the shepherd Attis, is handed down in several versions. According to the tradition related by Ovid (*Fasti* IV. 223 ff.), Cybele met the handsome youth Attis in the forest, was captivated by him, and having fallen in love with him, wanted to keep him for herself. Then when Attis met the bewitching nymph Sagaritis, fell in love with her, and broke the vow that he had made to Cybele, the goddess was seized by a fierce rage and killed Sagaritis. Attis, however, went mad; he emasculated himself, crying out that he had thus received the punishment he deserved, and was transformed into a pine tree (which, as the tree of Cybele, symbolizes the dead Attis). Yet he did not remain dead, but was awakened to new life and, enthroned beside Cybele, made a speeding tour of triumph driving a team of four lions.

The performance of the cult of Attis and Cybele consisted of the event of emotional intoxication of the mystai, who in their ecstasy felt seized by the divine power and in their worship cried out with the words: "I have eaten from the tambourine and have drunk from the cymbal, and I have thoroughly learned the secrets of religion," or "I have become a myste of Attis" (Firmicus Maternus 18.1). The musical instruments are named because it is through them that the ecstatic condition is produced in which the intoxication seizes the mystai and allows them to experience the sacramental celebration. In addition to the sacred meal observed by the mystai, there was still another noteworthy act of initiation. A deep pit was dug, a priest descended into it, and then the pit was covered with boards with holes in them; a bull then was slaughtered on this platform, so that its blood would drip down through the holes. The priest who was in the pit let the blood flow over his body and drank it. When the animal was dead, it was dragged away and the priest came out, covered with blood, to be hailed by the crowd and greeted as one reborn (Prudentius *Peristephanon* X. 1011–1050). While in the pit he himself experienced the deity's fate of death and was instilled with divine powers that would impart to him salvation and life.

Struggle and victory were the message of the *religion of Mithras,* which came from Persia and found numerous adherents in the Roman Empire, particularly in the second and third centuries A.D. Only in Greece, where ever since ancient times anything from Persia had been received coolly, was the cult of Mithras unable to gain a foothold. Mithras, who was worshiped as the god of light, was always pictured as a fighter who kills the bull, and who, as a victorious hero, possesses the light that drives out the darkness. Many soldiers joined the Mithraic cult and carried it with them to the boundaries of the empire, even to Germany. In contrast to the other mystery religions, only men were eligible for initiation into the mysteries of Mithras, and they were branded on the forehead with a hot iron, as his warriors. They were admitted to the company by means of a baptismal act and then were permitted to participate with the rest of the community in the observance of the sacred meal. Since Mithras' warriors fought beside their god for the victory of light, they were obligated to observe ethical commandments. It was expected that after death and before the gates to the world of light could be opened to any believer, everyone would have to account and be judged for his deeds. Because of Mithras' emphasis upon the struggle that must be waged against the darkness and for the light and because of the ethical-obligations placed upon all believers, the religion of Mithras exerted a powerful influence on the populace and came into sharp conflict with expanding Christianity, a conflict that ended in the fourth century with the victory of Christianity. In many places, then, Christian churches were erected over Mithraic shrines to signify the triumph of Christ over Mithras.

In the time of Christianity's inception, there were communities of followers of the mystery religions throughout the whole Roman Empire. Mithras was worshiped in Trier, and on the Rhine and the Danube, and wherever Roman legions had been encamped. Isis was venerated in Rome, Italy, Greece, and also Asia Minor. The cult of Attis and Cybele had adherents not only in Rome, Spain, and Gaul, but also in Britain and Africa. The question of how man could gain protection from the evil powers and salvation from the deity was answered by the mysteries, in that they promised the attainment of salvation, not through following a sophisticated set of teachings, but through the cultic experience in which only the initiated mystai were allowed to participate.

The ideas of these mystery religions exerted an influence upon many an infant Christian community; this happened in part through the Christian community's unconscious interpretation of worship activities in accordance with the example offered by the mystery religions, but in part by the conscious reference to views of the mystery religions. The consequence of the cultic drama in which the myste participates—that is, his incorporation into the destiny of the cultic deity—was also the interpretation given to the Christian baptism. Anyone who is baptized into Christ is incorporated into his death and resurrection, so that the powers of immortality flow through him. Paul is repeatedly obliged to combat the view that the Christian has already been raised to a life that cannot be lost (Rom. 6:1-5), or that in baptism and the Lord's Supper he has received a tangible, material salvation that now sets him free to do or not do, as he pleases (I Cor. 10:1-13). Just as it was thought that a permanent bond was established between the mysta-gogue who imparts the initiation and the myste who receives it from him, so also many Christians thought that the person baptized was forever linked with the one who had baptized him, because of the imparting of salvation. Thus a Christian could boast of the name of the one who baptized him (I Cor. 1:12). Such ideas must have surreptitiously crept into the faith; but in some places Christians arrogantly claimed that the saving power imparted to the believers in Christian worship was a possession which they could employ at will. Paul very sharply opposes these views and emphasizes that baptism and the Supper do not—as is assumed of the mysteries—bestow a material gift of salvation, but rather subject the Christian to the lordship of Christ, in order that one day they might be raised from the dead and be united with him. While for the myste the initiation into the mysteries joins him to the fate of a nature-deity and imparts to him a divine vital power, through baptism the Christian is related to the historically unique event of the death and resurrection of Christ. Allegiance to Christ as Lord is to be demonstrated by a Christian's way of life. It is not through cultic observance (in which irresistible power is supposedly derived from correctly performed ritual) but through the preached word (which proclaims the crucified Christ as the savior) that the offer of salvation is made to everyone on the condition of faith and obedience.

4. Popular Philosophy

When Paul gave his testimony concerning Christ to the Greeks in Athens at the Areopagus, he was confronted—according to the book of Acts—by Epicurean and Stoic philosophers (Acts 17:18). The scene is altogether fittingly sketched in this last respect, because at that time these two schools dominated philosophical conversation. The emphasis in philosophy was upon thinking through practical questions that needed answers in the light of human activity in the world. For example, in the Hellenistic period the strong link between city and citizen from which people derived a sense of belonging was destroyed. With the victorious campaign of Alexander the Great, the political history of the great cities came to an end and a world empire infused with Greek culture emerged. Philosophy, therefore, no longer saw itself confronted with the task of inquiring into the proper political conduct for the city commonwealth, but of accounting for the profound transformation of life that had come about with the end of the Greek polis and the spread of Hellenism. It had to show the individual man, who no longer felt truly bound to a commonwealth to which he belonged, how he should conduct his life and comport himself in everyday affairs.

In view of the new political situation as it prevailed in the Hellenistic era, *Epicurus* (*ca.* 342–270 B.C.) advised men to withdraw from public life into the quiet of private existence, because there is nothing better for a person to do than to enjoy his life. Enjoyment here is understood as the condition of human well-being which is achieved when one gains true wisdom and, therefore, is able in every situation to find the right thing to do. Since immoderate desire could disturb and destroy this condition, it was of crucial importance to investigate, by wise reflection, what action was best chosen or avoided and to eliminate anything that might disturb a well-balanced life of the soul. The fulfillment of life's meaning does not occur upon the entrance of man's soul into another world, but is either experienced or missed in this world. Since a reflective life can only be found and experienced solely by each individual, each person has the right to strive for this goal without regard to the community. Epicurus did not deny the existence of gods, but he did not expect gods to be concerned with the lives of men; hence neither do men need to concern themselves with the gods.

Epicurus' teaching was advanced by his pupils and because of its simplicity and clarity was accepted by many. But it also met with resistance because it had nothing to say about the tasks of political life and was exclusively oriented to the achievement of happiness for the individual. In the polemic that was waged against the Epicurean philosophy, Epicureans were reproved for striving for pleasure in this life without thinking of a hereafter. In Judaism "Epicurean" became an epithet given to those who, like the Sadducees, did not have faith in a resurrection of the dead and therefore sought to see the meaning of life realized in earthly existence alone (cf. p. 74).

In contrast to the Epicureans, the *Cynics* scorned any and all pleasure in life. Diogenes in his barrel was a vivid example of how a man could be frugal and self-denying.

Like the Cynics, the *Stoics* also refused to regard the pursuit of desires as the way to realize life's meaning. Nevertheless they held to a milder ethic than the Cynics, which they derived from a doctrine of nature that had already been developed by Zeno (*ca.* 336–263 B.C.) and Cleanthes (*ca.* 331–232 B.C.). In the course of the centuries the Stoic school underwent several transformations. The later Stoicism, whose teachers were active in the first and second centuries A.D., is distinguished from the earlier and the middle Stoicism primarily by the fact that it expressly emphasized the preeminence of ethics. In so doing, however, the connection of ethics to the view of the world and the view of nature was maintained without alteration.

Stoic teaching posits the entire world as a great unity. The universe is filled with the divine logos and its power, and the rule of the logos is discernible in the works of the cosmos. The deity, who can also be called by the traditional name of Zeus, is praised by Cleanthes in his famous hymn with these words of praise:

> Zeus, loftiest of the immortals, many-named ruler of the universe,
> Thou the source of nature, who dost rule all things by law,
> Hail! To call upon thee is fitting indeed for all mortals.
> For they stem from thy race. To men alone
> Of all that lives and moves on the earth didst thou give speech.
> Praise to thee, and thy power shall ever be my song.
> Willingly obedient to thee is the world that circles the earth,
> It follows thee wherever thou dost lead, submissive to thy mighty
> will.

The deity that governs the universe sends reason to guide men and directs discerning persons to the proper conduct of their lives. Anyone who recognizes the ordered coherence of the cosmos will therefore join in praise to the deity:

> For no more splendid calling is given to gods and men
> Than worthily to praise the eternal law of the universe.

The Stoics did not attack traditional religion, rather they interpreted the myths with the aid of the allegorical method of exposition, in order to introduce into the traditions its pantheistic teaching about nature and the ethic that followed from it (cf. p. 134). Because the divine power flows through the universe, man shares in it in that he reverently considers the order of nature, recognizes its laws, and follows them.

Man therefore has to understand himself as a part of all-encompassing nature and to order his life accordingly by striving to live in harmony with it. The divine logos that is everywhere operative is divided into many creative spiritual forces which are at work throughout the universe as emanations from the one deity. Since man is affected by them, he becomes aware of the conformity of all life to the law and thereby comes to comprehend where he belongs and what is expected of him. For the Stoics the differences among men are not of ultimate importance, since all men—whether rich or poor, slave or free, Greek or barbarian, male or female—

participate in the cosmic order. The Stoic ideal of humanity is cosmopolitan in orientation and acknowledges an obligation to act humanely toward persons of both high and low social strata. It is true that no effort is made to do away with existing social distinctions, but the regard that is owed to every man is to be shown even to the slave. Man is destined by nature for a communal life, so he is to regard marriage, family, and state as the sphere in which he has to prove himself and fulfill his tasks. The foundations of the law that regulates the life of men in society are likewise to be inferred from the laws of nature, so that the specific legal order will manifest the natural law in conceding to every man what is rightfully his.

The ideal of leading a life that corresponds to the order of nature is actualized by the Stoic sage, who is inwardly independent of all that artificially binds man to the world. Since external existence does not concern him, he is not after property and goods, wealth or family to call his own; and he is not affected when sickness or suffering comes upon him. Because nothing can assail him, fate may do with him what it will; whatever happens to him he accepts as an expression of divine will, and he submits to divine guidance from the hand that gives everything. In this inner freedom, which cannot be limited by any exterior circumstance, the wise man is fortified against all that might be inflicted upon him. And if he should someday get the feeling that his time is at an end, he can depart from this life without bitterness and resentment. Just as in unshakable calm he has achieved and preserved the peace of his soul, so also may he look calmly and composedly toward death.

The practical outlook of Stoic ethics, which teaches man to recognize that the tasks of his life should be accomplished in harmony with nature, exhibits various similarities with the Cynics' view that man should behave modestly and dissociate himself from his needs. Cynic and Stoic teachings were combined into the popular Cynic-Stoic philosophy which was offered by itinerant teachers as an aid for conducting one's life. People were reminded of where they had previously acted unsuccessfully or wrongly, were advised to practice self-reflect and were offered a sturdy morality according to whose direction they could order their lives. This teaching was not developed in complex intellectual exposition, but in lively dialogue, in order to compel even the simplest hearer to follow the train of thought and to persuade him of the logical character of the argument. The "lecture" (Greek *diatribe*) usually took the form of an exchange between two persons representing opposite view-points, the expectation being that the contrast would inevit-ably produce the correct conclusion. This form of the Cynic-Stoic diatribe, reflecting oral discourse, is evidenced chiefly by the teaching lectures of *Epictetus* (*ca.* A.D. 50–138), in which a question is often posed and then immediately followed by an answer. To quote:

A man posed the question of how one could be convinced that every one of our deeds is observed by God. Epictetus responded: "Do you not believe that the universe is a unity?"—"Certainly."— "Further, do you not believe that the earthly and the heavenly influence each other?"—"Of course."—"Indeed, otherwise how would everything be so ordered as to function at a command of God? When he commands the plants to flourish, they flourish; when he commands them to sprout, they sprout; when they are to produce fruit, they do so. . . ." (*Discourses* I. 14. 1–3).

Epictetus had come to Rome as a Phrygian slave and while there had been sent by his master to the school of the Stoic Musonius. Epictetus viewed his instruction in philosophy as the crucial event in his life, surpassing by far the importance of his emancipation from slavery which also was later granted to him. In his lectures, which were recorded by his pupil Arrian, Epictetus strives to explain to his listeners that they are to understand themselves as creatures of the deity that rules over nature and should live their lives accordingly. From the insight by which he viewed both his life and his life-long task as gifts from God's hand, Epictetus concludes that nothing else is as important for man as to recognize that which is within his power and that which is not. Nothing external— body, possessions, acclaim, social position—is controlled by man, so he must accept what is allotted to him. But it is in his power to determine his own thoughts and desires, his deeds and actions. The more he realizes he is free and independent in these matters, the happier he will be in his life. The little booklet compiled by Arrian from sayings of Epictetus is introduced with the fundamental sentences:

> Of all that is, some things are in our power, and other things are not. In our power are opinion, the impulse to activity, desire, dislike; in a word, everything that is our task. Not in our power are the body, possessions, honors, offices; in a word, everything that is not our task. That which is in our power is by its nature free; it cannot be stemmed or hindered. What is not in our power is weak, unfree, hindered; it is alien property. Always keep this in mind: if you regard as free that which by its very nature is not free, and alien property as your own, you will meet hindrances, fall into grief and confusion, and make accusations against gods and men. But if you regard as your property only that which belongs to you, but regard as alien that which is just that, namely as belonging to someone else, no one will be able to constrain you or hinder you, you will reproach no one, accuse no one; you will do nothing against your will, no one will be able to harm you, you will have no enemies, and nothing will happen to you that can be injurious to you. (*Manual* § 1)

Therefore man must strive to achieve that inner independence in which he will find true freedom. By submitting to the divine law, he will succeed in destroying the appetites that awaken wrong desires and entangle one in a state of dependence. The sage has gained the knowledge of good and evil and possesses the freedom to make right decisions, so that he is in a position to avoid the evil and to act ethically. He is conscious of being guided by the task of serving mankind and is ready at any moment to relinquish his life and all that he owns to the deity who entrusted them to him. In acceding to the cosmic order, the "I" of man is absorbed into the totality to which it belongs.

The sober ethic and the cosmopolitan breadth of the Stoic teaching made it especially attractive and useful to the Romans. Their practical mind adopted the ideas of the Stoics in order to use them to define anew the task of Rome. The Roman Empire was described as potentially the epitomization of a cosmopolitan community in which every man would understand and fulfil the task assigned to him by a divine commission. The doctrine of natural law could be connected with the legal thought and practice of the Romans and would provide for these the conceptual basis from which they could develop further. Hence the Romans reformulated the Stoic ideas into politically practicable rules as, for example, in the writings of Cicero. The philosopher Seneca served for some years as tutor of the Emperor Nero, and in the second century A.D. the ideal prevailed that the ablest and best should become the ruler and should be the servant of all (cf. pp. 207–8). In the shape of Marcus Aurelius, a philosopher ascended to the imperial throne—one who constantly accompanied his actions with critical reflection in order to ascertain whether he had followed the correct insight and then properly translated it into deeds.

Since the sage apprehends his life as worship, philosophy acquires for him a genuinely religious significance; in every situation it offers man such comfort and assurance that Seneca can describe its value in these laudatory words:

> Philosophy . . . forms and shapes the mind, it orders the life, it determines actions, it shows what is to be done and what is to be left undone, it sits at the helm and guides the ship of life through all dangers. Without philosophy no man can live free of fear and without cares. . . . One must philosophize! Whether the rule of fate fetters us with inexorable law, whether God as governor of the universe has determined everything, whether human life is set in motion by accident, without a plan, and is determined by a throw of the dice—philosophy must be our protection. God willing, it will exhort us daringly to obey fate. It will teach us to accept chance. (*Epistle XVI*)

Stoic ideas also found acceptance in Hellenistic Judaism, since people sought to identify the Creator and God of Israel as the deity that directs nature and to link as well the natural law that imposes ethical obligations upon all men with the Law of Moses (cf. pp. 123–24). Thus various Stoic conceptions were also transmitted by the Hellenistic synagogues to early Christianity. Thus in the speech at the Areopagus, explicit reference was made to the idea that men partake of the divine nature and therefore are of a divine race (Acts 17:28). God, who created all things and gave the nations their order, has placed in the hearts of all men the will to seek him. But this seeking attains its goal through the removal of ignorance and by man's realization of the correct insight as to God's governance. If man considers the works of creation in the context of the laws of nature he will comprehend that God directs nature and hence also guides the life of man. Paul also refers to this idea. However, he reverses the direction, not arguing in terms of a natural knowledge of God, but saying, conversely: Because all men could have known God, but have refused to give him the honor that is his due, all are without excuse (Rom. 1:19-23). Stoic expressions are echoed in primitive Christian confessional statements when it is said that all things are from God, through him, and to him (Rom. 11:36; cf. also I Cor. 8:6; Eph. 4:6). Just as the sage can consider it unimportant whether he is a slave or a free man, a Greek or a barbarian, and can see freedom grounded solely in an inward independence, so also Paul can say that ultimately it does not matter whether one is a servant or a lord. The freedom of the Christian, however, does not result from an inner imperturbability, but is the freedom of those whom Christ has called to freedom (I Cor. 7:17-24; Gal. 5:1-13; *et passim*). Paul frequently employs the manner of argument of the Cynic-Stoic diatribe, by developing the train of thought in rapidly alternating dialogue (cf. I Cor. 7:17-24). In the Epistle of James, also, references are made to nature (James 3:1-5). As one puts a bit in a horse's mouth to make it obedient, and ships are guided by the rudder, "so also is the tongue"—it is concluded from these allusions—"a little member and yet it can utter great things" (James 3:5). Rules advocating a prudent life and prudent conduct were incorporated into Christian instruction and recur both in the so-called *Haustafeln* (literally "housetables," i.e., a set of injunctions for a household; cf. Col. 3:18–4:1) and in the passages which urge acknowledgment of the civil authorities as the divinely established order and obedience to them (cf. Rom. 13:1-7).

In addition to the Epicureans and the influential Stoic movement there were other philosophical schools which influenced the intellectual life of late antiquity. Pythagorean ideas were operative in the teaching held by the famous itinerant preacher *Apollonius of Tyana* (cf. pp. 227–28). He urged an ascetic manner of life, preached repentance to high and low alike, reproached all who pursued soft lives of pleasure, and admonished people faithfully to honor the gods, to care for the temples, and to offer sacrifices. The life of the saint was not, to be sure, to manifest a norm obligatory for all, but it was to provide all with a stimulus and encouragement. Many saw in Apollonius the embodiment of divine power, visibly attested also in miraculous deeds, so that legends soon clustered around his life and were recorded in the account of his activity composed by Philostratus. In many places itinerant preachers like Apollonius traveled through the country. Many were filled with a genuine zeal to convert people, but others set forth their teaching with the intention of using it to gain an advantage and to earn their livelihood. In order to avoid being confused with such people, Paul emphatically points out, in his first Epistle to the Thessalonians, that he had worked among them in the power of the Holy Spirit, had not sought honor from men, and had labored with his own hands, in order not to be a burden to anyone (I Thess. 1:1–2:13).

Plato's ideas about the cosmos and his understanding of man and his immortal soul were, to a considerable extent, common knowledge among educated persons, as is shown by a little writing with the title "On the world," which was attributed to Aristotle but actually dates from the first century A.D. In it the unknown author develops the view of the creation of the world by God, who "sits enthroned in the highest place, whose power however penetrates and permeates the whole cosmos . . . free from trouble, free from concern and free from any and all bodily exertion. Sitting enthroned in the realm of the immovable, he moves all things by his power and causes them to move where and as he will, in various forms and beings." The Platonic view of the world was adopted also by many educated Jews, who read this view into the biblical texts and strove in this way to harmonize their particular beliefs with philosophy, so that even Philo of Alexandria could speak of the divine Plato (cf. p. 134). The idea that this world is a copy of a celestial prototype was appended to the biblical belief in creation in the Hellenistic synagogues as well as in early Christian communities (cf. Col. 1:15; 2:17; Heb. 8:5; 10:1; *et passim*). Platonic thought also guides the extensive literary activity of Plutarch (*ca.* A.D. 50–120), who through his studies in Athens and his wide travels acquired great knowledge and a rich education. As priest of the Delphic Apollo he opposed the widespread superstition and urged a proper worship of deity by striving to bind together the ideas of the great philosopher with the worship of the gods and true religion. Since man is given the task of striving after the good, the educated man will understand how, in a respectful attitude toward the traditional religion, intellectually to penetrate the religious ideas developed by the people and to develop a morality that is guided by philosophical reflection.

The efforts of the philosophers to achieve a positive relationship to religion was met by many contemporaries with sarcastic criticism. In the second century A.D., Lucian of Samosata loosed his biting ridicule upon religion and the veneration of the gods. It is true that the philosophical opinions which he expressed nowhere transcend views that were commonly held, and they do not exhibit any independent powers of thought; but his accounts contain instructive information about the civilization and the history of the times. Moreover, they speak the language of a skeptic who will not let himself be persuaded by traditional religious views and who holds the Christians whom he occasionally meets to be representatives of a curious superstition.

CHAPTER 3
Gnosticism

1. The Basic Structure of Gnosticism

The phenomenon of gnosticism has been much disputed since the days of the early church. The church fathers set themselves in sharp polemic against gnostics who followed a doctrine that denied the world, engaged in mythological speculation, and often practiced a libertine ethic. They were accused of distinguishing the God of the Old Testament from the Father of Jesus Christ and of falsifying the Christian message. Gnosticism appeared as a cluster of heretical groups who, as heretics, had to be separated and removed from the great Church. For a long time, therefore, people regarded gnosticism as an intra-Christian phenomenon that had stemmed from the encounter of early Christianity with the Hellenistic world and belonged to the history of Christian sects. This picture changed, however, when people began to look at the beginnings of the Christian church against the background of the history of religions. In this process it became evident that gnosticism was by no means a creation derived solely from within the framework of early church history; rather it was a movement with many branches in the Hellenistic world that had incorporated influences from a variety of religions and intellectual movements, was disseminated before and alongside primitive Christianity, and then in various ways combined with Christian elements to form a large number of Christian-gnostic communities.

By means of religio-historical investigation the picture of gnosticism became, on the one hand, clearer, but on the other hand, significantly more complex. The question had to be asked, therefore, as to when Iranian, Babylonian, Egyptian, and Old Testament-Jewish ideas could have been combined with ideas of Greek philosophy into a remarkable structure exhibiting a variety of colors on all sides. The various influences could be combined only because they were held together by a particular view of existence that attempts to offer an interpretation of the world and of man. The basic feature of dualism, which pervades all the conceptions and utterances of gnostic groups, points indeed to kinships with Iranian perspectives. However, through the true man's denial of the world and striving for redemption is expressed a new understanding of life which condemns the world as alien and seeks for a way to salvation that will enable the soul to return to its true home, which has long been lost to it.

In modern research the question of the Gnostic understanding of human existence was finally placed in sharper focus when previously unknown texts were discovered and traditions that had long been known could be explained more precisely with the aid of thorough analysis. In that process particular attention was directed to analyzing various phenomena characterizing the foundations and periphery of ancient Judaism, which by no means formed so unitary an entity as later Pharisaic-rabbinical teaching would like to claim. At any rate it is now beyond question that a not inconsiderable quantity of Jewish traditions significantly different from those informing the developing Jewish orthodoxy contributed to the complex phenomenon of gnosticism. Yet although scholarship has been intensively concerned with explaining the origins of gnosticism, it has not yet been able to arrive at conclusions in every respect about the rise of that movement; many problems—as, for example, that of the gnostic redeemer-myth (on this, see below, pp. 258–61) — are still vigorously disputed. Today, however, it is generally recognized that gnosticism is of pre-Christian origin, that it circulated as a broad movement alongside early Christianity, and that it frequently was combined with Christianity. The long known texts in which the church fathers waged a polemic against gnostic doctrines and in so doing gave some fragmentary quotations from them have been supplemented in modern times (1945/46) by important discoveries which brought to light a large gnostic library in Nag Hammadi in Upper Egypt. Apocryphal gospels, didactic writings, epistles, and apocalypses show how Christian gnostics in Egypt undertook to offer a gnostic exposition of the Gospels and to set forth true knowledge as the way to salvation. It is true that here we are dealing, without exception, with Christian writings, which therefore cannot provide us with any direct information about the shape of pre-Christian gnosticism; but the abundance of texts lets us look deep into the world of gnostic communities, which now speak to us with their own words, rather than viewing them through the refraction given by the church fathers' polemical quotations. To this extent, then, the discovery of these texts at Nag Hammadi can illum͏ ͏te the many-layered characteristic of gnosticism at ͏͏͏portant points. Yet in describing gnosticism we still must exercise caution, because there are very few literary attestations of pre-Christian gnosticism; its beginnings, therefore, cannot be readily deduced or reconstructed.

If one wishes to offer, at the present stage of the investigation, the most appropriate presentation of the basic structure of gnosticism, it is recommended that one begin with the question of what gnosticism purported to be according to its own interpretation. The word *gnosis* means "knowledge." However, this does not mean, as in Greek philosophy, an insight gained by way of scientific investigation and critical reflection. Moreover, it does not mean the true knowledge which either, as in Jewish apocalyptic, offers a glimpse into the relationships of the divine plan of history or, as in the Qumran community, signifies the correct understanding of the divine law (cf. pp. 108–9). But this knowledge is imparted through revelation, which bestows upon man the knowledge of God. According to the definition which the Valentinian Gnostic, Theodotus, gave to the concept of gnosis, gnosis has the following content:

> Who we were, what we became;
> where we were, whither we were thrown;

whither we are hastening, from what we are redeemed;
what birth is, and what rebirth. (*Excerpta ex Theodoto 78*)

The arrangement of these phrases in pairs points to the dualistic character of gnosticism. The first two pairs describe the downward movement from the original home of men into the world into which they were thrown. The last two pairs, on the other hand, pose the question as to the liberation by which men are delivered from imprisonment and led to salvation. If this insight is not granted to them, they must be lost, because they can neither become aware of their imprisonment nor discern the way to freedom. "He who has knowledge"—[thus the so-called Gospel of Truth from Nag Hammadi describes the concept of gnosis]—"knows whence he has come and whither he is going. He knows this like someone who was intoxicated and has turned from his drunkenness, who has come to himself and has restored what is his own" (22:13-20).

This knowledge comes to man by virtue of his having been grasped by the object of knowledge, that is, by God himself. As the "Unknown One" God is utterly unreachable; there is no direct road leading to him. But he prepares the way leading from himself to the soul, and the soul perceives him in an ecstatic vision. In this vision the soul becomes aware of its situation in the world and, thereby, sees that it is imprisoned in matter. But at the same time, this knowledge enables the soul to begin the homeward journey to the heavenly world to which it originally belonged. From this knowledge, therefore, is born a negative attitude toward the world; for the world is formed of material substance, is disposed toward evil, and is hostile toward the divine light-force that slumbers in man.

In the Hellenistic-Roman world there was widespread esteem for the strange, bizarre elements that occurred in the religious traditions of the Orient. People sought to discern in the ideas of those traditions mysterious divine knowledge and consequently readily appropriated various mythological traditions from which they then strove to perceive God's revelation. This attraction to strange and unfamiliar sounding religious discourse played a large part in molding the language of gnosticism. The myths that were told in gnostic circles are artificial constructions whose components are of diverse origin and are combined in such a way as to make the revelation of knowledge appear as attractive as possible. The myths were intended to make comprehensible why this world has become as it is, why man is in his present situation, and, finally, how the way to salvation can be discovered. Through gnosticism's eclectic approach toward the task of elucidating the contents of its knowledge, there actually arose, through the melting process, something new, the language of gnosticism.

The inner coherence of the world can be comprehended only when its origin is explained. Gnosticism speaks of this in the descriptions of the cosmogony, the details of which are variously presented, but whose basic features consistently recur. The *creation* happened because a portion of the divine fell from the divine sphere of the pure world of light into the lower regions and then united with matter. Because the world came into being through a fall, it is not the true work of the deity; it is an alien work that now is governed by hostile powers. For gnosticism, therefore, the cosmos is not God's good order, and the works of creation do not—as the Stoics claimed—verify that God himself rules over it and in it. Rather, the cosmos is entangled in darkness and is subject to perdition; it is the prison in which the fragments of light are held captive. While according to Stoicism divine providence orders and guides all things throughout the wide world so that God's will is done in great things and in small, gnosticism perceives the law of the world as a coercive power that wishes to keep everything under its dominion.

Old Testament-Jewish ideas also have been incorporated, in considerable measure, into the myth of the creation; but these have undergone profound alteration. For in the creation all things were not accomplished for the good; the world, in fact, is evil. Primal man did not precipitate the situation in which men now find themselves, but came into the world through a fateful fall and has since been held captive there. The powers that watch over the world overpowered him, caused him to become intoxicated, and put him to sleep, so that he forgot that he came from the heavenly home. The description of the creation reaches its climax—in this respect altogether consistent with the Old Testament accounts—in the narration of the creation and fate of man, who finds himself in a world that is wholly opposed to him. When he becomes aware of this, the first step is taken toward his return home, for the return can be achieved only by turning away from the world.

Thus comprehension of the gnostic view of *man* is dependent upon understanding the creation. For the myth which tells about the beginning explains the present situation of man by setting before his eyes the truth about whence he came and whither he has been cast. Since a divine spark continues to slumber within man, everything depends on whether this spark can be fanned into life again, or whether it will finally be extinguished. The cosmic forces have a vital interest in preventing its liberation from imprisonment in sleep, drunkenness, and self-forgetfulness; for if the fragments of lights were to be again withdrawn from the cosmos, the cosmos would disintegrate, because matter is nothing but darkness. Therefore the powers want to anesthetize the soul, which is the real self of man, so that it will not learn the circumstances of its origin and its future.

The divine spark that is concealed in the soul of man cannot, by its own power, free itself from this imprisonment. In the "Naassene Hymn"—a text of the gnostic community of the Naassenes—there is a description of the soul's desperate attempt to discover a way out:

> Now it wears the crown, and beholds the light;
> now it is plunged into wretchedness;
> now it mourns, and once again rejoices;
> now it weeps, and at the same time exults;
> now it is judged, and suffers death;
> now it is born anew;
> and a labyrinth of woes, with no escape,
> surrounds the unhappy wanderer.
>   (Hippolytus *Refutation of All Heresies* V. 10. 2).

Fear, anxiety, and yearning for liberation are useless. Since the gate leading to freedom and home can only be opened in the manner designated by God, knowledge must include not only the facts of birth, but, above all, of rebirth as well.

The problem of *salvation* is treated in the gnostic soteriology. Because God (who sits enthroned far above and remote from the world) and the divine substance that rests in the soul of man belong together by virtue of their natural affinity, the soul must therefore reascend into the higher world from which it once fell. While in the initiation performed in the mystery religions man is imbued with a deifying power that grants him immortality, in the gnostic understanding the rebirth signifies the restoration of the original state. Thus it is not, as is the case in the mystery religions, a matter of endowing man with a gift of salvation that is something essentially new; rather, it is a matter of returning to man what was originally his and has continued to be present in him, though hidden. In order for this to happen, man must be shaken out of his sleep and his drunken condition and must realize that the world is alien to him. This awareness comes to man through the call which greets him as divine revelation.

The call, which makes man conscious once again of his heavenly origin, is described in vivid fashion in the "Hymn of the Pearl" in the Acts of Thomas (108–113). The hymn tells of a king's son who disguised himself and went to Egypt to seek a valuable pearl, but in the strange country forgot both his origins and his mission. Thus is portrayed the fate of the soul, which has fallen asleep in the world and no longer knows whence it came and what is its destiny. The "Hymn of the Pearl" then continues: when the parents of the royal son, who had remained at home, discovered with sorrow what had happened to their son in the foreign land, they wrote a letter to him, conveying to him the following message: "Arise from your sleep, and listen to the words of our epistle. Remember that you are the son of a king. Look at your slavery; consider whom you serve. Think of the pearl for which you went to Egypt." An eagle carried this letter to the king's son, who at the voice and the noise of the eagle awoke and arose from his sleep. The words have a liberating effect: "The words of my epistle were written altogther in harmony with what I had in my heart. I have reflected on the fact that I am a king's son and long for the freedom that is mine by nature. I thought of the pearl for which I was sent to Egypt." Now he succeeds in wresting the pearl from the fearful dragon that guards it, begins the homeward journey and returns rejoicing to his parents with the pearl in his possession.

Thus the redemption takes place in the course of his return to his origins, in the liberation of the hidden divine kernel of man and his restoration thereby to his true destiny. The knowledge that is awakened by the call not only makes man conscious of his situation, but also bestows upon him the ability to outwit the guardians of the prison and to begin the homeward journey. Gnosis makes it clear to man that he does not belong to this world and demands that he detach himself from this world. This detachment from the world can work itself out in such a way that the gnostic turns away from the world and in asceticism renounces everything the world offers; or, on the other hand, it can lead a person who has attained true knowledge to the view that nothing he enjoys in the world can affect his true self. Thus contempt for the world can evoke an attitude of libertinism that rests on the principle that anything one chooses to do is permissible because nothing worldly can touch the "I" of the gnostic, which belongs to the divine sphere.

In the gnostic systems that were eventually developed the communication of the call that brings man to knowledge is variously described. This call, which comes from the divine sphere and reaches man where he is sojourning in the world, comes to him through an embassy, through the awakening word, and shows him the way to the heavenly home. The bearer of this knowledge can also appear in the shape of a redeemer who comes from God; disguised, this figure subjects himself to the conditions in which men live, is able to escape recognition by the cosmic guards and then to communicate to men the redeeming message. In Christian-gnostic teaching Jesus Christ is the redeemer who bears the divine message to men. He appears in human form so as to avoid being noticed prematurely by the forces in power, but he is not actually man and, therefore, does not take upon himself suffering and death. The question of whether pre-Christian gnosis was already acquainted with a redeemer-figure cannot be answered with certainty. Since the call to redemption can be communicated in various ways, the gnostic myth is in principle open to the adoption of a redeemer-figure. But, on the other hand, it does not necessarily require a heavenly deliverer; the call can be uttered directly as liberating knowledge. Hence it is not impossible that the clearly sketched figure of the redeemer could first have arisen under strong Christian influence which thereafter led to the formation of the Christian-gnostic systems. Judaism was familiar with "Wisdom" as the mediatrix and content of revelation, and Philo of Alexandria calls the Logos an intermediate being between God and man (cf. pp. 137–38). These motifs undoubtedly had an impact upon gnosticism and contributed to the clarification and illustration of the idea of the divine revelation by means of the conception of a heavenly redeemer.

The gnostic myth does not treat a particular history (as is proclaimed in the Christian message) but expresses an eternally valid truth that cannot be grasped as an historical or an apocalyptic event. The truth of the myth is revealed in the explanation of human existence which it imparts as a result of knowledge. Therefore a conflict between gnosticism and the Christian faith was bound to arise in the arena of the early church. Was it permissible to understand Jesus of Nazareth as a mythical being that remains separate from the world and history, that did not become man and was not nailed to the cross? Was it the guilt of the primal man or a hostile fate that brought the penalty of death upon all men? Did the creation come into being through a fall, as a work that is not God's own, or did it issue from the creative word of God, who calls into being things that are not? Is there a spark of light slumbering in man, a spark that in essence belongs to God and therefore must be called back to its true nature; or does redemption occur in the forgiveness of sins, whereby the new creation in Christ is accomplished? Will the souls of men return to their heavenly home, or will God raise the dead and unite his people with Christ? Does gnosis open up a tangible, palpable salvation, which remains the inalienable possession of the gnostics, whatever they may do, or is salvation experienced only in faith, which is joined to love and hope? The intellectual struggle which Christianity had to undertake to answer these questions required the church on its own part to formulate more clearly the doctrine of creation, of man, and of salvation, in order to define their opposition to the gnostic teaching.

2. The *Corpus Hermeticum* as a Witness to Pre-Christian Gnosticism

Gnostic thinking dominates the collection of eighteen tractates which are collected in the so-called *Corpus Hermeticum*. The Greek god Hermes is called the "thrice great" (Greek: *trismegistos*) and is identified with the Egyptian god Thoth. Hermes, who was, according to the Greeks, the messenger of the gods and in the Hellenistic period was regarded as the god of wisdom, appears as a revealer who brings divine information to men and leads them to knowledge. The instruction occurs chiefly in a dialogue between man and god, in which the man inquires and the god answers him with secret directives which may be passed on only by word of mouth.

The *Corpus Hermeticum* does not represent a unitary literary entity; for several authors, whose views do not always agree, had a part in writing the eighteen tractates. It is true that most of the parts were not written down until the time between A.D. 100 and 200, but the traditions which were recorded therein had previously circulated for a long time by oral transmission. They exhibit features of Iranian, Babylonian, Egyptian, and Greek religion; they incorporated philosophical ideas from Plato, the Pythagoreans, and the Stoics; and in many places they were unmistakably influenced by Old Testament-Jewish conceptions. Nowhere, however, does this colorful picture betray any sign of contact with the Christian message. To this extent the *Corpus Hermeticum* represents an extremely significant and instructive example of the gnostic world view which had not yet become interwoven or involved with Christianity.

The collection opens with the tractate entitled

Poimandres, which by far surpasses all the other writings in terms of the significance of its contents. The name *Poimandres* probably comes from the Egyptian, in which it originally meant "the knowledge of God." It has been given a Greek form, and now serves as a designation of the mediator of the revelation. The first tractate of the *Corpus Hermeticum* presents a compact summary of the cosmology, anthropology, and soteriology of gnostic doctrine and in so doing employs a variety of mythological traditions to describe the beginning of the world, the creation of man, and the redemption which is supposed to liberate him from earthly imprisonment.

At the outset the mediator of the revelation introduces himself to the recipient of the revelation with the words, "I am Poimandres, the spirit of the most high power" (2). To him is addressed the petition: "I wish to become acquainted with that which is and to understand its nature, and I wish to know God" (3). This wish is granted, and the beginning of the world is treated in a mythological discourse. God is light,

and from the light . . . came a holy word about nature, and an unmingled fire shot up into the heights out of the moist, damp substance; the fire was light and keen and powerful; and the air, which was light, followed the breath of fire; it ascended from the earth and the water to the fire, so that it appeared to be suspended from the fire. But earth and water remained in their place and mingled with each other, so that the earth could not be separated from the water. They were stirred by the glowing word which audibly rested upon them. (5)

God, who is in the heavenly heights, emanated "another spirit as creator of the world, who is the god of fire and the breath of spirit, and [he] created seven governors that embrace the true cosmos in circles" (9). These rule over the world, and this means that they determine the fate to which the world is subject. The creator of the world who stands below the supreme God caused the works of creation to rotate eternally. Living beings were brought forth by this rotation; the air was populated with fowls and the waters with fish, and the earth brought forth animal life: four-footed creatures, snakes, creeping things, and wild and domesticated animals. Thus the entire cosmos is the work of the creator of the world (i.e., the demiurge) and is subject to the destiny that is imposed upon it.

The creation of man is described in solemn-sounding words that exhibit certain contacts with biblical phrases: "But the spirit who is light and life, the father of all, begot a man similar to himself, whom he loved as his own son; for he was very beautiful, since he had the reflection of the father, so that God loved his own image. God handed over to him the whole creation" (12). The primal man beheld the work of the creator of the world, but the glimpse of the creative activity made him jealous, so that he too wanted to engage in creative activity. The powers that rule over the cosmos loved him, and each one of them gave him a share in its own position. Then came the event that was to govern the destiny of all men:

> And he who had all authority over the world of mortal beings and of beasts without reason bent down through the harmony [of the spheres], broke through the encirclement, and disclosed God's goodly form to the lower nature. When she [the lower nature] saw him who had in himself infinite beauty, all power over the governors, and the form of God, she smiled in love, because she beheld man's most beautiful form reflected in the water and in the shadow upon the earth. When he beheld in the water the figure like himself that was to be found in [the lower] nature, he loved it too and willed to dwell there. But the fulfillment followed at once with his intention, and thus he took his abode in the form devoid of reason. And nature [thereby] received the beloved and wholly embraced him, and they were united and loved each other. (14)

Thus occurred the fall of the primal man, who was drawn from the higher world into the lower world and then entered into a slavelike relationship with nature. Through nature he produced the earthly man, who, consequently, is indeed distinguished from all other living beings but, nevertheless, is subject to mortality:

> Therefore man, in contrast to all other living creatures on earth, is a dual being, mortal, to be sure, because of the body, but

immortal because of the essential man. Although he is immortal and is given power over all things, he suffers the lot of a mortal and is subject to fate. Although he is placed above the harmony [of the spheres], he became a slave within this harmony. Although he is bisexual, because he is born of a bisexual father, and although he is sleepless, because he comes from one who is sleepless, he is under the dominion [of desire and the longing for sleep]. (15)

From this time on, all people live as male and female, like the animals. They are given the commandment from God to multiply—a commandment which once again is clearly reminiscent of the biblical creation narrative: "Increase and multiply abundantly, all you that have been made and created" (18). In obedience to this divine word, "all things multiplied each after its own kind" (19). Thus the myth of the creation and the fall of the primal man explains the present situation of man, whose body is formed out of inanimate matter, but whose divine kernel is of heavenly origin. A person who on the basis of this revelation comes to know himself will be able to ascend to the Good and thus belongs to the elect. But anyone who is filled with love for the body and for matter will remain lost and wandering in the darkness and will experience death in the body. When a man comprehends who he is and who he is to be he will renounce all passions and desires and will liberate himself from all that binds him to the body and hence to the world.

Along with the discovery of true knowledge arrives insight concerning the only possible way to salvation. In death the body once again falls victim to the dissolute nature of matter, so that even the perceptions of the bodily senses come to an end. The soul, however, which can undertake the journey to the heavenly home, will undergo a purification in the course of its ascent; for in every sphere through which the soul passes, it divests itself of something that has previously burdened it: first the capacity to grow or to diminish, then the design to do evil, then deceitful lust that leads nowhere, then the desire to dominate, then godless boldness and deliberate audacity, then evil desire for wealth, and finally cunning falsehood. Liberated from all these passions, the soul enters into the eighth sphere, which lies above the seven spheres, and hears the songs of praise of all the powers and souls there, who join in praising the Father. The soul has reached its goal, that of "being deified" (26).

Knowledge about the real being of man, about the fallen state of the cosmos, and about the way to receive redemption awakens in those who have attained knowledge the desire to disseminate the gnosis. Therefore the recipient of the revelation must proclaim the beauty of piety and of knowledge:

> You earthborn men who have surrendered yourselves to drunkenness, sleep, and ignorance of God, awaken and become sober, cease your revelry, bewitched as you are by sleep devoid of reason. . . . Why, you earthborn men, have you surrendered yourselves to death, when you had the power to become partakers of immortality? Repent, you who have become fellow travelers with error and have had fellowship with ignorance; rid yourselves of the dark light, become partakers of immortality, and forsake corruption. (27-28)

Anyone who has gained the divine knowledge is to become a guide for other men so as to direct them to the way of redemption and to show them "how and in what way they are saved" (29).

The tractate *Poimandres,* like the other writings of the *Corpus Hermeticum,* does not say anything of cultic actions or of religious observances. Nothing is said of any assembly or community; instead, a teaching about divine knowledge is set forth. Anyone who hears and heeds it can and should draw for himself the necessary implications. While nothing, is mentioned in the *Corpus Hermeticum* of a religious group, it is also altogether possible that the gnostic knowledge was combined with the outward forms of a believing fellowship and in some cases was transmitted via adaptation to existing forms, and in others through newly created ones. Gnostic conceptions therefore frequently influenced the manner of cultic celebration employed by the mystery communities or took on Christian features, possibly causing the rise of communities which strove to supersede or surpass the gospel by means of the gnostic myth. But gnostic ideas also may simply take the form of a sermon that is addressed to the insight of any persons who wish to be informed about saving knowledge. Thus the literature for edification in the Hermetic writings apparently is not addressed to particular groups that are assembled for worship; it is intended to awaken individual readers and to summon them to enter upon the way of knowledge.

The basic themes touched upon in the first tractate are variously repeated throughout the rest of the tractates. The thirteenth tractate, which deals with the rebirth of man, is particularly noteworthy among them. Therein is no thought of a sacramental act, but only of the knowledge of God. At the outset the thesis is stated that no one can be saved until he is born again (1). Hence it is necessary to learn the doctrine of rebirth, which sets one free from the deceptions of the cosmos. The person reborn experiences a miraculous change; he "is God's son, the All in All, consisting of all the powers" (2). The process of rebirth, which signifies deification, cannot be perceived with the physical eyes, but takes place as a total transformation in a mystical and ecstatic vision. The transformation is so thorough that the reborn person can say that he is someone different (3). One enters upon the way to regeneration by a deliberate decision, by putting aside the passions which one bears within oneself. These passions—twelve in number—did their work through the mortal body and the senses, which kept the soul imprisoned. But when there is knowledge, which as the knowledge of God illumines the condition of man and shows him the way back to God, ignorance comes to an end (8). Where gnosis is attained, unrighteousness is put to flight and man becomes righteous. This means that a physical transformation takes place in him and with him, whereby he is deified. The ten virtues that are imparted to him expel the twelve vices, so that man becomes God, son of the One (14). The gnostic maintains silence about this miraculous mystery, to guard the event against profanation. Those who possess insight, however, will, by presentiment, join him in experiencing what has taken place in the rebirth—the rebirth which leads him to the true religion and to the rational sacrifice that is offered in the prayer of thanksgiving and praise (18–19).

The writings of the *Corpus Hermeticum* precisely clarify

the concept and the content of gnosis. The knowledge is not attained by means of one's own effort and application, but arrives through the revelation of God, who wills to be known by those who are his own. Hence gnosis is, by its very nature, knowledge of God which cannot be achieved in philosophical reflection, but which results instead from a transformation of the whole man, who is now filled with the divine power that has combined with his latent spark of divinity and will be guided to true life.

3. The Spread of Gnosticism in the First Century A.D.

The New Testament itself bears witness to the existence of a pre-Christian gnosis and to its wide dissemination. Thus we are provided with an important datum in the history of religions, because the writings of the New Testament arose in the second half of the first century A.D. or, for some portions, in the beginning of the second century A.D. Hence when definite allusions to gnostic ideas or debates with gnostic views appear in these precisely datable documents, we derive a sure reference point for dating gnostic motifs which later become more pronounced in the second century A.D. in the gnostic communities formed at the time of the early church.

In the book of Acts we are told that soon after the beginnings of the original community the Christian message was carried into the region inhabited by the Samaritans. There the early apostles encountered a *magician* named *Simon* who practiced sorcery and led the people of Samaria astray by claiming that he was someone great (Acts 8:9). His activity is said to have had extraordinary success: "For all, great and small, followed him, and they said, 'He is the Power of God that is called great'" (Acts 8:10). According to the account in the book of Acts, Simon was a magician who was impressed by the Christians' ability to perform extraordinary signs and wonders, and therefore he joined them (Acts 8:9-24). The account as presented by the book of Acts discloses an early dispute between gnostic doctrine and Christian proclamation. For the claim to be "the Great Power" cannot be understood simply as the expression of opinion of a magician; instead, it represents the claim to be the bearer of divine revelation. The polemical accounts directed against Simonian gnosis in the second century A.D. by the church fathers Justin, Irenaeus, and Tertullian show, on the one hand, that from this Simon who appeared in Samaria a movement issued which soon gained adherents not only in Palestine but even in Rome, and on the other hand, the expressly gnostic character of this teaching. If one ignores the various elaborations appended to the tradition, there emerges in all the descriptions the basic and strictly dualistic feature of Simonian gnosis. The divine *Ennoia* ("Thought") originally stood alongside the Father of the universe as the female principle; but then she fell into the captivity of the demonic powers and migrated from one female body to another, until at last she came into the body of Helena, who was in a brothel in Tyre. The imprisonment of the human soul, which is hopelessly lost if outside help is not given to it, is portrayed in Helena's misery and wretchedness. Then the most high God had mercy and he himself came down to redeem her; in Simon the divine power descends, who liberates the Ennoia in the form of Helena and leads it back to its heavenly destiny. Even though it cannot be determined with certainty to what extent the features of Simonian gnosticism can be traced to the historical Simon of Samaria, still the brief statements in the book of Acts illustrate the basically gnostic feature of his teaching. It was not accidental that the Simonian movement arose on Samaritan soil, where various religio-historical influences could combine with Jewish traditions that did not correspond to the strict standard of Jewish orthodoxy and, therefore, could develop more freely. The example of Simonian gnosticism clearly shows that ideas that developed on the periphery of Judaism significantly contributed to the emergence of gnostic teaching. Nevertheless it may not be asserted that the widely diverse movement of gnosticism derived from a single source which was situated in Samaria; for the structure of gnosticism is too multi-layered for its origin to be traced to a single place or even to a particular founder. From the earliest reports about Simon, however, we can arrive at the picture of an early form of pre-Christian gnosticism which soon was bound to come into sharp conflict with Christianity.

Gnostic views also influenced the various baptist movements that existed in the Syrian and Palestinian area. The Gospel of John presupposes that followers of John the Baptist worked alongside disciples of Jesus and that there developed a certain rivalry between the two groups. The emphatic statement that John was not himself the light, but had come as a witness to the light that came into the world as Jesus Christ (John 1:6-8, 15, *et passim*), is unmistakably directed against certain groups who wanted to see in the Baptist, himself, the eschatological savior. The sect of the *Mandeans* also belongs in the context of these baptist communities. Remnants of the sect, totaling about five thousand adherents, still live in small groups on the lower Tigris and Euphrates rivers. Their sacred writings first came to be known to modern scholarship about fifty years ago, and they have inspired a lengthy discussion which has not yet led to sure conclusions on all points.

The designation of the sect is derived from the word *manda* meaning "gnosis," and thus it signifies "the gnostics." The community itself, like the Syrian Christians, chiefly uses the name "Nasoreans," thus providing a hint that in the course of its history it has come into contact with Syrian Christianity. Their books were written in the seventh and eighth centuries A.D., because under the rule of Islam, sacred writings had to be presented if a religious community sought official recognition. The traditions that are preserved in these writings, however, are of much earlier origin; yet it cannot be said with certainty just how far back they go.

The teaching of the Mandeans speaks of God as the great life who dwells in the realm of light. Under him are numerous intermediate beings or "uthras," which play a mediatorial role between God and men. The most important of them is called Hibil-Ziwa or, frequently, Manda d'Hayye, which means approximately "gnosis of life." While Ruha and the planets that rule over the world want to hinder men from attaining knowledge and seek to hold them captive in error, Manda d'Hayye brings them the true knowledge through which they may comprehend their situation and enter on the road to freedom. The soul is equipped for the journey to the heavenly home by the ablutions and the baptism in which it receives the initiation. Baptism, anointing with oil, and celebration of communion are observed in the community in order to strengthen the souls and to make them capable of the journey to heaven, since only by decisive withdrawal from the world can redemption be gained.

Alongside the name of Manda d'Hayye and designated, as well, in the Mandean writings as a mediator of the knowledge that leads to redemption is John the Baptist. More careful scrutiny of the texts that mention John the Baptist, however, has demonstrated that his figure was inserted into the tradition during a later stage of its development. In the Islamic period the Mandeans not only had to appeal sacred writings, but to a prophet as well, and it was then that they referred to John, with whom they were already familiar through Christian narratives. Hence under no circumstances can the Mandeans be regarded as late descendants of a group whose founder could have been John the Baptist himself. It is likely, however, that the history of the community, insofar as its features can be distilled from its literature, can be traced back to its origin in the region of the Jordan. Presumably the Mandean sect arose on the periphery of Judaism and belongs in the category of the various groups which sought to purify and to gather together the holy community by means of baptism and ablutions. Toward the end of the first century or the beginning of the second century A.D., then, the sect migrated to Mesopotamia, settled there, and maintained itself through the centuries (even to the present time). Its long history evidences a variety of influences. At first Mandean doctrine was developed in accord with the gnostic world view; then the rite of baptism was developed on the basis of influences from Syrian Christianity; and in the Arab period the Mandean teaching was expanded with such features as were necessary for its survival in the encounter with Mohammedanism. If one eliminates the various layers of interpretation which in the course of time have been superimposed upon the original basic deposit of the Mandean cultic activities, one can very cautiously say that the rise of the Mandeans approximately coincides with the beginnings of Christianity. The mythology which the Mandean tradition gradually developed in ever-increasing measure, however, may be cited for comparison with New Testament texts only with extreme caution. The great antiquity of the gnostic ideas expressed in that mythology can be asserted only to the extent that these ideas are attested by other texts that can be dated with certainty.

The first Christians, who originally proclaimed the gospel in Palestine and Syria and soon in other parts of the ancient world also, spoke the language of their time. Therefore gnostic motifs were quickly appropriated for use in explaining the *Christian preaching*. Thus the idea is repeatedly expressed that this world is ruled by demonic powers and that forces of darkness practice their craft in it, forces that wish to create an irreconcilable rift between God and men (cf., Rom. 8:38-39; II Cor. 4:4; John 12:31; 14:30; 16:11). In order not to be detected prematurely by the rulers of the cosmos, the redeemer had to come into the world secretly and unobtrusively; "for if they had known him, they would not have crucified the Lord of glory" (I Cor. 2:8), because precisely thereby they pronounced judgment upon themselves. The fact that the fate of death is imposed upon all men is nowhere attributed in the New Testament to a fateful fall of the primal man; instead, it is said that sin derives from transgression and, hence, in its very existence as well as in its consequences remains the fault of man (Rom. 5:12-21). Therefore redemption is not the result, as in gnosticism, of a natural kinship between God and men that strives for a future consummation, but only of the forgiveness of sins that is promised for Christ's sake.

In many early Christian communities, gnostic self-understanding was soon combined with the Christian consciousness of freedom and was expressed in the proud feeling of those who are seized and sustained by the Spirit. Such enthusiasm appears first in the community founded by Paul in Corinth. Here the "pneumatics" professed that they had already been perfected by the Spirit, that the time of salvation was already present (I Cor. 4:8), that an inalienable power flowed from the sacraments of baptism and the Supper (I Cor. 10:1-13), and that a future consummation which

would come with the resurrection of the dead was no longer
to be expected (I Cor. 15:12). In their exuberance they
held the opinion that Christian liberty knows no bounds,
and everything is permissible (I Cor. 6:12; 10:23). What a
person does and experiences with the body does not matter,
because only the spirit matters (I Cor. 6:12-20, *et passim*).
Paul, on the other hand, emphasizes that the future consummation is yet to come, liberty can be experienced only
in obedience, and therefore the body belongs to the Kyrios
(I Cor. 6:13).

Similar manifestations of enthusiasm appeared very early
in other places besides the Corinthian community. It is true
that nowhere is a fully developed gnostic myth recognizable
in the debates which Paul conducted with such opinions;
but the proud self-consciousness with which people withdrew
from the world (were, in fact, indifferent to it) and attributed
great value only to the effects of the Spirit, exhibits similarities
to later descriptions of gnostic groups. Hence the fanatics of
Corinth as well as the group that appeared in the community
at Philippi may be characterized as early forms of Christian
gnosticism.

The more or less strong influences of the gnostic world
view and life-style upon the Christian communities are soon
demonstrated in Asia Minor also. In Colossae there appeared
teachers who promised protection against the hostile elements of the world (Col. 2:8, 20). These world-elements
were envisioned as powerful angelic beings that not only
govern the cosmic order but also guide the destiny of the
individual man. Therefore (thus these teachers sought to
persuade the Christians to believe) one can be brought into
a right relationship with these powers only through a cultic
veneration which bows to their authority. This means that
one must precisely observe the sacred seasons that are set
apart—feast days, new moons, and sabbaths (Col. 2:16) —
and must strictly avoid certain foods and drinks (Col. 2:21).
This teaching exhibits a distinctive combination of cosmological speculations whose legalistic nature intensifies Jewish
prescriptions, and it shows that not only in Palestine and
Syria but also in Asia Minor a considerable Jewish influence

contributed to the development of early forms of the gnostic understanding of the world.

Toward the end of the first century A.D. the Christian communities in Asia Minor were still further exposed to the influence of gnostic ideas in considerable measure. The Pastoral Epistles have to use sharp language to refute false teachers who think that the resurrection has already occurred (II Tim. 2:18) and that one should renounce the world by abstaining from marriage and from certain foods (I Tim. 4:3). And in the letters to the churches in the book of Revelation mention is made of the Nicolaitans (Rev. 2:6, 16), who apparently were of the conviction that some had learned the deep things of Satan (Rev. 2:24), and because of this knowledge had received the liberty to eat without hesitation meat that had been sacrificed to idols and to commit fornication (Rev. 2:14-15). Thus gnostic insight is coupled with a libertarian ethic—a typical feature of gnosticism, which also surfaces in the polemic of the Epistle of Jude against those people who defile the flesh, utter blasphemy about everything, and live in accordance with their own ungodly desires (Jude 8, 10, 18).

The *Gospel of John* and the Epistles of John stand clearly in opposition to gnostic falsification of the gospel. As these writings presumably arose in Syria, they are evidence that about the end of the first century gnosticism must have been sufficiently widespread in this area to cause the Christian communities to take a stand against it. In opposition to the gnostic contempt for the creation and the flesh it is emphatically declared that all things were made by the Logos and that the Logos became flesh (John 1:1-3, 14). The fact that the cosmos lies in the darkness is not the consequence of a fall caused by fate, but of guilt, because men have not accepted the light (John 1:5, 10). In I John the community is instructed that the right spirit confesses "that Jesus Christ has come in the flesh" (I John 4:2). This sentence is directed against a docetic Christology that holds the world in contempt and therefore does not wish to bring Christ into connection with the world. John emphatically maintains (in opposition to the view that Jesus appeared in the world only in disguise, not actually in the form of human flesh) that

Christ became true man, having come by water and blood
(I John 5:6), and that therefore all who belong to him are
bound to their brethren in love.

Hence it is firmly attested by the New Testament writings
that in the second half of the first century A.D. gnosticism
clashed with the Christian proclamation. The rise of the
Simonian teaching in Samaria, which soon reached even to
Rome, the beginnings of the Mandean baptist movement,
the appearance of fanatical arrogance in the communities
of Corinth and Philippi, and the conflict with gnostic teaching in Asia Minor and Syria all belong to the first century
A.D. Although there are no existing accounts of the emergence of the first Christian communities in Egypt, it may be
safely assumed that the early Christian mission also arrived
in Egypt as early as the latter half of the first century A.D.
In the second century A.D. several Christian-gnostic groups
were located there. It must often have been difficult in that
context to discern the difference between gnostic teaching
and orthodox confession. The fact that the boundaries must
have remained fluid for a long time is attested by the extensive library of Christian-gnostic texts discovered in Nag
Hammadi in 1945/46. Primitive Christian tradition, as preserved in many sayings of the Lord, is peculiarly combined
in the Gospel of Thomas with explicitly gnostic renuncia-
tion of creation and world. In various passages the sayings
and parables of Jesus take a form that is very close to the
versions found in the Synoptic Gospels. However, the entire
collection of sayings is placed under the rubric: "Whoever shall find the true meaning of these words will not taste
death." Gnostic ideas issue from the lips of Jesus when he
speaks of the heavenly origin of the soul to which it is to
return: "Blessed are you lonely and elect ones, for you shall
find the kingdom; indeed, you come from it [and] you shall
[consequently] return to it" (Saying 49). Or, again, it is
stressed in typical gnostic fashion that correct insight imparts
the knowledge that the resurrection of the dead has already
occurred: "His disciples said to him, 'When will the resurrection of the dead follow and when will the new world
come?' He said to them, 'What you expect has [already]
come, but you do not recognize it'" (Saying 51). Redeemer

and redeemed become one: "Jesus said, 'Anyone who drinks from my mouth will become like me. But I shall become himself, and the hidden will be disclosed to him'" (Saying 108).

Gnostic piety could live and be expressed in genuine and profound faith. This is impressively demonstrated by a collection of hymns from the second century A.D. that has been given the title "Odes of Solomon." In one of these songs the one praying is offering his thanks for the redemption that has come to him; this he accomplishes by combining Old Testament expressions with the gnostic view that the redeemed person puts on a body of light over which the darkness has no power and which is transported upward into the imperishable fellowship of the light-world:

> My arms I lifted up on high
> To the grace of the Lord,
> because he cast off my fetters from me
> and my helper lifted me up to his grace and redemption.
> I put off darkness
> and put on the light.
> And my soul acquired members
> in which there was no sickness,
> nor misery, nor pain.
> And extremely helpful to me was the counsel of the Lord,
> and his imperishable fellowship.
> And I was lifted up into the light
> and I passed before his face
> and I came near to him
> praising and confessing him.
> He made my heart overflow, and it was found in my mouth
> and arose upon my lips.
> And upon my face the exultation over the Lord and his
>   praise increased.
> Hallelujah!

(Ode 21)

In the encounter with gnosticism it had to be decided how the Christian message was to be properly expressed. In order to make the gospel comprehensible as the answer to the open questions men ask about the meaning of their lives and the liberating redemption, it had to be expressed in words and conceptions that were familiar to men. But through the adoption of these words and conceptions no change or falsification in the content of the Christian message was allowed to enter. How one could become a Jew to the Jews and a Greek to the Greeks without adversely affecting the truth and freedom of the gospel was often difficult to decide in complex matters and could be accomplished only after long and sometimes laborious reflection. The challenge which gnosticism presented for the early church demanded intensive concern for the correct understanding and exposition of the message of Christ which was owed to all men, Jewish or Greek.

CONCLUSION

The people who lived in the time of the New Testament were filled with anxieties and hopes, doubts and expectations, like the people of all ages. The Jews lived according to the Law, some aspiring to unyielding strictness, others to compatibility with Greek thought. In spite of the great multiplicity of groups and movements present in the Judaism of Palestine and in the Diaspora, the Jews were united in the conviction that the Law had been entrusted to Israel as God's gracious gift and was intended to show Israel the way to life. The hope with which they looked for the coming messianic age anticipated simply the continuation and heightening of what Israel was already experiencing in obedience to God's commandment. For even the Messiah would live under the Law and would rule the community belonging to the time of salvation according to the Law's direction. Since, as God's anointed one, the Messiah must show himself to be in agreement with the Law, in order to bring about the time of salvation, the Jews looked for signs which would infallibly illuminate God's work.

The Greeks, too, posed the question regarding salvation. The variety of intellectual and religious ideas and movements exhibited by Hellenistic-Roman world indicates how intensely the people of the ancient world searched for the ultimate meaning of their lives. The way they hoped to find it was through wisdom. The philosophers, for example, sought to fathom wisdom by rational thought, in order to mold life in accordance with its norms. But in the mystery fellowships

and in gnostically-minded groups, wisdom was understood as a mystical-ecstatic experience which seized man
by means of divine revelation and transformed him into a
new being which is lifted above corruption and decay into
the heights of celestial light. Knowledge and insight which
teach one to comprehend God and the world, man and his
destiny would open the door to deliverance and salvation.

"The Jews demand signs and the Greeks seek after wisdom"
—writes the apostle Paul—"but we preach the crucified Christ,
an offense to the Jews and folly to the Greeks" (I Cor. 1:22-
23). For the people of the ancient world it was not at all
easier than it is for the people of our own day to accept the
message of the crucified Christ as the truth. Rather the word
of the cross seemed to the Jews a challenge which simply
contradicted the Law, so that people turned away from it
offended. And the Greeks were bound to regard this proclamation as an absurd contradiction of all wisdom. But God's
wisdom does look different from the way people have imagined
it; and his power does not appear in signs that confirm for
people what they already knew. Only the word of the cross,
preached to Jews and to Greeks, opens the way of deliverance
and salvation to all who accept it in faith. Hence the crucified
and resurrected Christ is proclaimed as God's power and
God's wisdom; for—as Paul says—the alleged foolishness of
God is always wiser than men, and the alleged weakness of
God is always stronger than men (I Cor. 1:25).

BIBLIOGRAPHY

Texts

Charles, R. H., ed. *The Apocrypha and Pseudepigrapha of the Old Testament in English.* 2 vols. Oxford: Clarendon Press, 1913.

Epstein, I., ed. *The Babylonian Talmud Translated into English.* 34 vols. London: Soncino Press, 1935–48.

Barrett, C. K. ed. *The New Testament Background: Selected Documents.* New York: Macmillan, 1957.

Hennecke, E., ed. *New Testament Apocrypha.* Third edition edited by W. Schneemelcher. English translation edited by R. McL. Wilson. 2 vols. Philadelphia: Westminster Press, 1963, 1965.

Gaster, Theodore H. *The Dead Sea Scriptures.* English translation with introduction and notes. Revised and enlarged edition. Garden City, N. Y.: Anchor Books, 1964.

Danby, Herbert. *The Mishnah.* Translated from the Hebrew, with introduction and brief explanatory notes. London: Oxford University Press, 1950.

Whiston, William, trans. *The Works of Flavius Josephus.* Nashville: Broadman Press, 1974.

Colson, F. H. and Whitaker, G. H. *Philo of Alexandria.* 10 vols. English translation. Cambridge: Harvard University Press, 1929–

Rahlfs, A., ed. *Septuaginta.* Eighth edition. Stuttgart: Privilegierte Württembergische Bibelanstalt, 1965.

General Treatments

Schürer, E., *A History of the Jewish People in the Time of Jesus Christ.* 5 vols. Second and revised edition. New York: Scribner, 1897–98.

Bultmann, R. *Primitive Christianity in its Contemporary Setting.* Translated by R. H. Fuller. New York: Meridian Books, 1956.

Jeremias, J. *Jerusalem in the Time of Jesus: An Investigation into Economic and Social Conditions During the New Testament Times.* Translated by F. H. and C. H. Cave. Philadelphia: Fortress Press, 1969.

Reicke, B. *The New Testament Era: The World of the Bible from 500 B.C. to A.D. 100.* Translated by David E. Green. Philadelphia: Fortress Press, 1968.

Foerster, W. *From the Exile to Christ: A Historical Introduction to Palestinian Judaism.* Translated by Gordon E. Harris. Philadelphia: Fortress Press, 1964.

In addition, the pertinent articles in standard reference works should be consulted.

Part I: Judaism in the Time of the New Testament
Chapter 1: The Political History of Judaism in the Hellenistic Period

Schürer, E. *A History of the Jewish People in the Time of Jesus Christ.*

Ehrlich, E. L. *A Concise History of Israel from the Earliest Times to the Destruction of the Temple in A.D. 70.* Translated by James Barr. New York: Harper & Row, 1965.

Beek, M. A. *Concise History of Israel: From Abraham to the Bar Cochba Rebellion.* Translated by Arnold J. Pomerans. New York: Harper & Row, 1963.

Noth, M. *The History of Israel.* Second edition. Translation revised by P. R. Acroyd. London: A. & C. Black, 1960.

Reicke, B. *The New Testament Era.*

Jeremias, J. "Samaria." *Theological Dictionary of the New Testament, VII,* 88–94. Translated by G. W. Bromiley. Grand Rapids, Mich.: William B. Eerdmans, 1971.

Hengel, M. *Judaism and Hellenism: Studies in Their Encounter in Palestine During the Early Hellenistic Period.* Translated by John Bowden. 2 vols. Philadelphia: Fortress Press, 1974.

Bickermann, E. *The Maccabees, an Account of Their History from the Beginnings to the Fall of the House of the Hasmoneans.* Translated by Moses Hadas. New York: Schocken Books, 1947.

Perowne, S. H. *The Life and Times of Herod the Great.* London: Hodder & Stoughton, 1956.

———. *The Later Herods: The Political Background of the New Testament.* London: Hodder & Stoughton, 1958.

Yadin, Y. *Masada: Herod's Fortress and the Zealots' Last Stand.* Translated by Moshe Pearlman. London: Weidenfeld & Nicolson, 1966.

Chapter 2: Religious Movements and Intellectual Currents in Judaism in the Time of the New Testament

Plöger, O. *Theocracy and Eschatology.* Translated by S. Rudman. Oxford: Blackwell, 1968.

Vielhauer, P. "Apocalypses and Related Subjects: Introduction." *New Testament Apocrypha,* II, 581–607.

Rowley, H. H. *The Relevance of Apocalyptic: A Study of Jewish and Chrstian Apocalypses from Daniel to the Revelation.* Third edition. New York: Association Press, 1964.

Eissfeldt, O. *The Old Testament: An Introduction.* Translated by P. R. Ackroyd. New York: Harper & Row, 1965.

Schürer, E. *A History of the Jewish People in the Time of Jesus Christ.*

Meyer, R. "Sadducees." *Theological Dictionary of the New Testament,* VII, 35–54.

Baeck. L. *The Pharisees, and Other Essays.* New York: Schocken Books, 1966.

Jeremias, J. *Jerusalem in the Time of Jesus.*

Meyer, R. and H. F. Weiss. "Pharisees." *Theological Dictionary of the New Testament,* IX (1974), 11–48.

Hengel, M. *Was Jesus a Revolutionist?* Translated by William Klassen. Philadelphia: Fortress Press, 1971.

Bruce, F. F. *The Teacher of Righteousness in the Qumran Texts.* London: Tyndale Press, 1957.

——. *Second Thoughts on the Dead Sea Scrolls.* Second edition. Grand Rapids, Mich.: William B. Eerdmans, 1961.

Allegro, J. M. *The Dead Sea Scrolls.* Harmondsworth, Middlesex: Penguin Books. 1958.

——. *The Dead Sea Scrolls: A Reappraisal.* Second edition. Baltimore: Penguin Books, 1968.

Schubert, Kurt. *The Dead Sea Community: Its Origin and Teachings* Translated by John W. Doberstein. New York: Harper, 1959.

Stauffer, E. *Jesus and the Wilderness Community at Qumran.* Translated by Hans Spalteholz. Philadelphia: Fortress Press, 1964.

Burrows, M. *The Dead Sea Scrolls.* New York: Viking Press, 1955.

——. *More Light on the Dead Sea Scrolls: New Scrolls and New Interpretations.* New York: Viking Press, 1958.

Dupont-Sommer, A. *The Essene Writings from Qumran.* Translated by G. Veremes. Oxford: Blackwell, 1961.

Cross, F. M. *The Ancient Library of Qumran and Modern Biblical Studies.* Garden City, N. Y.: Doubleday, 1958.

Lohse, E. "Rabbi." *Theological Dictionary of the New Testament,* VI (1968), 961–65.

Lietzmann, H. "The Jewish Diaspora." *The Beginnings of the Christian Church,* pp. 75–103. Translated by Bertram Lee Woolf. London: Lutterworth Press, 1949.

Hengel, M. *Judaism and Hellenism.*

Chapter 3: Jewish Life and Belief
in the Time of the New Testament

Moore, G. F. *Judaism in the First Centuries of the Christian Era: The Age of the Tannaim.* 3 vols. Cambridge: Harvard University Press, 1927–30.

Ringgren, H. *Israelite Religion.* Translated by David E. Green. Philadelphia: Fortress Press, 1966.

Jeremias, J. *Jerusalem in the Time of Jesus.*

Foerster, W. *From the Exile to Christ.*

Schrage, W. "Synagogue." *Theological Dictionary of the New Testament,* VII, 798–852.

Schrenk, G. "To hieron," *ibid.* III, 232–47, 262–65, 268–72.

Meyer, R. "Krupto." Supplement on the Canon and the Apocrypha, *ibid.* III, 978–87.

Mowinckel, S. *He that Cometh: The Messiah Concept in the Old Testament and Later Judaism.* Second edition. New York and Nashville: Abingdon Press, 1959.

Part II: The Hellenistic-Roman Environment of the New Testament
Chapter 1: Politics and Society in the Roman Empire in the First Century A.D.

Rostovtsev, M. I. *A History of the Ancient World.* 2 vols. Oxford: Clarendon Press, 1945.

———. *The Social and Economic History of the Roman Empire.* Second edition. Revised by P. M. Fraser. 2 vols. Oxford: Clarendon Press, 1957.

Carcopino, J. *Daily Life in Ancient Rome: The People and the City at the Height of the Empire.* Translated by E. O. Lorimer. New Haven, Conn.: Yale University Press, 1955.

Stauffer, E. *Christ and the Caesars: Historical Sketches.* Translated by K. and R. Gregor Smith. London: S. C. M. Press, 1955.

Chapter 2: Religious Movements and Intellectual Currents in the Hellenistic-Roman World in the Time of the New Testament

Cumont, Franz. *Oriental Religions in Roman Paganism.* New York: Dover Publications, 1956.

Bornkamm, G. "Mysterion." *Theological Dictionary of the New Testament,* IV (1967), 813–17.

Wagner, G. *Pauline Baptism and the Pagan Mysteries: The Problem of the Pauline Doctrine of Baptism in Romans 6:1-11 in the Light of its Religio-Historical "Parallels."* Translated by J. P. Smith. Edinburgh and London: Oliver & Boyd, 1967.

Vermaseren, M. J. *Mithras, The Secret God.* Translated by Therese and Vincent Megaw. New York: Barnes & Noble, 1963.

Chapter 3: Gnosticism

Bultmann, R. "Gnosis." *Theological Dictionary of the New Testament,* I (1964), 692–96.

———. "Gnostic Motifs." *Theology of the New Testament.* Vol. 1, pp. 164–83. Translated by Kendrick Grobel. New York: Charles Scribner's Sons, 1951.

Jonas, H. *The Gnostic Religion: The Message of the Alien God and the Beginnings of Christianity.* Second edition, enlarged. Boston: Beacon Press, 1963.

Haardt, R. *Gnosis: Character and Testimony.* Translated by J. F. Hendry. Leiden: Brill, 1971.

Bauer, W. *Orthodoxy and Heresy in Earliest Christianity.* English translation edited by Robert Kraft and Gerhard Krodel. Philadelphia: Fortress Press, 1971.

van Unnik, W. C. *Newly Discovered Gnostic Writings: A Preliminary Survey of the Nag Hammadi Find.* Studies in Biblical Theology No. 30. Naperville, Ill.: Allenson, 1960.

Foerster, W., ed. *Gnosis: A Selection of Gnostic Texts.* English translation edited by R. McL. Wilson. Vol. 1: Patristic Evidence. Vol. 2: Coptic and Mandean Sources. Oxford: Clarendon Press, 1972, 1974.

Wilson, R. McL. *Gnosis and the New Testament.* Philadelphia: Fortress Press, 1968.

CHRONOLOGICAL TABLE

722 B.C.	Destruction of Samaria by the Assyrians		
587 B.C.	Destruction of Jerusalem by the Babylonians		
		539 B.C.	Conquest of Babylon by Cyrus
		333 B.C.	Victory of Alexander the Great over the Persian King Darius III at Issus
		323 B.C.	Death of Alexander the Great
End of the 4th century B.C.	Palestine under Egyptian rule		
End of the 3rd century B.C.	Palestine under Syrian rule		
175–164 B.C.	Antiochus IV king of Syria		

169 B.C.	Plundering of the temple in Jerusalem by Antiochus IV
167 B.C.	Cult of the Olympic Zeus in Jerusalem
164 B.C.	Restoration of the temple cultus by Judas Maccabaeus
160 B.C.	Death of Judas Maccabaeus
153 B.C.	Jonathan high priest
143 B.C.	Murder of Jonathan
140 B.C.	Offices of high priest, military commander, and leader of the Jews confirmed as hereditary for Simon's heirs
134 B.C.	Murder of Simon
134–104 B.C.	John Hyrcanus
128 B.C.	Destruction of the Samaritan temple
107 B.C.	Conquest and destruction of Samaria
104–103 B.C.	Aristobulus king of the Jews

103–76 B.C.	Alexander Jannaeus king of the Jews		
76–67 B.C.	Salome Alexandra queen of the Jews; conflict between her sons Hyrcanus and Aristobulus		
64/63 B.C.	Pompey in Syria and Palestine		
		48 B.C.	Death of Pompey
		44 B.C.	Murder of Caesar
		42 B.C.	Defeat of Caesar's murderers at Philippi
40–37 B.C.	Invasion of Palestine by the Parthians; Antigonus high priest and king of the Jews		
37 B.C.	Herod conquers Jerusalem		
37–4 B.C.	Herod king of the Jews		
		31 B.C.	Octavian's victory over Antony at Actium
		27 B.C.	Establishment of the principate of Octavian

		12 B.C.	Augustus pontifex maximus
		2 B.C.	Augustus pater patriae
4 B.C.–A.D. 6	Archelaus ethnarch in Judea, Idumea, and Samaria		
After A.D. 6	Archelaus's territory under the rule of Roman governors	A.D. 14	Death of Augustus
4 B.C.–A.D. 39	Herod Antipas tetrarch in Galilee and Perea	A.D. 14–37	Tiberius
4 B.C.–A.D. 34	Philip tetrarch in northern Transjordania	A.D. 37–41	Caligula
A.D. 41–44	Herod Agrippa king of the Jews	A.D. 41–54	Claudius
After A.D. 44	All of Palestine under the rule of Roman governors		
A.D. 52–60?	Felix governor in Palestine	A.D. 54–68	Nero
A.D. 60?–62	Porcius Festus governor in Palestine		
A.D. 66–70	Jewish War	A.D. 69–79	Vespasian

A.D. 70	Conquest and destruction of Jerusalem		
A.D. 73	Conquest of the fortress Masada	A.D. 79–81	Titus
		A.D. 81–96	Domitian
		A.D. 96–98	Nerva
		A.D. 98–117	Trajan
A.D. 132–135	Revolt of the Jews under Bar Cochba	A.D. 117–138	Hadrian
		A.D. 138–161	Antoninus Pius
		A.D. 161–180	Marcus Aurelius

INDEXES

a) Index of Names

b) Index of Subjects

c) Index of New Testament Passages

I Thessalonians		Hebrews		9	70, 173, 182
1:1	123	7:1–10:18	157	10	274
1:1–2:13	251	8:5	252	14–15	69
2:9	116	10:1	252	18	274
II Thessalonians		James		Revelation	
1:1	123	3:1-5	250	2:6	274
3:8	116	5:17	173	2:14-15	274
I Timothy		I Peter		2:16	274
				2:24	274
4:3	274	5:12	123	9:20-21	180
II Timothy		I John		11:1-2	50
				12:7	182
2:18	274	4:2	274	13:1-18	206
3:8	173	5:6	275	17:12-17	206
Philemon		Jude		17:14	220
				19:16	220
10–16	213	8	274	20:1-10	194

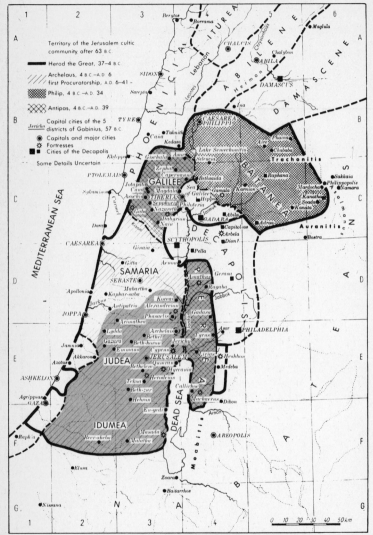

Fig. 1. The Kingdom of Herod the Great and His Sons

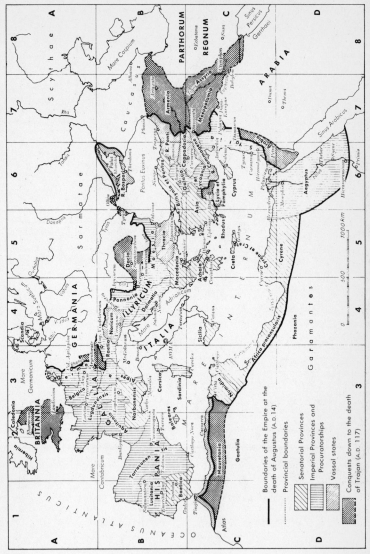

Fig. 2. The Roman Empire in New Testament Times

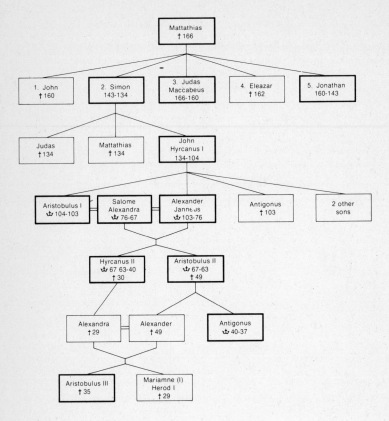

Fig. 3. The House of the Hasmoneans

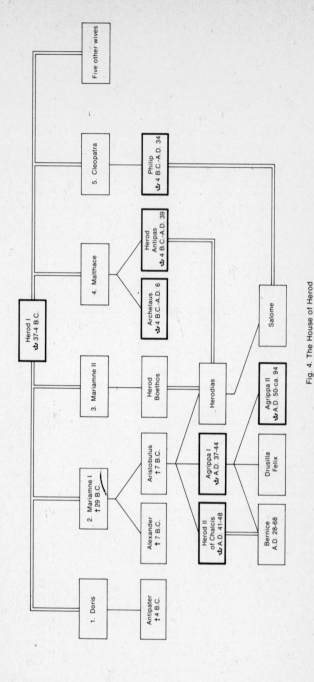

Fig. 4. The House of Herod

Figs. 1-4 are taken from: Biblisch-Historisches Handwörterbuch.
Hrsg. v. B. Reicke und L. Rost. Vandenhoeck & Ruprecht, Göttingen